PORTRAIT OF
AN OBAMA NANNY STATE

IF IT CAN HAPPEN TO THE BRITS,
IT CAN HAPPEN TO US

F. LaGARD SMITH

Portrait of an Obama Nanny State

Copyright © 2012 by F. LaGard Smith

Published by Cotswold Publishing
cotswoldpublishing@gmail.com

ISBN-13: 978-1475087710
ISBN-10: 1475087713

Printed in the United States of America

Note about Format

In the pages ahead, you will find a mixture of British and American spellings, punctuation, and style consistent with the dual aim of local flavor and readability.

The many so-called "News Reports" throughout this book are summaries of facts and events adapted from actual articles, appropriately footnoted. Apart from length, the various "Comments" and "Editorials," are only minimally edited from the originals so as to eliminate any potential distortion.

The bureaucracy is expanding to meet the needs
of the expanding bureauracy.

—*Oscar Wilde*

Contents

Introduction

The Looming Nightmare of a British-style Nanny State

British Newspaper Headline: "Christians have no right to wear cross at work, says Government"

U.S. Newspaper Headline: "Church complains to Obama administration that 'Obamacare' trumps religious conscience"

Which is more predictable: prophecy, or 20/20 hindsight? Thanks to our British cousins across the Pond, we have the best of both worlds. It won't matter what government happens to be in power by the time you read this book. The point is that we have a 13-year track record under Britain's former Labour Government (only moderately changed under the current Conservative/LibDem Coalition), which is the closest thing possible to the current Obama administration, or any other Left-leaning administration that might follow. At this point in history, no one who has experienced the hyper-regulatory, militantly-secularist state in Britain needs a crystal ball to predict America's bleak future. Given the bedrock liberal assumptions of the ruling elite in both countries, the garden path down which we're being frog-marched cannot help but end up in the same demise of individual freedoms that cowering British citizens have been forced to accept.

The headlines at the beginning of this Introduction alone tell the story. Listen to President Obama, and you'd think his administration's recent attempt to force the Catholic Church to compromise its stance on birth control was merely an attempt to guarantee women (including

Catholic women) access to contraceptives. Don't you believe it. It's about the power to will and the power to control, even when that means running roughshod over religious freedoms. For decades, the Brits have seen the liberal-Left's sexual agenda relentlessly enforced through the Trojan horse of Britain's sacrosanct National Health Service. But that's the least of the problems. The same forces of the liberal-Left have a far more sinister agenda: Militant secularism. Today, it's all about being able to wear condoms. Tomorrow, it's all about *not* being able to wear crosses.

It's a package deal. Buy one, get one free...with a nightmarish twist. "You WILL buy one!" and "You WILL accept the other!" Ever noticed that those screaming most loudly about Choice are the very folks who give you no choice? Or that those who insist on tolerance are themselves the least tolerant? Despite all the liberal talk, Obama is the poster child for intolerance.

The conventional wisdom during the run-up to the 2012 elections? The Republicans would be well advised to put their social issues on the back burner and focus solely on jobs and the economy. At the very least, that is a false dichotomy, wrongly suggesting that in the battle for America's mind a pincer movement is somehow less effective than in a normal war. More important by far is the inconvenient truth that America's most serious threat is not a flagging economy and joblessness but an assault on individual freedom and initiative. Have you ever stopped to think that under communism in the Soviet era there was total employment...but no freedom? And total employment...but little productivity?

If forced to decide between high unemployment and a loss of individual freedoms, which would you choose? In truth, that too is a false dichotomy. Where there is a flourishing of freedom, economies also flourish. Where freedom is curtailed, economies tank. So the real issue facing the American electorate comes down to but a single, simple question: Which leadership is congenitally-disposed to thinking that they can run our lives better than we can, and which leadership believes as a matter of principle that beyond limited legitimate concerns, government ought to stay out of our face? On that hook hang both the crucial social issues of our time and the current economic challenges created in large measure by the self-same hyper-regulatory mentality that Obama and his fellow-travelers insist we must employ to solve the problem. Any problem.

If you haven't yet sensed the crisis looming on this side of the Pond, there's a political and cultural tsunami fast approaching our shores caused by a tectonic shift in fundamental values on the European continent. Already it has fully engulfed Britain and we are as vulnerable as an unsuspecting, now-devastated northern Japan. Let the incredible pictures of that devastation play in your mind. All you need do is translate the chaos of huge ships being tossed onto multistory buildings into images of unimaginable political and economic chaos when liberalism's full force hits home.

Speaking of the British, where is Paul Revere when we need him? "One if by land, and two if by sea," and all that. Even if his historic cry, "The Regulars are coming!" doesn't quite pack the same patriotic punch as the more popular version, "The British are coming," either way it was the dreaded British redcoats who were threatening to upend the American experience before it ever was birthed. Never since those opening volleys in 1775 has America been so threatened by its Mother Country, with whom more lately we have a much-celebrated "special relationship" (or at least Obama's subtly-downgraded "essential relationship").

This time around, the threat has nothing to do with His Majesty's warships and red-coated British soldiers. In this battle, there will be no occupying forces, and not a shot will be fired. In fact, hardly anyone will even notice when our nation has been overrun. And how ironic that will be. For just as in 1775, the stealth battle even now being waged goes to the very core of what the Revolutionary War was all about—the preservation of individual liberties and religious freedoms in the face of tyrannical government.

This is not to say that Britain consciously intends to wage war against us. It's just that there's more to our "special relationship" than meets the eye. For "two countries divided by a common language," as George Bernard Shaw famously put it, the surprise is how very undivided we are—perhaps especially because of our common language. For their part, the Brits readily acknowledge the broad influence America has had on their own culture, military obligations, and—these days especially—their economy. "When America sneezes," so it is said, "Britain catches a cold."

For all the reasons why the Brits might hate us (and they cite many), they can't seem to get enough of us. Though few Brits would admit it, there is a fair amount of sibling rivalry going on. Call it envy, to be precise. If you're looking for evidence of America's influence on Britain, merely turn on the "tellie" over there. Or consider who typically follows whom into combat against mutual enemies. Or simply drive to a local super-store in Britain these days. American-style mega-stores have all but killed off the village shops so integral a part of Britain's once-vibrant village life.

Naturally, the traffic across the Atlantic has not all been one-way. If perhaps the charm of afternoon tea never quite caught on, nor, thankfully, the quintessential but inscrutable game of cricket, it would be hard to overestimate the influence of the Beatles on the American music scene. Or Britain's own film-making contribution to Hollywood. Or the burgeoning interest in soccer (which for Britain and the rest of the world is the only *real* football). In a myriad of ways, the American experience has "Made in Britain" indelibly stamped all over it.

Never is that more true than when one considers America's system of government and laws. Compare England's unwritten Constitution with our written one, and you're sure to find a host of similarities, despite the historic royal connections which now are virtually reduced to window-dressing. Which came first, America's House of Representatives and Senate, or England's House of Commons and House of Lords? And where do you think we got our laws? From the

English Common Law, of course—complete with presumptions of innocence, burdens of proof, and definitions of crimes. Yet it is in the arena of law and government that we are now most threatened by the very hand that has fed us so sumptuously in the past. Merely consider two key factors.

First, ironically, is the fact that the United States of America itself has given birth to the notion of a "United States of Europe"—now fast on its way to becoming federalized in the form of the European Union, having its own Constitution and wishful superpower status. What goes around comes around. So when we speak of modern Britain, we're talking about a nation rapidly devolving into merely one of many sister states, having foolishly relinquished her once tightly-guarded sovereignty like a tipsy virgin on prom night. The days when Britannia ruled the world are but a fading memory. No less than with the Queen herself, Britain's political center has shifted, not only from Buckingham Palace to Westminster, but now from London to Brussels—a political journey almost as fast as the Eurostar.

As a result, the British Parliament is now little more than a rubber stamp to mostly-unelected European bureaucrats who churn out policies, edicts, rules, and regulations subjugating British citizens as surely as any satellite nation under Soviet rule. Even British courts must now kowtow to the European Court of Human Rights, with its secularist-liberal agenda for all the world to see. To say, then, that "The British Are Coming!" is almost as much to say that "The Europeans Are Coming!" *Almost*, but not completely. What Brussels busily invents, Britain happily invites with a relish not seen in any of the other EU nations. Unlike anywhere outside of openly totalitarian societies, intrusive government regulation is just her cup of tea.

The second crucial factor threatening America is a growing reciprocity of influence from Europe to America, seen perhaps most shockingly in the previously-inconceivable citing of European law by America's Supreme Court—as if any foreign law should have any bearing whatsoever on legal decisions affecting domestic issues. Writing for the majority in *Lawrence v. Texas*, a landmark decision supporting gay rights, Justice Anthony Kennedy noted that the European Court of Human Rights and other foreign courts have affirmed the "rights of homosexual adults to engage in intimate, consensual conduct."

This unprecedented appeal to "the world community" (as it is put euphemistically) is a predictable foretaste of further appeals to other countries' opposition to the death penalty, their emphasis on foreign prisoners' rights and even their acceptance of same-sex marriage. It won't be long before American courts and legislatures will be importing without a license a host of social and legal policies conceived, drafted, and enforced in the European community—wholly outside the American experience and incompatible with America's core values.

Ask most Americans about government regulation and you're likely to get an ear-full of complaints that we're already over-taxed, over-governed, and dangerously overboard. Yet despite a monolithic federal government sticking its nose into everything from small businesses to education to religious freedoms, we have yet to touch the hem of the garment of Britain's omnipresent nanny state.

And thanks largely to the Leftist-agenda-driven American Civil Liberties Union (ACLU)—once a principled defender of individual liberties—we've already been fighting once-unthinkable culture wars right here at home for decades. Already, America has been forced to retreat from the faith-based social values that made it strong, as evidenced by prayers banned in public schools, displays of the Ten Commandments all but shut down, Christmas celebrations kicked out of the public square, extremist gay rights shoved in our faces, and, of course, the wholesale killing of babies in the womb. But if you think this liberal onslaught is alarming, take a deep breath. We ain't seen nothing yet! Ours is but a prepubescent awakening compared with the secularist totalitarianism in which our British cousins are already enslaved.

"You couldn't believe it unless you'd seen it," one often hears. Hence the purpose of this book...to help you see it. To take you up close and personal into the everyday world of British life. To read the daily reports in Britain's newspapers and be appalled. To be forewarned and forearmed. To resist the seemingly inevitable before it's too late. To follow in the footsteps of our brave forefathers...if that's still possible....

Were Paul Revere and his compatriots confronted with today's British nanny state, there's little chance they could pull off a repeat performance. Merely consider Longfellow's "trembling ladder steep and tall" leading up to the tower of the Old North Church. Today, church sextant Robert Newman and Captain John Pulling wouldn't even get to the bottom rung before discovering the whole thing was shut down tight by Health and Safety. No risks allowed, thank you very much. Nor is there a chance in Her Majesty's queendom that anyone would be permitted to light one lantern, much less two, in the belfry of any church having the word "old" as part of its name. In fact, there's an increasing possibility that the word "church" itself would fall afoul of the hyper-sensitive political correctness required of today's British citizens. You can safely bet that "mosque" would pass muster, but "church" does tend to suggest something far more Christian, and thus suspect by definition—even in a nation with an official (Christian) state church!

Then there's Revere himself flying recklessly across hill and dale in the middle of the night...spreading alarm. Just how alarming is that! Worthy of an ASBO[1] wouldn't you think? And no prizes for guessing what Health and Safety would say about any "steed flying so fearlessly and fleet" that "the spark struck out by that steed kindled the land into flame with its heat." Can't have sparks flying about, now can we! What's next? Banning fireworks on the Fourth of July? Although that might have some appeal for the Brits (who speak wryly of also

---

[1] Anti-Social Behavior Order, designed for drunken louts and howling hooligans but increasingly applied to upright citizens, including Christians daring within the privacy of their own homes to debate Muslims on the merits of Islam. More on that later.

celebrating our Independence Day, if for different reasons!), one can only wonder how much longer all those dangerous fireworks can be lit on Guy Fawkes night. (The short-lived rebellion by England's own "Paul Revere" proved to be a singular disaster.)

Pardon the more-than-slight stretch here, but it hardly bears imagining what the British government (whether Labour, Conservative, or Liberal Democrat) would have to say about Revere and his fellow nightriders trying to stir up the "Middlesex population." It would be perfectly fine for them to wake up every five-year-old to the joys of sex and supply hormone-happy teenagers with condoms, but to dare suggest that it's not perfectly Yankee Doodle dandy to engage in any kind of twisted "middle" sex (take your pick: lesbian, gay, bisexual, transgender) will get you fired faster than Revere's breakneck ride between Boston and Lexington. In Britain's current climate of radical egalitarianism, the no-holds-barred gay lobby gives new meaning to "Rule Britannia."

How very far Britain has come from anything like Longfellow's ode to Paul Revere, lauding as it does the "cry of defiance, and not of fear" where there's "a voice in the darkness, a knock at the door." In today's inexorably-evolving police state, the Brits have reason to fear not only the knock at the door by notoriously undeterred criminals, but even more so the knock at the door by the local police themselves, demanding to know why a mother dared threaten her child with a spanking for misbehaving. Or maybe by officers wanting to interrogate children outside their parents' presence to see if home schooling (now considered nigh unto seditious) is just a cover-up for child abuse. Or perhaps the police are interested in that highly dangerous eight-year-old who called one of his classmates a name deemed to be socially intolerant. In modern Britain, the police are more a tool of social engineering than the first line of defense they ought to be against real harm to its citizens.

So what would Revere have thought about a Big Brother surveillance society with its moment-by-moment intrusion into every aspect of its citizens' lives, right down to the contents of their rubbish bins?

It's not simply Britain's budget-bolstering speed cameras Revere would have reviled as he sped through the night. In the most CCTV-monitored society on the globe, Revere couldn't have blinked without a uniformed official in some secret control room observing every minute detail. Naturally, the authorities would justify their interrogation-level snooping as a means of catching nefarious terrorists such as Revere. But even the most loyal and innocent of British subjects would not have been spared the camera's scrutiny on that night of nights. First it's security cameras, then mandatory identity cards, and finally a totalitarian regime without the slightest pretext of benign, democratic governance.

If ever a society gets to that point, of course, maybe, just maybe, history might play out as Longfellow describes: "how the British Regulars fired and fled," and "how the farmers gave them ball for ball, from behind each fence and farmyard wall." Not that such a scene could ever unfold in modern Britain, mind you. With gun regulation so tight that only petty criminals now get away with carrying guns, there could never be an armed rebellion by outraged citizen soldiers. As for those stalwart farmers with their trusty muskets, in Britain there wouldn't even be many *farmers* left these days after decades of over-regulation from Westminster, Whitehall, and Brussels.

In case you're wondering, this admittedly-contrived parody is intended merely as a teaser for the serious message that lies ahead. In the chapters to come, true-to-life anecdotal evidence will paint a graphic picture guaranteed to grab the attention of even the most cynical reader. Because outside observers often are in a better position to appreciate the approach of danger than those who already are embroiled in it, there's even a remote chance that this comprehensive portrait of the Great British Loonyfest might even catch the attention of the locals. With any luck, it's not too late to rout the madness and force its hasty retreat all the way back across the English Channel.

In the pages ahead, we're going to witness not only Britain's fully-entrenched laws and policies that defy any possible definition of common sense, but also the ongoing radical agenda even now being pushed by activists fresh out of the asylum. If the present scenario is scary enough, just how disturbing is it to think that the current madness was once only a distant blueprint for extremist social change in the minds of an elitist ruling class? As with all radical social planners, creeping incrementalism is the preferred way forward. The slower the process, the less noticed it will be. The less noticed, the less challenged.

If you've never heard the story of the frog in the kettle, it's time you did. Drop a frog into a pot of boiling water, and he'll jump right out. But if you plop the frog into a pot of cold water and gradually turn up the heat, the frog won't take the slightest notice...until it's too late. Only a short time ago, Britain herself was the unsuspecting frog in the kettle. By now the water is bubbling and boiling, and Britain is virtually cooked. In a case of froggie see, froggie do, America is now the frog in the kettle, wholly oblivious to the same dangers headed our way. Heaven help us if we don't jump now, and fast!

For all that's lovable about the glorious history, rich traditions, and incomparable beauty of truly *Great* Britain, there's nothing lovable about its present loony liberal madness, spawned by the promiscuous seed of a progressively amoral society and gestating with sinister effect in the womb of a virulently bureaucratic, arrogant, and secularist European Union. One need only follow the same line of logic to conclude that, despite her own unique history, traditions, and beauty, the America we so dearly love is already running headlong into the same bureaucratic, arrogant, and secular abyss. Having a loony cousin across the Pond might just be oddly quaint. Becoming a loony nation ourselves would be a tragedy of the highest order from which we could never survive.

It's not just Obama, of course. Quite deservedly, he is the symbolic name and face of the current problem, but there are loony folks at every level of American government from top to bottom. Some might not even be left-wing Democrats, as you might expect. There are politicians, civil servants, and bureaucrats of every stripe who are heady with power and seemingly born with the irresistible urge to tell the rest of us what we must do. Sometimes, they're even on the religious-Right, thinking that they're not only politically Right, but invariably *right*! Dare suggest that they share that same arrogant perspective with Obama and they'd surely shriek.

What you get when you double-click on Barack Obama is a mixed-bag of professional busybodies, most of them philosophically certain that they are acting in the name of freedom, liberty, and equality, but completely delusional about the counter-productive results of their efforts.

And don't be fooled by the God-talk more common in American politics than in Britain (where famously it has been said, "We don't do God"). Like Obama at the National Prayer Breakfast, liberal loonies may even cite "what Jesus would do" in aid of socialist redistribution of wealth. Like Obama, they may invoke, "God bless America," all the while pushing policies that are a breathtaking affront to God. Militant secularism is at its very best when clothed in pious God-talk.

Want a graphic picture of where America is likely to be in less than a decade under the present Obama trajectory? No more striking a portrait could be painted than this microscopic view of the nanny state even now fully entrenched in Britain and fast headed to the heartland of America.

1

When the Nanny
Steals the Kids

*Give me the children until they are seven
and anyone may have them afterwards.*

—St. Francis Xavier

News Report—*A mother left her children (the oldest being nine) playing in a park while she did a quick bit of shopping. All this was observed by police officers who logged "the incident" with the Criminal Records Bureau. When the woman later volunteered in a Sunday school, a criminal records check popped up, indicating her to be a risk to children.*

The Criminal Records Bureau collects information on people who apply for jobs working with children, including so-called "soft information" where police have questioned someone but released them without charge. The woman was never told she was being placed on a criminal database and never had an opportunity to comment on the allegation that she was a risk to children simply because she had briefly left her own children alone playing in a public park.[1]

This shocking story—repeated often throughout Britain with variations on theme—raises several critical questions along a number of fronts. For the moment, the immediate concern has to do with the State's right to interfere with the role of parents. What constitutes good parenting, who is to decide, and what role if any ought the police to play in protecting children from harm? In Britain today, the Government has insinuated itself between parents and children as if the State were an all-knowing, all-wise Super-Nanny. Instead of "Father knows best," by official British reckoning, it's "Nanny knows best."

Anyone familiar with the legal concept of *in loco parentis* will appreciate that the State has a legitimate role to play in protecting the nation's young from malevolent parental abuse. Rarely have Americans had any problem with government intervention in cases where children are subjected to physical harm by cruel parents. Presumably, even the beleaguered woman in the news report above would be among the first to agree—which makes it all the more outrageous that such a conscientious mother and Sunday school teacher should be lumped unceremoniously into the same category as criminal child-abusers.

Could we have a show of hands, please? Is there any parent who hasn't made a dumb parenting decision, or taken some embarrassing action they'd love to forget? Are there any parents who couldn't have been second-guessed on occasion for how they treated their children? In America, thank God, we haven't yet sunk to the level of having the police place parents on a national criminal database for nothing more than what some wooly-headed police officer might consider to be a lapse in good judgment. To reasonable folks, the only lapse in judgment in this case was on the part of the police themselves...and any government that would create and maintain a system capable of such unthinkable results.

Unfortunately, this is not the only intrusive interference with the family heading our way fast. In Britain and Europe, even the most benign corporeal punishment is regarded as being only slightly less objectionable than waterboarding and the torture of terrorists. (After all, haven't you heard folks refer to children as "little terrors"...?)

Spare the rod and spoil the nation

News Report—*Smacking a child is the equivalent of using an electric fence to control an animal. So argues the attorney acting for Northern Ireland's Children's Commissioner, Patricia Lewsley in an attempt to introduce a smacking ban. Miss Lewsley believes that smacking is "illegitimate violence," and her lawyers are appealing to the UN Convention on the Rights of the Child under which children are protected from torture or degrading treatment. Lawyers are trying to say that smacking falls within that definition. When asked by the court whether it would be okay to smack a child throwing a tantrum when being strapped into a car seat, Miss Lewsley's lawyer said that such a situation would constitute "illegitimate violence."*

When asked by a reporter if she would make any distinction between physical abuse and smacking, Commissioner Lewsley replied: "No." The reporter then asked: "Even if someone is setting out to deliberately harm their child and obviously cares nothing for them, and a parent who has the best interests of their child at heart—albeit you may think misguided—you think that's entirely the same thing? The Commissioner answered: "Yeah."[2]

The good news is that the Court of Appeal rejected this daft attempt to ban any and all corporeal punishment. The bad news is that you can be sure all four Commissioners in Britain will continue knocking on the courtroom door until one day they have beaten it down and had their way with Britain's parents. It's only a matter of time.

For now the British Government says it opposes a full ban on corporeal punishment. Being politically savvy, they're biding their time until a younger generation who've never had a hand laid on them think that there must be some law against it—and then suddenly there will be!

Want an interesting analogy? In America, the same founding fathers who provided that there shall be no cruel or unusual punishment had not the slightest objection to capital punishment. But when in time courts began to buy the liberal notion that capital punishment might be cruel and unusual, the result was fewer and fewer instances of executions—providing anti-execution advocates with the perfect evidence that capital punishment, if not cruel, was at least *unusual*.

Given this same progression of logic and events, one now could argue with increasing force that capital punishment is no real deterrent (one of its original justifications). Interesting how all this works out. Consistent with time-honored parenting, a slap on the hands or a brief stinging of the bottom was always intended to have similar deterrent effects. So what might we reasonably guess to be the result when such punishment is no longer allowed for an entire generation of children? Are alternative forms of discipline really equal to the task? What seems to be the overwhelming evidence so far?

Maybe the problem with the Brits is their unfortunate choice of words. To American ears, *smacking* has a somewhat harsher ring than *spanking*. After all, you *smack* a baseball! "And did you see that guy *smacking* the poor woman upside the head with a shovel handle?" Not exactly the same as something that's "lip-smacking" delicious! On this side of the Pond, *smacking* is certainly not the first image that comes to mind when we hear the word *spanking*. Typically, we associate *spanking* with altogether-proper parental discipline of children; *paddling* with what once was the dreaded use of a wooden paddle by schoolteachers on unruly boys; and a *beating* with merciless, unjustified, excessive force.

Even when Scripture suggests the more familiar adage, "spare the rod and spoil the child," there is no hint that the "rod" is to be used for a *beating*. More important is the connection the half-dozen "rod" proverbs make between the absence of corporeal punishment and the moral ruination of a child. But secularists wouldn't understand that connection, nor the wisdom behind it, nor certainly the divine authority by which is was given. Disdainful of Scripture, they have little appreciation for parental authority. For secular humanists, it's all about human rights and children's rights.

Strangely, you hear little talk of parental rights these days. If there *were* such a thing, parental rights invariably would be trumped by children's rights; and both would be trumped by the authority of the State—blithely supplanting parents so as to gain control over the next generation of citizens. Enter Mao, stage left.

Even now, it begins

News Report —*A 34-year-old mother was shopping at a Southampton supermarket when she warned her children, ages eleven and four, that if they continued to misbehave they would get a "hiding" when they got home. An off-duty officer overheard the conversation and followed the woman home to determine where she lived. Two weeks later, uniformed officers appeared at the mother's home and advised her to use a "naughty step" or to withdraw treats as discipline instead of smacking. This was followed up by a letter from social services which said no further action would be taken "at this time," but added: "We would like to advise you that we do keep the information on record."*

The shocked mother said: "The local authorities have told me they're keeping my family on record until my kids leave school. My daughter is only four. If she ever falls over and has to be taken to a hospital, I'm worried about what conclusions they might come to. I feel I'm being kept on record as an abuser, so I will always be looking over my shoulder. It was an amazing intrusion. I was doing what parents should do, and what thousands do every week—setting moral boundaries for how children should behave. If no one stands up to this oppression—this political correctness—parents will lose responsibility for their kids and the state will take over."[3]

Again we encounter an unfamiliar term: "a hiding." But it's nothing more than code for *spanking*—as in, "Keep that up, and I'll tan your hide." Guess that sounds cruel to today's liberal do-gooders, but it was common language and practice among those we now look back on with deep respect as "the Greatest Generation." They were all the better people and citizens because of an occasional "hiding." And none of them died as a result...only courageously on the field of battle, giving Hitler his own good hiding.

Did you catch what the police told the woman about using a "naughty step" and withdrawing treats? Can someone explain what in the world gives police the authority (or special insight!) to give instruction in good parenting? And don't forget it's the same police who complain about violent, disrespectful kids acting out in anti-social and criminal ways. Do they not have a clue? Are the police the only ones who can't connect the obvious dots? As it happens, they're *not* the only ones....

News Report —*A woman was fired as a school nurse after smacking her child at home. Her worst nightmare began in 2007 when her eleven- and sixteen-year-old sons started misbehaving. She said, "We were having quite serious teenage rebellion problems with our eldest son, and our middle son started swearing at me. After warning him that I would smack him if he did not stop, he continued swearing so I smacked him."*

The older brother reported the incident to the police, who promptly removed the woman and her husband to a jail cell and questioned them on abuse charges. The children were placed on the Child Protection Register, and their mother was suspended from her job. The school said it was reluctant to allow unsupervised contact with pupils who might be vulnerable.[4]

Have you noticed how similar the stern action of social services is to the very offense at which they get so outraged? Parents who spank their children are not merely given a "naughty step" warning, but immediately subjected to arrest and jail cells and blacklisting—all of which amounts to an abusive "legal smacking" having the most serious and lasting repercussions.

Are you ready for the police to show up at your door within hours of your using physical force of any kind against your rebellious teenager? Or to be taken to jail and interrogated? Or to be "marked for life" as a child abuser? If you don't think that could happen soon in America, think again. The British are coming! The loony British are coming! Not in red coats this time, but in blue uniforms.

Need a further example to be convinced...?

News Report —*A father spent a night in jail after smacking his seven-year-old son, Harry, for wandering off alone after dark. The boy had been told by his father to stay with him as they shopped in Plymouth. But when the young lad wandered off, his father smacked him once.*

A witness reported the incident, and four police officers quickly arrived at the man's home to arrest him. Young Harry was forced to strip to his underwear for an examination, following which the father was taken to the police station where he was kept overnight. Released the following morning after the witness withdrew the complaint, Harry's father said that the police's response was "massively over-the-top."[5]

Four police officers? In every respect, "massively over-the-top" is an understatement. What do you suppose young Harry will remember for the rest of his life: an appropriate, timely spanking by a loving parent, or being forced to strip down in front of police officers, then seeing his father hauled off to jail? No lawsuit against the police could ever undo the psychological damage. Worse yet, no lawsuit against the police likely would succeed—such is the convoluted sense of priorities in Britain these days...and soon to come to our own shores if we don't nip the nanny-state state-of-mind in the bud before it becomes full-bloom.

Robbing the cradle

If you can't trust parents to exercise judgment in disciplining their children, can they possibly be trusted to exercise good judgment regarding their children's education...?

Breaking News —*All parents are to be encouraged to send their children to school at the age of four under Government plans, despite fears they are being* *pushed into education too early. At the moment, children in England must start school at five, although most are enrolled aged four during the reception year. The proposals will reignite the debate over the school starting age, just days after a major report recommended delaying formal education until six.*

The Cambridge Primary Review said all children should be given a play-based curriculum at a young age to allow pupils to develop emotional and social skills. Children in the UK already start school earlier than most other European countries, where formal education is delayed until six. Children in Scandinavian countries do not start lessons until seven but often outperform those in UK schools.

This report of October 19, 2009 by *The Daily Telegraph's* Education Editor, Graeme Paton, highlights just how dearly the nanny state would love to raise Britain's children. The sooner the better; the younger the better. Naturally, this will be done through a curriculum of lessons and activities determined by the same enlightened intelligentsia mandating early sex education, outlandish political correctness, and other liberal propaganda.

Home-schoolers beware!

Breaking News —*New measures are being introduced to regulate the way parents educate their children at home. According to Norman Wells, of the Family Education Trust, the new plans signal "an unprecedented level of intrusion into family life."*

Under the measures, local authority officials will visit families and interview children away from their parents to ensure that they are providing a "suitable" and "efficient" education. Parents will have to provide their local authority with "a statement of approach to education" and a twelve-month plan outlining what they will teach.

Graham Badman, who is calling for the new measures, said there must be changes in the way home schooling is regulated. He said that home schooling lacks "the correct balance between the rights of parents and the rights of the child—either to an appropriate education or to be safe from harm."[6]

If requiring a teaching plan from home-schooling parents seems not all that ominous, read more carefully between the lines. Recall what Badman said about the rights of the child to be *safe from harm*? What possibly is he implying? Nothing less than that home-schoolers must surely be using home-schooling as a cover-up for child abuse! That's right. Child abuse.

Lest you wonder if that's a fair interpretation, consider the apology offered after Vijay Patel, a policy adviser at the National Society for the Prevention of Cruelty to Children (NSPCC), told the *Independent* (February 26, 2009): "Some people use home education to hide. Look at the Victoria Climbié case. No one asked where she was at school." (Eight-year-old Victoria—*who was not home-schooled*—died after suffering months of torture despite being in regular contact with police, doctors and social services, who together missed at least 12 chances to save her life.)

As if Patel's home-schooling slur weren't patently contrived and outrageous, it just so happens that the NSPCC itself was among the social services ignoring the warning signs leading to Victoria's death! Compounding the felony, the NSPCC was forced to explain why there were two different versions of vital documents unearthed in an official inquiry.[7]

When it comes to a cover-up associated with child abuse, home-school parents are not the dastardly villain, but rather the liberal establishment itself. One is tempted to say it's the pot calling the kettle black, except that the "kettle" in this case (home-schooling) was never black. Only the collective pot of *illiberal* liberal social workers and officious government intermeddlers deserve that dubious honor.

If only it were a single case of abuse driving this bus. Even local commentators are highlighting the nefarious "clipboard state" that Britain has become....

Editorial —*We are about to see the next stage in the onward march of the clipboard state into every aspect of our lives. Today, the consultation period ends on government plans to impose new restrictions on the thousands of parents who educate their children at home.*

Just as adults wishing to volunteer to help children in a range of activities are to have their suitability decided by a state agency, parents themselves will soon need to satisfy a government functionary that they know how to bring up their own children. These plans are deeply sinister. For the first time, local councils will have the power to enter family homes and question young children without the presence of their parents—something even the police are not allowed to do unless the parent is the suspect.

So observes Philip Johnston (*Daily Telegraph*, October 19, 2009). So again, let's see if we've got this straight. Why will the Government be interrogating home-school children? To determine if there is any child abuse going on. And why will that interrogation take place outside the parents' presence? Because there is a deep-seated suspicion on the part of the liberal establishment that home-schooled children are the victims of child abuse, and so every home-school parent is automatically a suspect!

Religious faith is the real target

But let no one be fooled. It's not really *physical* child abuse that's in the cross-hairs of Britain's secular warlords. Not unlike more-militant extremists, just listen to the heightened level of "chatter" before the bureaucratic bombs begin exploding....

News Item —*A BBC radio host, Roger Bolton, has said that some evangelical parents need monitoring by the state because they may "intimidate" their children with ideas about God, sin and hell. Bolton spoke* *of "authoritarian" evangelical fathers of "Victorian periods" who threatened their children with theology. He went on to say, "Some people will worry that this is possible now under home tuition. And you would not be able to do anything about it because people would just say, 'We're simply telling them what we believe.'"[8]*

Now do you see where this freight train is headed and what it's loaded with? The "abuse" the liberals are worried about is *psychological* abuse caused by parents teaching their children about God. Sound the alarm! The (secular-humanist) British are coming! And even now, their fifth-column compatriots are in the streets and by-ways of our own homeland, conspiring toward the demise of Christian education in the home....

American News Report —*In New Hampshire, a child educated at home by her mother, a Christian, was ordered to attend a public school so she can learn about other belief systems. The court conceded that the ten-year-old is bright, sociable and academically advanced for her age, but decided she should no longer be home-schooled. The reason, says her mother's attorney, is simply that the girl's "religious beliefs are a bit too sincerely held" and need to be "mixed with other worldviews."*

The girl's divorced mother has been educating her at home since first grade with a curriculum that exceeds required academic standards. However, when the terms of the child's parenting plan were re-negotiated recently, the official representing the girl's interests raised concerns about her religious beliefs. The guardian ad litem told the court that the girl "appeared to reflect her mother's rigidity on questions of faith" and that the girl's interests "would be best served by exposure to a public school setting."[9]

Considering what's already happening in Hampshire across the Pond, nothing's new in *New* Hampshire.

And in Britain there's more ways than one for officials to talk with children outside their parents' presence....

Everyone knows but the parents

News Report —*A pilot scheme is being introduced by Oxfordshire County Council after the county saw a sharp rise in pregnancies among girls aged 18 and under. Text messages are being sent to schoolgirls as young as 11, encouraging them to request the morning-after pill. Parents are not informed of their daughter's requests and are only alerted if a girl under 13 actually uses the service. Oxfordshire County Councillor Louise Chapman rejected all concerns, claiming: "We'd be foolish to think there was something we could do to stop young people having sex."*[10]

Amazing, isn't it? Assuming government officials like Ms. Chapman are serious about minimizing teenage sex, just what message is being sent by schools providing the morning-after pill? In any other context of abuse and dependency, all the talk would be about *enabling*...and *enablers*.

Of course, the greater threat by far is that the Government's scheme seriously undermines the role and authority of parents over the lives of their children. At no point are parents to receive notice that their 11-year-old is receiving text messages urging her to request the morning-after pill. The school knows, and the child protection staff know, but not the parents. Apparently it's none of their business. After all, they're only the parents, once foolishly thought to be responsible for the children they sire. Guess that's just one more outdated notion these days, what with the state assuming that role.

And since Ms. Chapman assures us there's nothing we could do to stop young people having sex, one can only suppose that parents soon will be barred from teaching their children that sex outside of marriage is morally wrong. No, surely that would never happen....

News Alert —*A new booklet, called "Talking to your Teenager about Sex and Relationships," is being made available at pharmacies nationwide. In it the Government tells parents to discuss sex with their children without "trying to convince them" of what is right and wrong. The booklet cautions:*

"Discussing your values with your teenagers will help them to form their own. Remember, though, that trying to convince them of what's right and wrong may discourage them from being open."

Similarly, the Family Planning Association has been given £530,000 by the Government to train parents in how to teach their children about sex. FPA was behind "Let's Grow With Nisha and Joe," a comic-style sex education booklet for six-year-olds, and promoted a video to schools along with a booklet telling teenage girls that warnings about the negative consequences of abortion are just "myths".[11]

Why all the liberal angst about teenage pregnancies? Is there something wrong with teenagers having sex? To juxtapose those two sentences is to put the cat of common sense among the leftist liberal pigeons. For fuzzy-minded liberals, there is a huge disconnect between *teen sex* and *teen pregnancy*. To the liberal mind, there's nothing wrong with teenage sex, only teenage pregnancy. But it's funny how it seems to work: a lot of young girls who have sex actually end up pregnant, can you believe?

Invariably, the liberal answer to that conundrum is to promote *safe* sex. Sex without consequences. So encourage the kids to have sex, but make sure they have access to contraceptives, morning-after pills, and—if all else fails—abortions. The last thing we want are all those unwanted babies being brought into the world to be mothered by mothers who are still children themselves.

Which only begs the question: Is there something morally objectionable about unwanted babies? Something morally wrong with having an epidemic of unmarried teenage mothers? Be careful how you answer. If you agree that there's a moral problem here, you are obviously appealing to some universally-recognizable set of values. Once you go there, you can't just whimsically cherry-pick which values you like and which you dislike. Parents who object to their teenagers having sex aren't merely concerned with unwanted pregnancies, but with the whole range of transcendent moral values shaping the character and souls of their children.

Liberal social planners who decry obvious moral crises like the epidemic of teen pregnancy are blind to the lapse in moral standards giving rise to those crises. Propagandizing parents to abdicate their role as moral arbiters teaching the right and wrong of sexual relations is merely to propagate a generation of young people set morally adrift. And if morally adrift about sex, then morally adrift about bullying, and drunkenness, and violence, and responsibility, tolerance, and respect.

Among the bedrock moral principles of all time is respect for parents. Sending text-messages to children behind their parents' backs not only shows breathtaking disrespect for parents on the part of liberal social planners but cannot help undermining respect for parents on the part of children who are encouraged to hide what they're doing from their parents. Why not just go ahead and take all children out of the grasp of any parents who might possibly stand in the way of the state's radical child-rearing agenda?

You're kidding, of course. Not in the least. Watch for it; wait for it. Coming soon to a social services agency near you....

Playing God with "the state's children"

News Report —*Social workers have halted the wedding of a pregnant young woman because they feel she is not sufficiently intelligent to marry, and her newborn baby will be taken away from her. The 17-year-old has mild learning difficulties. She will be allowed a few hours with her son before he is taken into foster care. Miss Robertson, of Dunfermline, Fife, who is 26 weeks pregnant, said: "I couldn't believe it. I am so upset—I can't stop crying. Mr. McDougall, an artist, said: "Social Services are ruining our lives. As we are not married—because social workers would not let us marry—it seems I have no rights as a dad at all."*[12]

Precisely when is someone too stupid to wed? Does any bride or groom fully "understand the implications of getting married?" And who is prepared to play God, deciding which parents are fit to sire children and which are not? God himself has never drawn a line, apparently being divinely grateful for omniscient county councils making such ponderous judgments on his behalf.

Today, it's the marginally-intelligent who fail to qualify as parents. Left to Leftists, tomorrow it will be misguided religious folks who fail to qualify. Think that's a bridge too far even for liberals? Consider the bridge of "emotional abuse" in the following cases...

Editorial—*George and Liz, parents of 12-year-old Emily, who is visually impaired, sought to move Emily from a local school where she was bullied, under-performing, and miserable, to the Royal Blind School in Edinburgh. The local authority rejected the request.*

There was nothing remarkable about the request and denial until the couple discovered the minutes to a series of secret child-protection meetings at which they had been accused of emotionally abusing Emily by persisting with the placing request. George and Liz were then told that they would be taken to the Children's Reporter, who decides whether to start care proceedings against abusive parents.

After the local MSP [Member of Scottish Parliament] took up the family's cause, proceedings were eventually put on hold, allowing George and Liz to pursue their court case, which they won in May last year.

Had it not been for the intervention of a member of the Scottish parliament, George and Liz could well have had their precious Emily taken away from them by the state. The grounds? "Emotional abuse"—the definition of which is in the eye of the beholder. In this case, it was nothing more than parents persisting in pursuing what they thought was in the best interests of their vision-impaired daughter.

In other cases, as reported in Heidi Blake's editorial above (*The Daily Telegraph*, October 21, 2009), parents risked losing their children merely by criticising professionals about their child's care being referred to social services for investigation. Or, in another case, by filing a complaint against a pediatrician who obtusely had reported a small red mark on a two-year-old's cheek as a "non-accidental injury," leading to a social services nightmare.

How, then, do parents in Britain get slapped with the charge of "emotional abuse"? Sometimes for nothing more than questioning the wisdom of the nanny state's autocratic demigods. Sometimes—as we've already seen—merely by teaching faith and morals out of line with secular liberalism's perversely-twisted agenda. When Nanny gets uppity, no parent is safe from her clutches. Indeed, no *child* is safe from her clutches!

When Green turns mean

No reporting of liberal thinking about families in Britain would be complete without at least passing mention of some rather shocking liberal "chatter" from the chattering classes. If it sounds a little "out there," the fact remains that it's *out there...!*

News Report —*Jonathon Porritt, chair of the Government's Sustainable Development Commission, has said that families should be limited to two children and that more babies ought to be aborted in order to protect the planet. Porritt was adamant, saying, "I am unapologetic about asking people to connect up their own responsibility for their total environmental footprint and how they decide to procreate and how many children they think are appropriate. I think we will work our way towards a position that says having more than two children is irresponsible."*[13]

In case you're not already familiar with the history of the abortion movement in America that culminated in *Roe v. Wade*, it all started with precisely this kind of talk among the intellectual elite. Right here in America, none less notable a personage than Alexander Graham Bell lent his support to the eugenics movement, arguing that—since congenitally deaf parents were more likely to produce deaf children— deaf couples should not be permitted to marry.

As the eugenics movement gained momentum, "imbeciles" were not only refused the right to marry but they also were sterilized to prevent their having offspring. As the world now knows to its horror, forced sterilization became an art form under Hitler's Nazi regime, eventually morphing into the genocidal death camps of the holocaust.

Connecting those dots is more than mere gratuitous conjecture, as are the tell-tale links with America's abortion movement. Margaret Sanger, avowed socialist and founder of what emerged as America's greatest abortion provider—Planned Parenthood of America—began by urging the legalization of contraception for the lower classes. Call it "soft eugenics." Her early objections to abortion ("life is already begun") did not derail the inevitable course of her organization.

Depending on whom you believe, Sanger and fellow "negative eugenics" campaigners seriously contemplated eliminating blacks and undesirable immigrants through the use of birth control. What's not in dispute is that Planned Parenthood is one of the greatest Orwellian oxymorons of all time. Left to the liberal elite, it's *non-parenthood* that's been planned—specifically to accomplish whatever social goals might be desired. Once such a wide-open agenda is declared, there's no logical end to it. Eliminate the unfit? Rid society of undesirables? Save the planet? Whatever their particular goal of the moment, activist social planners on the liberal Left have little regard for human life, parents, or children.

In the context of this discussion it's worth noting that in both Britain and Europe the environmentally-radical Green Party wields political clout to a degree unknown in the United States. Yet with every passing year, the prospect of the Greens gaining support here in America increases exponentially—especially among a younger, environmentally-conscious generation. Make that also a pro-choice generation. And if you think this generation won't eventually put two and two together to get five, you are Pollyannaish to the max. The First Commandment (Thou shalt save the planet at all cost) ensures that, unless this generation shifts dramatically away from being pro-choice (actually, there are surprising signs it might!), fewer and fewer Americans would have any scruples whatsoever about the state virtually mandating abortions in aid of population control.

There's more than one way for Nanny to steal the children. And just how ironic is that? When radical environmentalism finally rules the day and the size of families is strictly limited by law, a once passionately pro-choice society will no longer have the slightest choice...nor any right of privacy. Inconvenient truths are vexing, aren't they?

The nationalization of childhood

Editorial —*The pressure organisation Action for Children worked out that successive British governments have made more than 400 major announcements relating to children and young people over the past 21 years, leading to 98 Acts of Parliament, 82 strategies, and 77 initiatives—many of which are no longer working. Three quarters of these policy changes and statements were made in the past decade under Labour. This is a sure sign of a governing class that has lost all sense of what are the proper limits of state activity.*

It is all of a piece with the nationalisation of childhood that has been going on for years now. It has become a displacement activity for a government that once was able to run large chunks of British national life when a good deal of our industry was state-owned but which now has to exercise its control-freakery in some other way.

Columnist for *The Daily Telegraph*, Philip Johnston, weighs in yet again in protest to what he calls "Barmy Britain through the looking glass" (September 28, 2009), an obvious reference to Lewis Carroll's captivating tale of the absurd. In a follow-on comment (October 19, 2009), Johnston further explains the bureaucratic mindset behind the absurdity in government policy towards parenting and children....

Editorial —*In his book* The Socialist Case, *Douglas Jay coined a now notorious observation that was once taken as gospel: "In the case of nutrition and health, just as in the case of education, the gentleman in Whitehall really does know better what is good for people than the people know for themselves." Although Jay often protested that he did not believe that civil servants know best, his phrase nevertheless captured an attitude of mind that the political Left has never shaken off.*

The idea that a compulsory registration scheme and all the other busybody paraphernalia that has caused such damage elsewhere in the public sector should now be visited upon people in their own homes is a step too far. The pied pipers of Whitehall are after our children and must be resisted.[14]

Whether Johnston is right about the motives and attitudes behind what he calls the "control-freakery" of the state in the affairs of the home, no one would dispute the high level of control currently exercised by the government over what once was the sacrosanct role of parenting. Nor would many dispute that the goal of EU bureaucrats, civil servants in Whitehall, local councils, and social services departments throughout Britain is to assume more and more responsibility for the care and keeping of Britain's young. What can that unseemly intrusion possibly suggest other than that the government is better suited to parenting than parents?

Or is it perhaps a corollary to the adage, "He who holds the purse strings, holds the power"—that he who controls the children, controls the nation? The communists certainly made no bones about it. The fascists just did it. And leftist liberals only barely disguise it—undoubtedly for purely pragmatic purposes.

It doesn't take a genius to figure out the plan. From time immemorial, the family has been the basic building block of society. As the family goes, so goes the nation. So you say you want to change the direction in which society is going? Then mold the children in that direction. How do you mold the children? Simply take that job away from the parents. The war of competing ideologies is fought on the battlefield of the young. Win that battle and you've won the war.

The "Thought for the Day" is sobering: The tragic loss of Britain's young men and women in the wars of Iraq and Afghanistan is penny-ante compared to the fierce battle being waged internally over Britain's young people. Already Britain is experiencing an unacceptable level of adolescent casualties (count the endless body bags one by one), and very nearly has lost the ideological war.

The decline and fall of the British family

Britain's "social Dunkirk"—it's most costly retreat from societal responsibility—came long ago when it abandoned the nuclear family. This catastrophic defeat occurred along three crucial fronts, the first being a failure to provide economic incentives to reward intact families. On the second front, the government was seduced into believing the liberal myth that any kind of mix-and-match family was equal to any other. Most costly of all was the third front, on which divorce became respectable and commonplace.

The economic front was a natural extension of Britain's notorious welfare state, producing a most unnatural result....

News Report—*Harriet Sergeant spent nine months researching Britain's most disadvantaged youngsters. Her report contends that single motherhood is encouraged by the Government's promise of benefits and rent-free accommodation, and that as the state takes the place of fathers as the family's main provider, more young men are growing up without a male role model.*

As one young man who had recently been released from prison told Sergeant, "If I had a father, I would have got a good hiding and I probably wouldn't be here now." Another young man (who is on the police list of top-ten troublemakers in his town) said: "You need a dad for growing up."[15]

In study after study, two things are abundantly clear: First, that Britain has disincentivized traditional marriages, giving financial encouragement for unmarried parenting. Second, that this policy results in a plethora of social ills, from crime to inferior education to job instability to future generations repeating the same destructive social patterns—all at a huge economic cost to the nation. The government price tag for police, education, health services, and child benefit payments made necessary by Britain's failed family policies is bringing Britain to its financial knees.

But it's not just about money. More importantly, it's about young men without fathers. And about young girls mimicking the destructive lifestyle of their unmarried mothers. And about a liberal culture that is more committed to non-judgmentalism than common sense when it comes to family structure and the indispensable role it plays in society. Some might say it's a "value-neutral" culture, but there's no such thing. Every culture has its core values—some solid, built on the conservative rock of faith and family; some built on the same shifting liberal sands into which they have poked their collective heads, ignoring the calamitous social train wreck they've caused in favor of hubristic self-delusion. But facts don't go away that easily....

Editorial —*The demise of the traditional family set-up is continuing despite growing evidence that children suffer when they are not raised by a married mother and father. Data published by the Office for National Statistics show that in 2007, 44.4 percent of live births were outside marriage. The proportion is the highest on record, up from 43.7 percent the previous year, and has risen from just 9 percent in 1976, when illegitimacy was taboo....Among British-born mothers the proportion of babies born out of wedlock is already likely to be above the landmark 50 percent.*

The marriage rate in England and Wales is now the lowest since it was first calculated in 1862, as the population increases but the number of people getting married falls. Critics say the declining popularity of marriage and the rising numbers of unmarried parents are partly the fault of Labour, which insists all types of relationships are equally valid and has removed financial incentives for couples to stay together.

In this column of March 27, 2009, Martin Beckford, Social Affairs Correspondent for *The Daily Telegraph*, highlights the ever-widening gap between conservative and liberal social values at ground zero. Sometimes Nanny doesn't steal the children outright, only robs them of the advantages they are due by the natural order of marriage, parenting, and a supportive, sympathetic government.

Without doubt, the more-liberal Labour party has contributed its fair share to the demise of the family, but the more-conservative Tories are not without fault. They too have countenanced a culture of tolerance for all things immoral—whether sexual promiscuity, shameless cohabitation, or civil partnerships (and now "marriage") for homosexuals. Insistence by the Conservative Party leader, David Cameron, that "family matters" is a sham. Along with Labour and Lib Dems, the Conservatives are still loathe to take on the gay lobby demanding gay marriage, or risk offending the significant voting bloc represented by the millions of heterosexual couples living out of wedlock.

America catching up fast, through No Fault of its own

Not every battle over the family has been lost in Britain. To its credit, in 2001 the Government pulled the plug on legislation adopting American-style "no fault" divorce—whereby no moral fault (such as adultery) need be proved in order to obtain a divorce. In the States, the "no fault" concept was dreamed up to minimize the acrimony typically involved in a divorce, and to speed up the process. Yet any initial thoughts that splitting up the family this way would avoid unhappy or abusive marriages have been overwhelmingly outweighed by messier divorces than advertised and long-term emotional damage to all concerned.

The result of "no fault" divorce (along with a host of other cultural factors weighing in) is that divorce in America has sky-rocketed, even among those professing to be conservative, church-going Christians. It's been a nightmare for husbands and wives, children, and the whole of society—but especially for the children. When the family splits, whether in the U.S. or in the U.K., Nanny is always waiting on the doorstep to take the kids—sometimes permanently (and often unfairly) from one spouse or the other; or perhaps from grandparents, denied access to their own grandchildren; or effectively from both parents through mystifying, nonsensical custody and visitation schemes. Seems that Nanny missed the point of the Solomon story and is all too eager to split the child.

America is also fast gaining ground on Britain in the number of couples living together outside of marriage and producing offspring from those unsanctioned liaisons. Whether resulting from cohabitation or otherwise, births to unwed mothers in America has reached an all-time high of 40 percent.[16]

If there is any good news, U.S. abortions have dropped to their lowest levels in decades. Those who might otherwise wish to attribute the decline to a greater use of contraceptives are generally the very same "safe-sex" campaigners who insist that we still need more and more sex education to stem teen pregnancies.

A more likely explanation for the decrease in abortions is that there are fewer and fewer abortion providers out there, owing principally to a growing awareness among physicians of the early viability of life in the womb. Rather curiously, the wedge was not so much a matter of *morality* as *technology*. Thanks to technical advances, we can now *see* the baby in the womb at earlier and earlier stages, making it increasingly difficult for even the most liberal pro-choice advocates to deny that Margaret Sanger was right when she acknowledged the presence of life in the womb from the moment of conception onward.

This may also explain the many criminal homicide prosecutions and wrongful-death civil cases that over the past couple of decades have been successful even in some of America's most liberal jurisdictions (such as California) where "non-viable" fetuses have been killed in the womb. If a mother *wants* it to be a baby, then the law *affirms* that it is a baby, and provides the fetus every protection of the law—making it all the more problematic for anyone not wanting a baby to deny the obvious.

The growing trend not to abort might also be due in part to high-profile cases like that of Bristol Palin, daughter of former Alaska Governor Sarah Palin, who decided to keep her baby despite being unmarried. Indeed, there is the model case of Governor Palin herself, refusing to abort a baby with Down's Syndrome. For whatever reasons, the public mood seems to have shifted significantly away from the formerly-unassailable acceptability of abortion. Which raises an interesting observation....

Do you remember the Viet Nam protest slogan: "Suppose they gave a war and nobody came?" In the evolution of the rancorous pro-choice/pro-life debate, *Roe v. Wade* has been modified, limited, and circumscribed, but never overturned. By and large, abortions are still very much legal today. But with every passing year it becomes increasingly clear that the pro-life camp may have lost its biggest battle (in the courts) but is now on the brink of winning the war for the hearts and minds of American women. Today's question—"Suppose abortion were absolutely legal and nobody had one?"—is the encouraging light at the end of a long, dark tunnel.

If the abortion wars are anything to go by, there is yet hope for America (and even Britain) when it comes to other political madness involving the family. Even when we have gotten it terribly wrong as a nation, nothing says we can't come to our senses and do an about-face.

Time to fire the nanny

For leftist liberals who consider themselves to be on the cutting edge of progressive thought, it is instructive to remember that they're merely pushing along a tired old ball which first got rolling with the ancients. There is, for example, the notion in Plato's *Republic* "that the wives of our guardians are to be common, and their children are to be common, and no parent is to know his own child, nor any child his parent." Radical stuff, eh? Communal living aside, the more disturbing thought among the philosophers of old was that children belonged to the state rather than to the parents. If by any chance you missed it, that's precisely the bottom line of this entire chapter: the ever-creeping nationalization of children. What goes around, comes around. Among Britain's elitist ruling class, it's (as Yogi would say) déjà vu all over again!

Dress it up as they wish, and masquerade all they want—the truth is that Britain's nannycrats, together with America's liberal-Left counterparts, are working night and day to confiscate your children and grandchildren for the benefit of the state, as surely as if they were parcels of property being acquired by eminent domain.

Whether it be micro-managing how parents rear their children and criminalizing even the most reasonable of spankings, or forcing adolescents into school at earlier and earlier ages, or clamping down on faith-based home-schoolers, or communicating with students behind parents' backs, or removing children from the home for spurious reasons, or daring to suggest a limit to the number of children per family, or formulating government policies which encourage parenting out of wedlock—the tapestry of twisted family policies being woven by the liberal-Left is not just irritating bureaucratic meddling, or even leftist loonies running amuck, but a deliberate, calculated treason against the very foundation of society.

Before Nanny steals any more of our kids, it's time we threw her out of the House...and the Senate, and the White House, and the State Capitol, and the City Council, and the courts, the regulatory agencies, the social service departments, the universities, the accrediting agencies, and even the churches, if necessary. It's not exactly a conspiracy theory, but already in America a very British-looking nanny is everywhere... watching and waiting...plotting and planning.

2

Giving New Meaning to
Liberal Education

Children are like wet cement.
Whatever falls on them makes an impression.

—Haim Ginott

Editorial—*No, really, this is it. Bring on the revolution. Man the Lego barricades! Devise 88 Pampers dirty-bombs! Send in stormtroops to smear puréed apple and vomit over the concrete barricades of Westminster! Ofsted, that giant mutant Godzilla of the education world, has finally stepped over the last line and shown how deeply the State despises us.*

Two young detective constables in Aylesbury became pregnant at the same time and agreed to apply for a job share. Each would look after the other's infant during the long, sometimes unpredictable shifts. It suited the police work and the children; the babies grew up in homely sibling amity for two and a half years. The officers, relaxed and reassured, were presumably all the better at tracking down Buckinghamshire felons.

Then, DC Leanne Shepherd sadly relates, "An Ofsted lady came to the door" and accused her of illegal childminding. Because the arrangement was deemed a "reward," she should have been registered, inspected and compelled to deliver and record the 65 targets of the new early years curriculum. Ofsted considered the private friendly swap no different from a commercial

45

enterprise. DC Shepherd says that she was not even given grace to go through the hoops, but had to put her crying, baffled child into a nursery to complete her police work. Result: unhappy child, anxious mothers, wasted fees.

[For goodness sake!] What has an "office for standards in education" to do with babies crawling around in their mums' friends' houses anyway? Government and its regulations exist to defend us from incompetent or bad strangers, not from our mates. Today, it seems, ordinary life has been made illegal. Do you remember voting for that?

So writes an angry Libby Purves in her *Times* column of September 29, 2009, along with a chorus of other outraged commentators and members of the fuming public. From the comfortable, unknowing distance of the States, one could be forgiven for wondering why the education watchdog, Ofsted, has anything at all to do with childcare arrangements. But that's the nature of unofficial political bodies in Britain ("quangos" as they're often called). There's a watchdog for this and a watchdog for that. Even watchdogs of the watchdogs! Like any other dogs, government-appointed quangos have a tendency to wander outside their appointed boundaries in search of greener grass. Or perhaps we should say *yellow* grass, given the manner by which they mark their territory. Are we surprised, then, that Ofsted should mark its own territory outside home base in a similarly crude manner?

Unlike many of the current outrages in Britain these days, this sad story has a different ending...at least for now. Due to overwhelming public outcry (it's never too late!), we have the following...

Breaking News—*The Children's Secretary has told Ofsted's chief inspector that reciprocal childcare arrangements should no longer be treated as childminding.*[17]

Well, thank goodness for at least one victory for common sense! If only this ludicrous incident were just a bizarre result of one petty-minded official going ballistic. Unfortunately, given the law's ambiguous wording, it was far more systemic than that. Had it not been for a rare public revolt in the press and across the air waves, other hard-working, law-abiding parents up and down the land risked running afoul of intrusive government regulation with their clean records and reputations forever blighted.

The obvious questions raised by this case are many indeed. In the first place, what kind of pervasive social attitude would encourage someone to report this benign childcare arrangement? Smacks of informant cultures typical of totalitarian regimes, doesn't it? Call it Neighborhood Watch on Marxist steroids.

And just how absurd is it to require background security checks for two mothers, both of whom are police officers! More interesting yet, how did Ofsted officials (burdened with the heavy duties of ensuring quality education in Britain) have the time to tackle this dubious violation of the education code, and then threaten even more time (and money) spent surveiling these two childcaring desperados? Still more serious, whatever happened to prudence and good judgment along the way, either in the legislation itself or in its administration?

Of course the overriding question always begging to be asked is the role of government in child-rearing and education. As we've already seen, the Government in Britain today assumes it knows how to rear and educate children better than parents who are directly responsible for their children's well-being. No wonder parents often have limited or no options when controversial programs are introduced in the educational arena.

News *Report—As part of new compulsory lessons in personal, social, health and economic education, sex education will now be compulsory in all schools. Faith-based schools will be permitted to teach sex education consistent with the "tenets of their faith," but must nevertheless teach the required curriculum, including lessons on same-sex relationships, contraception, and abortion.*

The Schools Secretary was reassuring, saying: "You can teach the promotion of marriage, you can teach that you shouldn't have sex outside of marriage.

What you can't do is deny young people information about contraception outside of marriage. The same arises in homosexuality. Some faiths have a view about what in religious terms is right and wrong. What they cannot do, though, is not teach the importance of tolerance."[18]

The Schools Secretary's grudging nod to religious beliefs must surely be cold comfort to Roman Catholic schools opposed to abortion, contraception, homosexual behavior, and sex outside of marriage. Can't you just hear the lessons now? "Contraception is a violation of divine law, students, and subject to eternal damnation. But if you insist, then here's how you use condoms...." Across a wide spectrum of moral issues, the dilemma would be equally problematic for many other faith-based schools.

So many troubling issues are raised by this Initiative that it's hard to know where to begin. The most basic question is: Why in the name of reason are five-year-olds (not all that far removed from potty-training) the target of state-imposed sex education? How many five-year-olds are involved in risky sexual behavior, or are getting pregnant, or turning up with sexually transmitted diseases? What possible good can come from talking explicitly about sex with adolescents?

Defying all sanity, the Family Planning Association in Britain (now known as "Brook") recently launched a sex-education comic book for primary school children. Included was a puzzle asking children to draw a line from the words *vagina* and *testicles* to the corresponding areas on pictures of a naked girl and boy.[19] With such sexually-graphic literature brazenly invading the public schoolroom, it will take all the steam that Thomas the Tank Engine can muster to pull this load of nonsense off the track before young innocents are forced to a premature and damaging coming-of-age.

To get a better idea of what kind of organizations are influencing the British government in formulating its sex-education guidelines, check out Brook's website where among other advice for teens is this blurb: "As you grow up, it's normal to think sexually about both the same sex and the opposite sex. Some people know exactly who they fancy, but others may experiment with sexual experiences, including those with members of the same sex, during the years they are exploring their own sexuality." And then there's this open-ended endorsement of homosexuality: "It can feel like you are expected to be straight and that being gay is somehow wrong. It's not. It's just you."

Even if heterosexuality is "just you," as it usually is, is that a moral license to express your sexuality any way you please? Secularists will never "get it," but *orientation* and *conduct* are distinctly separate issues. You can be sure such careful moral distinctions never get the slightest passing mention when teens and younger adolescents are being sexually indoctrinated. And don't forget how this works. Private-sector bodies such as Brook act as cozy advisors to the Government, pushing an extremist sexual agenda that ends up being law and policy. Can you imagine the furor if faith-based organizations here in America wanted to proselytize students with the message that homosexual conduct and sex outside of marriage is immoral?

It was this self-same Brook, incidentally, that recently announced a program whereby boys of 13 would be issued with "credit cards" allowing them to pick up free condoms at football grounds and scout huts.[20] Sex for teens? Bring it on! Just y'all be careful now, you hear?

When will Britain (and America) wake up to the obvious—that the increase in sex-education programs has served only to promote an increase in sexual activity, with its attendant spin-offs of teen pregnancy and sexually transmitted disease? The problem is not that young people don't know enough about sex. The problem is that they already know too much! From television and radio to every billboard, magazine, newspaper, and internet site, sex is the omnipresent goddess of our modern culture. Who needs kindergarten teachers spelling out the details? If five-year-olds can figure out computers and the mysteries of cyberspace, they can jolly well figure out human anatomies and the mysteries of sex, all in good time.

Far from grasping the hard truth that sex education is both a failure and destructively counterproductive, the Teenage Pregnancy Independent Advisory Group, involved in pushing for compulsory sex-education lessons, is calling for sex education (buckle your seat belts) to "include teaching children about sexual pleasure in order to cut teenage pregnancies"! Yes, you read that right.

Among the members of TPIAG is Professor Roger Ingham of the University of Southampton, one of the authors of a National Health Service (NHS) sex-education leaflet recently distributed to teachers throughout Britain. The leaflet, titled *Pleasure*, urges that children need to be taught about sexual pleasure and encouraged to discuss "experimentation in sexual relationships," including how condoms can be used "to enhance sexual pleasure."[21]

Is it any wonder that the Government's "forward-thinking" Teenage Pregnancy Strategy has fallen dramatically short of its target to halve teenage conceptions? Sadly, it's the sex-obsessed sex activists who have absolutely no conception!

News Report—YouTube has banned a *graphic NHS video for teenagers depicting a schoolgirl giving birth on a playing field. The video was produced as part of NHS Leicester City's drive to encourage teenagers to use contraception. The video shows a screaming teenage girl giving birth at the centre of a shouting and jeering crowd of pupils.*

A spokesperson said the video was intended to "raise awareness for all under-18s getting pregnant in Leicester." The home page of the Leicester City Teenage Pregnancy and Parenthood Partnership is designed to look like an open diary, with calendared phrases like, "Matt dumped me;" "period late;" "go with Sarah to chemist to get condoms (should get pregnancy test as well)."[22]

While local government has been reduced to lurid sensationalism in battling an epidemic of teen pregnancy, the collective wisdom of Britain's brightest sex mandarins is to stem the problem by teaching children about the pleasures of sex! Oh, yes, certainly they'll be taught about the risks as well, but those can be minimized through contraception and other safe-sex practices. And of course if all else fails, there's always abortion as a back-up. Today, half of all teenage pregnancies in Britain end in abortion. Which only begs the question: With sex education having been taught in the schools for years now, how did all these girls manage to get pregnant in the first place?

Pop quiz: What in the world did the world do before mandatory sex-education classes for adolescents? Answer: It kept spinning along nicely with a combination of parental guidance, church teaching, and societal expectations—all contributing to a world in which there was no epidemic of teen pregnancy, abortion, and STDs. You say that's ancient history prior to television, R-rated movies, the decline of faith, and the breakdown of the nuclear family? Bingo!

Co-opting parents by limiting opt-outs

Returning briefly to the newly-mandated sex-education curriculum, the Government grudgingly has given concessions to objecting parents...up to a point.

News Report—*Thousands of parents lose the right to opt their children out of sex-education lessons when those children turn 15, according to the government's new sex-education guidelines.*

Chris Keates, general secretary of the NASUWT teachers' union, said that "allowing parents to withdraw their child from sex and relationship lessons up to the age of 15 does not sit well with statutory entitlement. If it is important enough to be a statutory provision, then it is important enough for every child to receive it."

Simon Blake, Chief Executive of Brook, urged that any opt-out provision for parents should be removed. "You cannot reconcile children's right to high-quality sex and relationship education with the parental right of withdrawal."[23]

So here we go again. If ever there were any doubt, children's rights clearly trump parents' rights. Or to put it more forcefully, children's rights trump even children's *responsibilities*. And we wonder why Britain has raised a generation of selfish, bullying, drunken, disrespectful hellions? If you take a close look at Britain's children who are *not* drunken, disrespectful, selfish bullies, you will find intact families, serious grounding in religious faith, parental authority, firm discipline... and a proper disdain for all things PC.

Also noteworthy in these news reports is the invariable pairing of "sex education" with "relationship education." As already mentioned regarding Brook's sexual-identity advice, behind every so-called "public health" initiative relating to teen sex you'll inevitably discover the gay lobby pushing its own agenda. Obviously nothing to do with teen pregnancy....

As for any right of parental opt-out, someone's clearly not thinking about the bigger picture. While the government is desperate to dampen rampant bullying among schoolchildren, it turns right around and hands the little rascals one more reason to bully their classmates. Forcing opt-out children to walk out of the classroom before all the sex talk begins is sure to bring a predictable barrage of scorn and teasing from fellow students. From that point forward, those hapless children might as well have leprosy.

Not just sex education

If perhaps one might dismiss all the controversy about sex-education courses as merely a philosophical difference between progressives and prudes regarding the nature and extent of giving school children appropriate information about the birds and bees, it still doesn't explain the obsession with sex nudging its way elsewhere into the British educational scheme. Consider, for example, the latest sexing up of the exam process known as GCSEs (General Certificate of Secondary Education), taken by students 14 to 16 years old. The largest of Britain's three exam boards, the Assessment and Qualifications Alliance (AQA), is soon to spice up the curriculum with a course of study guaranteed to attract many (particularly male) students.

Breaking News—*It has emerged that GCSE pupils could be analysing sexually explicit lads' mags as part of a Media Studies course. Teens could be asked to compare the "style and tone" of sexually lurid magazines, many of which display semi-nude women on their covers.*[24]

No one will ever accuse leftist liberals of being overly-fussed about consistency. They righteously decry the objectification of women, listing that mortal sin near the top of secularism's own Ten Commandments of "Thou shalt nots." Yet the unfettered sexual freedom demanded by these same liberals inevitably comes full circle back to the objectification of women. No surprise, then, that the progressive educrats put in charge of evaluating Britain's secondary students would come up with such a debauched idea as using pornography for GCSE training and testing.

And what a grand irony. For all the current hyper-mania over pedophilia in Britain, now requiring police background checks for a substantial percentage of the adult population, the most widespread sexual abuse of Britain's children comes at the hands of sex-obsessed social planners robbing entire generations, first, of sexual innocence and then of sexual responsibility. Worse yet, in the process they contribute in no small way to the sexually-saturated, sordid minds that actually end up being the very sexual predators Britain so much fears. Go figure.

Maybe it's time someone ran a background check on Britain's elitist educrats. Odds are that you'd discover a common genetic trait: control-freak socialist hubris. The warning for America is that such elitist arrogance among government and social planners knows no national boundaries.

Liberal agenda shrinking traditional curriculum

In case you're wondering how a chapter on education got derailed into a discussion of sex, the answer is: Exactly! More to the point, how in the world did schools designed for teaching English, history, science, and math get derailed into teaching anything and everything *but* English, history, science, and math? Britain's national curriculum is an ever-shrinking set of core courses, once deemed fundamental to a quality education. It hasn't escaped the notice of such luminaries as Prince Charles.

News Report—*As the Government pushes ahead with proposals for the biggest overhaul of lessons for under-11s since the National Curriculum was introduced 20 years ago, Bernice McCabe, who runs the Prince's Teaching Institute, said teaching by "theme" risked undermining basic knowledge of key subjects such as history, geography and science.*

Prince Charles has warned that the "voguish" drive towards fashionable teaching "denied youngsters an understanding of their place in history."[25]

It only gets worse. Even the traditional core subjects still permitted to remain in the curriculum have been excised of serious content in favor of the "vogish fadism" referenced by Prince Charles.

Breaking News—*Ofqual [the regulator of Britain's qualifications and exams] has warned that standards in new-style GCSEs had been compromised by the introduction of a "21st Century" science curriculum, which now includes global warming, recycling, GM crops, mobile phone technology and bird flu—all designed to make the subject more relevant to teenagers.*[26]

What may be "more relevant" is no less in need of careful analysis than the subjects thought to be less relevant but indispensable to the development of critical thinking. One would think that the still-controversial issue of global warming, for example, could benefit from a thorough working knowledge of hard science. And that mobile phone technology would be greatly enhanced by some expertise in math. Beyond that, who knows what other "relevant issues" will arise during one's lifetime for which a firm grounding in fundamental subjects will be crucial? Undeterred by reason, the Government plows blindly ahead, pandering to whatever is trendy or the most talked-about hot topic. Sound familiar even here in the States?

But the problem is deeper than merely a penchant for the latest and greatest. Liberal change-agents are keenly aware that fact-based history has a way of exposing the shallowness and fraud of fashionable government initiatives. To the truly educated thinker, "inconvenient truths" fostered by the government (about, say, the environment) might not be true at all. That being the case, an understanding of math, science, and history could well prevent social brainwashing—a prospect which for leftist liberals intent on reinventing society is too great a threat to ignore. Better to dumb down the proletariat, creating a mental vacuum begging to be filled with trendy progressive rubbish.

Editorial—*The latest initiative by our "Children's Secretary," Ed Balls, is to abolish what remains of fact-based teaching of history and geography in our schools....The ruthless drive of educational progressives to eliminate history-teaching from schools has been under way since the 1960s. The aim is to ensure that children know nothing about their country's past or how the world came to be as it is, leaving their minds blankly open to whatever vacuous progressive claptrap is fed to them.*

In his desire to chuck history onto what Lenin called "the scrapheap of history," Mr Balls may have to make an exception, however. A campaign is now being mounted in the European Parliament to make it compulsory for children to be taught the history of the EU. According to Mário David, the Portuguese MEP leading the campaign...it is vital to counter all the "lying, cheating and mistrust" that surrounds the EU in the minds of the peoples of Europe. Our children must therefore be indoctrinated accordingly.

Christopher Booker's comment (Daily Telegraph, November 21, 2009) underscores the way in which education has been viewed in all totalitarian states as a tool of social manipulation. In order to re-write history, you have to abolish history. Under the Soviet regime, even music and art fell victim to statist thought control. If it can happen in Russia, it can happen in Britain. If it can happen in Britain, it can happen in the good ol' US of A.

Not just religiously neutral, but anti-religious

If there is any truth supremely inconvenient to Britain's educrats, it's Truth with a capital "T". Whereas many folks easily confuse the words *relevant* and *relative*, educrats are all too aware of the distinction. They know that, while *relevant* and *relative* have become more and more intimately interdependent these days, to keep it that way the very concept of Truth has to be guarded against with all possible vigor.

In terms of moral absolutes, *truth* is the sworn enemy of *relative*. When it comes to abortion, for example, what's true in fact must be overcome by talk of that which is only relative. Those who rightly demand absolute truth about weapons of mass destruction in Iraq do an abrupt U-turn when it comes to absolute truth about life in the womb. Or the real causes of climate change. Or even when it comes to fraudulently claiming Parliamentary expenses. (For any Americans who might have missed it, Britain has been rocked by an embarrassing expenses scandal involving Members of Parliament.)

So what do you do when *truth* threatens the *relativity* needed to push a socio-political agenda that is progressive and thus *relevant*? First of all, make "Truth" lower-case, as in *truth*. Better yet, pluralize it to *truths*, as if there might possibly be more than one truth about any given matter. At that point, abracadabra, *truth* magically becomes *relative*.

Of course, there's a huge hurdle to cross in reducing capital-T Truth to lower case. For if there is no Truth with a capital "T," then no single individual's truth can be appealed to as being superior to anyone else's truth. The terrorist's truth is as valid as the gang member's truth; and his truth is as true as a cheating MP's; and hers is as true as the abortionist's; and his as true as the anti-abortionist's; and hers as true as the homosexual's; and his as true as the anti-gay campaigner's; and so on down the line. To what truth can any of us appeal? The fickle finger of political correctness? The current party-line? Opinion polls? Majority rule? The latest decision of the Court of Human Rights?

Any serious truth claim of any kind intrinsically assumes an Ultimate Truth out there somewhere. Which itself assumes a universal standard of morality naturally associated with the transcendent, the divine, and the eternal. Which is to say God. Which, for secularists (whether outright God-deniers or those merely paying lip-service to God), presents a huge problem. For secularist educrats, in particular, it is a double dilemma. How can you hold students to absolute standards of learning and conduct without tacitly admitting the inadmissible? If "facts" are deemed to be true, and truth ultimately is associated with a problematic God, what can you do but denigrate facts? Especially fact-statements concerning faith in God...?

News Report—*A school principal has said that it was right for a school to chastise a five-year-old girl who expressed her beliefs on heaven and hell, because children must not be permitted to present faith as fact. The comment followed an investigation against a receptionist at the school after she sent an email to her church friends asking them to pray for the situation involving her daughter Jasmine.*

The problem arose while Jasmine was talking with her friend about God and heaven. When an older classmate asked Jasmine how a person could go to hell, young Jasmine answered: "By not believing in Jesus." For that, Jasmine was reprimanded by her teacher, and her mother, the school's receptionist, was also called on the carpet.

The head of the school said that Jasmine was entitled to talk about her faith, but that her answer was unacceptable. "What we don't say is 'this is the truth,' because I think that is unfair to children, and it doesn't help them in the long run when they have to make up their own minds when they're adults."[27]

Forget the lunacy of expecting a five-year-old to carefully nuance a discussion of faith so as not to cause offense to her classmates. The larger question is: How does a head teacher know with any certitude what is *unfair*? Is his idea of fairness any more than his own personal opinion? For that matter, was it *fair* to rebuke Jasmine's mother? If so, on what basis apart from objective truth is anyone to make such a judgment?

Lest it pass unnoticed, the most crucial issue of all was the truth-claim presented by Jasmine's statement that a person could end up in hell by not believing in Jesus. If her belief is true—really, actually, and factually *true*—wouldn't that be a truth worth knowing? If it is false (having no basis whatsoever in fact), what have secularists to fear?

Of one thing you can be sure: it wasn't *how* Jasmine said what she said, but *what* she said that provoked the reaction from school officials. You can safely bet the farm that the teacher would not have taken the slightest notice of Jasmine's opinion had it not involved a statement of faith; nor would Jasmine's mother have been called on the carpet had not her email involved a prayer request. In education as elsewhere, secularism in the name of "diversity" has sunk to an all-time low. In Britain today, everyone has a seat at the table...except Christians vocal about their faith. And that, apparently, includes five-year-olds.

Was this shocking episode merely an over-reaction from one insensitive teacher under unique circumstances? If only....

News Report—*A new GCSE course titled Religon and Belief in Today's World will include studies in Druidism, Rastafarianism and the "rise of atheism." Students will also study the influence of religions such as the Order of Bards, Ovates and Druids. Religious attitudes towards medical and sexual ethics, including areas such as same-sex relationships and cloning, will be covered. The "groundbreaking" new syllabus largely excludes the Bible and other religious texts.*[28]

Back home in the States, the American Civil Liberties Union has little need to worry about any genuine church-state conflict—first, because there never has been an established national church, and second, because the established (indeed entrenched) Church of England has proved no defense against the rise of secularist religion in Britain. It is only owing to its official ties with the Church of England that Britain has maintained Religious Education in state schools for as long as it has. The surprise is that it's lasted this long before being watered down beyond all recognition.

The difference between Britain and America (putting it starkly and not altogether fairly) is that Britain is a faithless Christian nation while America is headed in the same direction, just lagging far behind. We may no longer have prayers in the public classroom, or the Ten Commandments on the wall, or the teaching of divine Creation, or the celebration of Christmas in many schools outside the Bible-belt. But at least to this point Americans are still very much a religious people, whose regard for the Christian faith held by a majority of citizens continues to have a beneficent influence throughout its educational system, both public and private.

The worry is America's eventual slide away from faith into the throes of British-style secularism, which in Britain is already threatening to gain control over even faith-based schools.

Breaking News—*Under the Liberal Democrats' plans, pupils who are "old enough to decide for themselves" could opt out of faith-based school assemblies, regardless of their parents' wishes. Not only that, but while state-funded faith schools may continue to select pupils that share their beliefs, atheists must be free to teach in any role other than Religious Education. The Lib Dems have been accused of wanting to ban all faith schools, but the party has denied the accusation.[29]*

Maybe the Lib Dems aren't yet at the point of banning all faith schools, but that's only because they haven't a prayer of ever becoming the majority party. Should some minor miracle occur, you can bet it wouldn't be long before banning faith schools would be a centerpiece plank in their platform. Nor are they the only ones bandying about that radical idea....

News Report—Vocal members of the National Union of Teachers (NUT) have called for faith groups being completely banned from running schools, saying that faith schools create "segregated schooling." In response, representatives of the country's 7,000 faith schools argue that their religious ethos is the reason why they consistently out-perform their non-religious counterparts.[30]

Fortunately, the aptly-named NUT organization will not have its way anytime soon, though surely it's only a matter of time before secularist educrats trim the sails of faith schools to such an extent that there will be little to distinguish them from non-faith schools.

While it would take much longer to shut down the venerable institution of private, faith-based schools in the States, even now the secularist trajectory bears close watching. The Achilles heel already being exploited by liberal social architects is the government's indirect financial role in making private education economically viable. Charitable tax deductions, federally-guaranteed student loans, and governmental grants of all kinds pave the way for the inevitable reality that whoever holds the purse strings also holds the reins of control. Ask any private school administrator about today's government regulation, and you'll quickly appreciate what road we're on. Ask them about the escalating political correctness mandated by their various accrediting agencies, and you'll begin to realize just how far along that road we've already traveled.

A road too far

Speaking of traveling, Britain has traveled so far down the motorway of political correctness that quite extraordinary concessions are being made for the children of those who call themselves travellers, Roma (Romani), or Gypsies. (Even what you call these fringe social groups is a matter of closely-scrutinized PC, with the correct terminology changing by the day. Shades of the same diversity language battles constantly being fought in the States.)

News Report—*A study published by the Department for Children, Schools, and Families urges that all of England's secondary schools should have a teacher trained to support pupils from Gypsy families. "For Roma pupils, having a member of staff who could speak their language and demonstrate good insight into their cultural experiences was comforting for pupils and their parents," the study said. It also urged staff to attend traveller events, celebrate key events in their history, and show sensitivity towards potentially contentious issues such as sex education.*

The study recommended that schools should exercise leniency towards pupils' homework and behaviour to increase their confidence and boost standards. Gypsy pupils are four times more likely to be expelled from school, and a low percentage of Gypsy, Roma, and traveller pupils performed as well on standardized tests as other teenagers nationally.[31]

First off, did you catch that line about showing sensitivity regarding potentially contentious issues such as sex education? You mean sensitivity for Gypsies, but not for Christians? Since there are conscientious Christians even among Gypsies, what a dilemma that must be for politically correct educrats.

This is not the place for a full-blown discussion of the complex issues surrounding Britain's unique Gypsy culture, for the most part foreign to the American experience. Suffice it to say that if you want a snapshot of Britain's current social lunacy, you could hardly do better than follow the whole Gypsy conversation. As with any sub-set of society, there is often less homogeneity among those who comprise a fringe minority than might be expected. Among Gypsies, Roma, and travellers, you'll invariably find the good, the bad, and the ugly.

Unfortunately, the bad and the ugly tend to dominate the travellers scene, giving the collective roaming populace its reputation for being violence-prone, tax-dodging thieves. Hiding behind the cover of human rights legislation, criminal-element travellers can make life miserable for unsuspecting land owners onto whose property these

PORTRAIT OF AN OBAMA NANNY STATE

hooligans forcefully make their way. For the worst of Gypsies, Roma, and so-called New Age travellers, fences are but invitations to come in and devastate the place. Backed by specialist legal experts, the anti-social travellers know precisely how long they can get away with terrorizing the locals before outrageously slow legal processes finally kick in.

The disreputable types are further emboldened, knowing that the police won't dare touch them. No matter how much damage they do to farms and nearby villages, not a single ASBO will be filed. Nor does it seem to matter how much rubbish, filth, and even human excrement they leave behind. If anyone else were to engage in such a lifestyle, you can be sure that Health and Safety would shut them down in a heartbeat. But not so with this lot. They are a law unto themselves. Indeed, Surrey Police have recently spent £15,000 ($25,000) producing a DVD telling officers that Gypsies are *not* "tax-dodging thieves." Good thing they have the DVD, otherwise they'd never come to that conclusion based on the evidence at hand.

Which brings us back to the children of many of these same travellers. Is it any surprise that they are four times likely to be expelled for behavior problems? Or that their chances for academic excellence are virtually nihl? It is loony enough that Britain should give *carte blanche* protection to travellers who so blatantly flaunt the law. To mollycoddle their children at school is merely to compound the lunacy, not to mention perpetuate the cycle of dissonance so characteristic of this socio-cultural population.

Do-gooder educrats rarely see beyond the trees to the forest. Whatever the particular concern, this is always the essential difference between liberals and conservatives (not necessarily to be confused with Lib Dems and Conservatives, nor yet Democrats and Republicans). It's not a matter of motives. Everybody wants to do the right thing. What matters is the approach. Whereas liberals tend to focus on individual hard cases (an admirable aim in itself), conservatives tend to focus on the bigger picture (which makes them appear uncaring). It's not that conservatives don't appreciate the pain of those in difficult circumstances, only that they believe hard cases make bad law and policy overall, and that by changing the larger frame the best interests of society, including all those lamentable hard cases, will be better served.

The point here is that no amount of politically-correct strategies in a nation's schools can ever overcome the underlying problems in society. It is an enduring myth of liberalism that more money and more education is the answer to every social ill. To the contrary, the most effective cure for a nation's social ills—character—is not formed by either money or education, at least not unless we're talking about genuine, faith-based moral education, which is the last thing secularist educrats want to happen.

Despite liberal social planners' best intentions, their artificially-contrived PC initiatives are simply no substitute for solid, fundamental values. When faith and morals are expelled from school and political correctness is brought in to fill the vacuum, such a misguided project can only fail.

Even more so is this the case when the larger culture is devoid of the bedrock values of faith and family. As we have already seen, Britain's liberal Nonsense Machine has already decreed it is unacceptable for parents to corporeally punish their children, even when done with moderation and restraint. And then there's the liberal lie that it really doesn't matter whether children are raised by two parents or only one. And also, quite incredibly, the growing notion that children receiving serious religious training in the home are as likely to be abused by that process as edified.

But then all of a sudden we see liberals wringing their hands over the lack of discipline in the schools. And bullying. And disrespect. So what's their answer? Punish any teacher courageously attempting to bring order to all the chaos they've created!

News *Report*— *After spending 31 years giving exemplary service to the cause of teaching, 62-year-old Michael Becker was preparing to retire. But* *all that changed when one of his students refused to stop telling racist jokes during a science lesson and Becker grabbed the boy by his belt and sweat shirt and removed him to an adjacent room. Becker was convicted of assault by beating and now departs his profession under a cloud of disgrace.[32]*

What? You mean to say there were no liberal activists rushing to defend Becker for standing up to racism? Can you imagine what they would have done if Becker had permitted such racism to go unchallenged in his classroom? Not surprisingly, Becker is not the only teacher who's run into the buzz saw of defiant pupils....

News Report—*Teacher Mark Ellwood asked one of his pupils to take off his coat and stop playing with his mobile phone. Responding defiantly "I will have you killed," the boy then threatened to stab Mr. Ellwood.*

If much of what we've reported in this chapter seems light-years away from the American experience, the lack of discipline and physical threats to teachers bears great resemblance to what's happening in school after school all across the land. Gangs, in particular, are high-profile terrorists in classroom these days.

And who, invariably, is waiting in the wings to press these bullies' cause in court? The ACLU, of course. The same ACLU that calls for greater and greater children's rights. The same ACLU that frustrates school boards and administrators seeking access to student lockers so as to control weapons and illegal drugs. The same ACLU that almost single-handedly has expelled faith and morals from America's schools. Most importantly, it's the same ACLU that is such a staunch ally of the loony liberal-Left in today's British government. If politics makes strange bedfellows, the ACLU and Britain's barmy social planners couldn't be more comfortable sharing the same cozy bed.

Time to get educated!

Still think the day won't come when the best and brightest of America's teachers are run out of the classroom by violent little squirts posing as students? When five-year-olds are no longer permitted to talk about faith in public schools? When sex-education will be dominated by lurid literature tantamount to porn? When reading, writing, and arithmetic are replaced by whatever might be the latest "relevant" hot topic? When faith-based schools are held hostage by secularist educrats and finally outlawed altogether?

If all of that never happens on this side of the Pond, it will only be because we've learned hard lessons from the British experience and stepped back from the brink.

3

A Nation of Pedophiles

So, first of all, let me assert my firm belief that
the only thing we have to fear is fear itself—
nameless, unreasoning, unjustified terror
which paralyzes needed efforts to convert retreat into advance.

—FRANKLIN D. ROOSEVELT

Editorial—*Have you been ISA-cleared? If you want a new job then you had soon better be. According to Sir Roger Singleton, head of the Independent Safeguarding Authority...a clean bill of health from his fledgling organisation will become as important as a professional qualification for any aspiring employee. It will announce to the world that you are not a paedophile, that you have not assaulted a child and do not pose a danger to vulnerable old people. The state will have decreed that you are not a monster.*

If you are coming around slowly to the view that this country is going mad then confirmation came yesterday with Sir Roger's comments in this newspaper. It is now, apparently, considered perfectly reasonable to regard the entire adult population as a potential pool of criminal suspects.

Even the NSPCC [National Society for the Prevention of Cruelty to Children] said it threatened "perfectly safe and normal activities" and risked alienating the public and discouraging volunteers.... Adults who volunteer their time to coach children in sports, or run Scout and Guide organisations, or adventure outings are being put off doing so in their thousands.

Philip Johnston's comment (*The Daily Telegraph*, October 29, 2009) introduces one of the most draconian laws ever enacted in a free society. It's Nanny gone ballistic. To get some sense of the scale of its reach, the law requires police background checks on a full quarter of the adult population of Britain. For anyone with minimal math skills, that's one out of every four grown-ups!

Who is subject to this nefarious ISA? Officially, it's anyone working with children under 18 (including everybody over 16 living in the house where contact with children is in one's home). And it's anyone working with vulnerable adults such as any over-18s with a physical or mental illness. And everybody but everybody in the health care professions—including doctors, nurses, dentists, psychologists, vets, pharmacists...and *midwives!* Checking midwives surely makes sense. As everyone knows, they're the first to abuse the little innocents the moment they arrive into this monstrous world. All that slapping around they do....

Anyone working within the financial services sector will also have to prove their innocence (for adolescent investors, presumably), along with wheel clampers (for all those infant drivers), doormen, security guards, customs inspectors, and even employees working in betting establishments (from which children are barred!).

Naturally, educators head up the list of those required to have background checks, but because children are always involved, even school visitors—such as an author or a politician—would have to be checked out first.[33] Authors? In the words of John McEnroe, you cannot be serious! But politicians? Hmmm. Maybe ISAs aren't such a bad idea after all—especially any politicians responsible for this insane legislation.

ISA-metrics, the invisible stretch

Well that's the *official* categories. But just listen to the *unofficial* ones....[34]

Letter to the Editor—*As chairman of a scout group, I was responsible for ensuring all leaders and assistants had CRB [Criminal Records Background] checks, including any parents who wished to help. The difficulty came when a CRB check on a parent came back negative [for stealing from a village sweet-shop many years previous]. This person was told he could not even enter the building to collect his own child.*

Letter to the Editor—*I have worked in dentistry for 41 years and am a grandmother. I have just had my first CRB check. We are told that most abusers are known to the abused, yet the new database will exclude family or private arrangements. I am also worried that under the ISA system an accusation could be enough to blacken a character—no conviction needed. This could be a wonderful way to square a grudge.*

Letter to the Editor—*Parents need to be aware that the ISA will regard them as potential abusers if they have ever taken a child to A & E [Accident and Emergency] or to their doctor with a physical injury.*

Letter to the Editor—*In contrast to the culture of distrust of adults now being nurtured in our children by legislators, across the Channel it is an offence not to help anyone, including a child, in difficulty and distress. I doubt if it would be prudent for an adult, especially a man, to help a child in distress on this side of the water. We have seriously lost the plot.*

Letter to the Editor—*Why doesn't the Government go the whole hog and install CCTV in every house, since nearly all child abuse takes place at home, behind closed doors?*

Letter to the Editor—*I cannot drive from home to work without being put under camera surveillance because I am a suspected criminal. I cannot draw euros from my local post office without handing over my passport* *because I am a suspected fraudster. I cannot catch a holiday flight without being screened and searched because I am a suspected terrorist. Now I cannot help out with my neighbours' children because I am a suspected child-abuser. How did I become an enemy of the state?*

Letter to the Editor—*The majority of child molestations are instigated by itinerant live-in partners of single mothers, a domestic arrangement encouraged by this wretched Government's crazed welfare policies.*

Letter to the Editor—*A convicted murderer, I read, is training to become a London taxi driver. Will the Independent Safeguarding Authority let him carry children in his cab?*

Do you get the idea that the public have had enough of Nanny? The wonder (or not!) is how out of touch the Government is with the pulse of the people. No, make that how out of touch the Government is with the *will* of the people. As in Britain, so in America—witness the recent actions of the Congress and President shoving through legislation clearly against the will of the American people. That would be the "people's elected representatives" in the "democratic model" we encourage all other nations to adopt.

Why is it that whenever the government starts abusing its own young in this perverse fashion their first victims seem always to be the Scouts...?

News Report—*Scout jamborees could be cancelled in Britain because of anti-paedophile vetting rules. Organising criminal record information and other checks on thousands of foreign Scout leaders was "just not possible" a spokeswoman said.*

In a letter to The Daily Telegraph, Judith Allen complained that, "as a favour to an old friend who is a district commissioner for Brownie groups in a Midlands city, I agreed to take notes at monthly meetings held in her sitting room along with other adult leaders. I have never, and never will, come into contact with a Brownie in my voluntary position. For me to start this voluntary note-taking I have had to be CRB-checked at a cost to the Brownie organisation. Is this really necessary?[35]

It's the Government that should be taking notes. No use complaining that bottom-rung lackeys are wrongly taking the legislation too far and applying the law in ways never intended.

At the end of the day, there is something quite predictable about all radical social legislation: Those who are the targets of protection invariably end up being the very ones victimized....

When children become the victims of...protection

News Report—*Because of the burden of the Government's latest child protection measures, a theatre company is to stop using performers under 18. The Loft Theatre Company said it might also be forced to scrap its youth theatre. A spokesperson for the company said the decision was forced upon it by the "legislative crassness bordering on insanity" of the Government's safe-guarding legislation.*[36]

So much for protecting children. Under the ISA regime, children are "protected" to such an extreme that they can no longer enjoy the special activities that help them bloom into maturity, or to participate in the exciting programs designed for their benefit....

News Report—*A European Union plan encouraging teens to spend a year in another country has fallen foul of Britain's child protection rules. It was hoped the scheme would include British pupils, giving them the opportunity to experience the culture and language of other EU states. But officials in Britain and Ireland have branded the scheme "utterly impractical" because it may expose young people to danger.*[37]

Does anything about that report strike you as odd? What does it say when British young people can't take advantage of an EU-sponsored program because of a British vetting and barring scheme? It is yet one more reminder of how Britain takes even the rare good idea from the EU (already sufficiently regulation-crazy), then immediately kicks it completely out of bounds! Make no mistake, among all the EU countries, Britain is the one most addicted to petty, micro-managing, life-intrusive regulations.

There are other ways in which those who are the objects of child protection are the very ones being victimized by the ISA requirements....

News Report—*More than 125,000 teenagers are now having their backgrounds checked each year, even if they just volunteer as mentors or sports coaches. Young people whose parents are childminders must also be vetted for criminal convictions because of the risk they pose to toddlers being cared for in their family home.*[38]

As if all that weren't crazy enough, here is the absolute prize-winner, where potential pedophiles are interacting with other potential pedophiles....

News Report—*Despite denials from the Home Office, the tradition of students visiting lonely pensioners for a chat or to help with housework is now potentially threatened because both the young people and the elderly may have to be officially vetted to check they are not potential abusers.*

John Claughton, chief master of King Edward's School, Birmingham, said the regulations were heading towards "madness." He added: "I went to a governors' meeting at a school where the head teacher was constructing a policy to ensure there were no unaddressed child protection issues in pupils showing prospective parents round at open morning. I didn't know whether to laugh or cry."[39]

Reader Comment—*What a sick country I live in. The very fabric of our society is being ripped to pieces by bureaucrats and teachers. Surely social cohesion is the key here! So now the old will be forgotten, and our children will care less about all aspects of society. Brilliant. So what are the police doing? Surely they should be out detecting and safeguarding us against deviancy. Honestly, this country disgusts me. I recall our local swimming* *pool has a spare lane which is used as a barrier to protect children—so it keeps adults and children separate. Is it me, or is this not a little creepy?*[40]

Care to cast your vote on that question? At the very least, what's creepy is the ever-creeping idea surely being formulated in young minds that adults (and even their own peers) are not to be trusted. That within every swimming pool, every park, every school, every doctor's office, and every candy shop, there are sexual predators just waiting to pounce on them. Or most certainly at 33,000 feet....

News Report—*British Airways is being sued over a policy that bans male passengers from sitting next to children they don't know. BA policy requires that cabin crew patrol the aisles before take-off checking that youngsters travelling on their own or in a different row from their parents are not next to a male stranger. If they find a man next to a child or teenager they must ask him to move to a different seat.*

Mr. Fischer and his wife were flying from Gatwick when the incident occurred. Fischer's six-months pregnant wife had booked a window seat to give her more room. Fischer was in the middle seat between his wife and a 12-year-old boy. After all passengers had been seated, a flight attendant asked Mr. Fischer to change his seat. Fischer refused, explaining that his wife was pregnant. The attendant then raised his voice (causing alarm among fellow passengers) and warned Fischer that the plane could not take off unless he obeyed. Fischer eventually changed seats, but is taking the BA to court for sex discrimination.

Mr. Fischer complained that "This policy is branding all men as perverts for no reason. The policy and the treatment of male passengers is absolutely outrageous. A plane is a public place. Cabin crew regularly walk down the aisles and passengers are sat so close to each other. The risk of any abuse is virtually zero. Furthermore, statistically children are far more likely to be abused by a member of their family. Does that mean that BA is going to ban children sitting next to their own parents?"[41]

The good news? Fischer won his case, and British Airways has now modified their hopelessly misguided "pervert policy."

Statistically, of course, it's as likely that the passenger in 16G is a terrorist bomber who will bring about the ultimate abuse of every passenger on board, not just the children. But are cabin crews patrolling the aisles visually profiling anyone who's appearance is far more likely to suggest a terrorist than a pedophile? They wouldn't dare!

You can understand the obvious fact that every man on board an aircraft is just waiting to abuse any kid within reach. (By now we all know the reputation of those oversexed British males in particular!) But who ever would guess that not even one's own mother and father are to be trusted...?

News Report—*In Watford, parents are being banned from supervising their children in public playgrounds if they have not undergone criminal record checks. Only council-vetted "play rangers" are now allowed to monitor youngsters in two adventure areas while parents must watch from outside a perimeter fence. Furious relatives have attacked the policy as insulting, and say they are being labeled as paedophiles.*

Mo mills, 62, a retired youth worker who has six grandchildren, added: "This is typical of the nanny state and I am furious. The council should hang their heads in shame at this political correctness gone mad."

The Council Mayor said: "Sadly, in today's climate, you can't have adults walking around unchecked in a children's playground, and the adventure playground is not a meeting place for adults.[42]

Actually, the time was when parks and playgrounds were just that— a meeting place for adults, children, families, friends, and strangers. How long will it be before public parks are off-limits to any member of the public without a police check?

Candid camera, but not too candid

Already public parks and other venues are risky places these days for anyone daring to take photos of children—even their own! The fol-

74

lowing editorial by Jemima Lewis (*The Daily Telegraph*, June 29, 2008) is lengthy, but well worth every word....

Comment—*While I was enjoying one of the many pleasures of maternity leave this week—sitting with my son in the dappled shade at Hackney lido, watching an enormously fat PE teacher from the local comprehensive attempting to teach the butterfly—a minor contretemps started up. A man who was sunbathing in front of me picked up his mobile phone, started tapping out a text message, and was immediately apprehended by one of the pool attendants.*

"I'm sorry, sir," said the attendant, in an embarrassed whisper. "It's against the law. Because of the children. You know, with phone cameras and everything..." He trailed away, looking hardly less uncomfortable than the object of his reproach, and a murmur of outrage went up among the rest of the sunbathers. It was, we all agreed, "ridiculous," "so depressing" and—above all—"terrible for the children."

I am naturally pusillanimous to a degree, but motherhood brings out the inner tub-thumper. I do not want my son to grow up in a world that... treats all adults as potential paedophiles, and thereby "poisons the relationship between the generations." I do not want to have to explain to him why certain do-gooders (like the very perverts they revile) consider a child in a swimming costume an indecent sight.

So I tapped the pool attendant on the shoulder and told him...that he was mistaken: there is no law against using cameras around children, or indeed openly taking photographs of them. I know this because I investigated the subject, after a similar incident at a christening.

It was one of those bumper ceremonies where they induct several babies at once. The three families were unknown to each other, but were casting shy smiles across the pews when the vicar coughed into his clip-on microphone. "Before we begin," he said, drumming his fingers together in the prayer position, "a little technical matter. Please don't take photographs during the ceremony. It's against the Child Protection Act. In case you accidentally get someone else's child in the background." As we frowned in bafflement, he attempted to explain: "It's all this digital manipulation you can do these days...."

There was no more smiling after that: only incredulous silence. What should have been a celebration of innocence had been invaded by the most sordid of spectres. As each baby, resplendent in white lace, received the blessings of Christ, all I could think was: is it really possible to fashion something so vile from an out-of-focus shot of someone else's infant dressed up like a frothy lavatory-roll cover?

In Britain these days, it doesn't matter if the law itself doesn't actually prohibit the photographing of children. Rumor and public capitulation up and down the ladder of society is doing the work of a thousand laws and statutes....

From loony legislation to public psyche

News Report—*A father taking pictures of his children playing on an inflatable slide suddenly found himself being accused of being a "pervert." The woman running the slide asked him what he was doing and other families waiting in the queue demanded that he stop. One parent even accused him of photographing youngsters to put the pictures on the internet. Nearby policemen confirmed that he had not violated any law, but that didn't cure the abuse the father had already received at the hands of prickly privacy police.*[43]

Ironic, isn't it? Over-the-top laws aimed at sexual perverts end up perverting the decent, common-sense values of an entire nation. The liberal-Left must really be proud of its new generation of disciples who spread the gospel of fear and suspicion and so eagerly become the petty-tyrant enforcers of nanny nonsense. Shades of the Third Reich brainwashing a nation into becoming complicit in Jewish persecution....

Of all the threats to America from the current loony mindset in Britain, one might suppose that the photographing of children likely would be the last frontier of liberalism to catch fire in the States. Given our obsession with photographing every moment of children's lives—from those first fetal ultrasounds, to the delivery room, to mandatory bath-tub shots, to every sports event exhausted parents can attend, to high school and college graduations, to weddings, and then (coming full-circle) to grandchildren's first fetal ultrasounds—American children are the most photographed generation in the history of photography. What would cell-phone cameras and Facebook be without them?

And yet...and yet...

American News Report—*An Arizona couple accused of sexual abuse after taking bath-time photos of their children (ages 18 months, 4, and 5) and then trying to have them developed at Walmart are suing both Arizona and Walmart. Lisa and Anthony "A.J." Demaree's three young daughters were taken away by Arizona Child Protective Services last fall when a Walmart employee found partially nude pictures of the girls on a camera memory stick taken to the store for processing. Walmart turned the photos over to police and the Demarees were not allowed to see their children for several days. Neither parent was charged with sexual abuse. After a month, they eventually regained custody of their children.[44]*

So it begins, even in the States....

Finally, some frustrated push-back

If there is any good news it's that even Britain's most liberal (often-leftist) educators are beginning to have second thoughts....

News Report—*An unprecedented coalition of head teachers, complaining of "disproportionate bureaucracy," has written a letter demanding sweeping changes to the anti-paedophile vetting rules, which they say threatens school activities such as foreign exchange trips, Duke of Edinburgh awards, parents helping at school plays and work placements. Some parents are even having to undergo criminal records checks simply to accompany their children to Christmas carol concerts.*

In the letter, the coalition warns that the system is imposing a string of "unintended consequences" and is heavy-handed but gives no guarantee of safety.[45]

In case any nannycrats dare attempt the argument, we'll hear no talk of "unintended consequences." If that excuse doesn't work for drunk drivers or rain-forest loggers, why should governments get a free pass on any quirky results for which they are responsible?

In truth, it can't even be said of the civil-servant oddballs who think up these schemes that the consequences are unintended. To the contrary, they are very much intended! For extremists of all stripes, no consequences are ever unintended. And even if they were, it wouldn't matter. Idealists can't be bothered by collateral damage. It's an all-out war out there! Gotta win, no matter the cost. Merely witness political terrorists, for whom the death of innocent victims is but the price of achieving the ultimate goal.

All that utilitarian social planners can see is "the greatest good for the greatest number"—as *they themselves* see that good, regardless of whether the greatest number of citizens agree in the least. No one is demanding that any regulatory system be one-hundred percent foolproof, only that any cure not be worse than the disease. With its penchant for extremist reactionism, the liberal-Left seems always to use the proverbial sledgehammer to crack a nut. If two or three children sadly are abused or killed by pedophiles, suddenly the civil liberties of every law-abiding citizen must be infringed...just in case.

The civil liberties conundrum

Speaking of civil liberties, are you listening ACLU? Which hat will you wear as we enter the Nanny zone in the States? There was a time when your high-minded founding principles—the defense of civil liberties—would have been outraged at the intrusive regulations of the nanny state. But since you've now joined forces with the same liberal-Left politicos pushing the pro-abortion, pro-gay, anti-religion agenda in Britain, you must surely be experiencing more than a little cognitive dissonance. The problem is, you can't play it both ways.

In fact, how would your liberal child-sex policies sit with the child-protection mania sweeping through Europe? What, for instance, would your rabid, anti-pedophilia cousins in Britain think of ACLU Policy 4, section (g)? "The ACLU views the use of children in the production of visual depictions of sexually explicit conduct as a violation of children's rights *when such use is highly likely to cause: a) substantial physical harm; or b) substantial and continuing emotional or psychological harm* [emphasis added]." Why the loopholes? Why give someone like pornographer Stephen Knox an "out" when he lewdly films girls as young as ten without their knowing it? No physical harm is done, and there's no psychological harm. But these young victims are having their privacy violated in a far more tangible way than the ludicrously-artificial "right of privacy" concerns touted by the ACLU in defense of abortion.

And how's this for protecting the young? ACLU Policy 4, section (d) 6) says: "Distributors, exhibitors and retailers should not be obliged to risk punishment by misjudging the age of a minor. Such persons should not be required to keep records of evidence submitted by minors; *and should be entitled to rely reasonably on a minor's statement of age* [emphasis added]."

Make no mistake. For all the ACLU's talk about "children' rights," the ACLU is no friend of children—whether born or unborn. If there's so little respect for babies in the womb that they can be destroyed at will, what chance is there of children being respected once they are born?

Bizarre liberal line-drawing

If you're wondering why the ACLU would stoop so low as to give such wiggle-room for kiddy-porn, it's partly because they're defending at all cost their pre-commitment to the indefensible cause of obscenity and pornography. And why defend to the death so unworthy a cause as obscenity and pornography? Ostensibly, because the only way to protect free speech is to take an absolutist position whereby nothing, but nothing can infringe on that sacred right (unless, of course, it happens to be *religious* speech).

You can see the same principle at work when the ACLU and their pro-abortion allies insist on the right of doctors even to perform so-called "partial birth abortions," which amount to nothing less than infanticide at a point in time when there can no longer possibly be any question about either viability of the baby or a potential threat to the mother's life. After all, where do you think the phrase *partial birth* comes from? Having been turned around so that it comes head-first, the baby is already emerging from the womb when a scalpel is cruelly inserted into the brain! While any normal human being would be repulsed and appalled by such a procedure, pro-abortion supporters feel compelled to defend it, lest they concede the slightest ground to their opponents.

Even if we grant that initially many pro-abortion supporters had legitimate concerns about women dying of backstreet abortions, we are now long past that sad chapter in history and yet the fight continues unabated. Ever stopped to ask yourself what motivates folks to get themselves out of bed in the morning and rush off to picket and scream for the right to kill innocent babies in the womb? Abortion is not a stand-alone issue. As attested to by the vocal support it gets from gay activists (who obviously would never be faced with an unwanted pregnancy), abortion is, above all, an icon you double-click on to preserve, protect, and defend unfettered sexual freedom.

Make one terribly bad decision and before you know it you're doing the unthinkable. In fact, make one wrong turn after another and one day you wake up unable to make any good choices whatsoever. Once you jettison an overarching moral framework, you are left without the ability to distinguish between good and evil, right and wrong, or even—as with Britain's liberal-Left-inspired pedophilia mania—between the reasonable and the absurd. That which is reasonable (the protection of children from abuse) quickly turns into the absurd (treating even upstanding citizens as potential pedophiles).

It gets worse. Far worse. For secularist liberals pushing all the outrageous "anti-pedophilia" legislation, there is the glaring ethical inconsistency that inevitably accompanies the moral vacuum in which they live. If half a dozen children are abused and killed, there must be extremist legislation to prevent its ever happening again. But if thousands of lives (indeed millions in America) are killed while still inside the womb, then the only protest you'll hear from the liberal-Left is a strident, vitriolic demand that it not be stopped! Go figure.

Which answers a question you might have as to how it can be said that those on the liberal Left live in a moral vacuum. Don't liberals speak out against child abuse, poverty, violations of human rights, environmental catastrophes, and genocide? Sure, but certainly not the ghastly, unseen genocide of abortion victims. And as we've seen in Britain recently, they're just as likely to get caught up in a parliamentary expenses scandal. Or seduce an entire generation of young people into sexual promiscuity while decrying its inevitable disastrous effects. Or promote the breakdown of the nuclear family by policies tearing it apart limb by limb. Or attack religious faith which threatens their own patently contrived, faux morality.

Selective morality is no morality. Maybe it salves the conscience. Maybe it makes one feel better about one's personal moral failings. Maybe political activism in aid of good causes is a convenient substitute for religious faith. Maybe it's even part of a genuine religious commitment which, in postmodern thinking, can accommodate simultaneously a belief in treating your neighbor as yourself while denying the very humanity of your neighbor in the womb. (Liberals are not alone in that. Slavery was once justified in precisely the same way.) Let no one be fooled: the smorgasbord, pick-and-choose "morality" of the liberal-Left is not the universal morality of the ages—divinely given, coherent and consistent, genuine and true.

"Disproportionate" is a word often heard in Britain these days in protest to the legislation, regulations, rulings, and bizarre applications under which the nation is suffocating. Not unlike the religious fundamentalists with whom they least would wish to be associated, leftist liberals have no appreciation for "the weightier matters of the law." Even *with* a moral code believed to have been handed down from God himself, religious zealots—whether Christians, Muslims, or Jews—find it hard to think in terms other than black and white. (They've never understood Jesus' teaching that "the Sabbath was made for man, not man for the Sabbath"—demanding more sophisticated moral thinking.) But certainly *without* any higher moral framework, secularist social planners are at a complete loss as to proportion. Proportion is a concept requiring the kind of moral judgment and maturity that prioritizes among a hierarchy of moral principles, some lesser, some greater.

There is yet another striking parallel. If the case of "the woman caught in adultery" were to arise today, you might be tempted to think that religious zealots would join as one in having her stoned to death, whereas liberal-Left zealots would defend to the death her right to sexual freedom. Yet funnily enough, secularist liberals would be among the first to pick up the stones...*if they themselves, in their near-divine wisdom, had enacted the law against adultery!* Among zealots of all kinds, nothing is different about their self-righteous, narrow-minded, let-them-eat-cake, legalism.

In theological terms, what legalists all lack is any sense of *grace*. In political terms, the legalistic nanny syndrome manifests itself as a lack of proportion...and restraint...and common sense. One thing is certain: When the general population is treated as sexually suspect, it's time to wonder if there isn't something terribly suspect itself about any perspective so ludicrously perverse.

4

Health and Safety, Risky Business!

Life is either a daring adventure or nothing.
Security does not exist in nature, nor do the children of
men as a whole experience it.
Avoiding danger is no safer in the long run than exposure.

—Helen Keller

News Report—*Old sailors from the 8th Destroyer Association were denied permission to march through the city of Scarborough due to new health and safety regulations that would have required these heroes to take out public liability insurance for over a million pounds, employ two lines of marshals in reflective jackets, and have an ambulance on stand-by.*

A police spokesman justified the action, saying, "The last thing we would want to do is cause upset among a group of people who have given so much for their country, but safety is of paramount importance."[46]

This indignity is a sign of the times. Thanks to the sacrifice of these brave souls, Britain had won the war against the Nazis, but who among these old sailors could have imagined their own homeland being invaded by bureaucratic totalitarians? And just how ironic is it when proud old sailors who fought to protect Britain's freedom are forced by harsh, arbitrary regulations to experience the loss of that costly freedom?

As with any war, there were other brave volunteers who stepped up to save the day. The coastguard provided an ambulance, local motorcyclists provided an escort, and an anonymous benefactor paid for the insurance premium and some jackets for the marshals. But don't forget why all this effort was necessary. Attempt almost any community event in Britain these days and you'll get a taste of the maddening Scarborough affair. "Why bother?" is the growing response from one volunteer after another. Just ask Diane Tovey....

News Report—*Diane Tovey has raised nearly £1000 for the Royal National Lifeboat Institution by selling tea and cakes from her home on bank holidays. Claiming Mrs. Tovey is running a business, council officials have said she must take out a £5 million public liability insurance policy. An exasperated Mrs. Tovey said: "I don't know what the world is coming to. I think it is quite disgusting. The council is even quibbling over our tables in the garden on planning grounds. How stupid can you get?"*

A council spokesperson insists they have no choice in the matter since the Toveys pay ground rent to the council for their chalet. "If we consent to something and the tenant is not insured and a customer submits a claim against the Toveys, as the land is ours and we are party to the agreement, we could be pulled into the proceeding and potentially be liable as well."[47]

And pigs might fly, and the moon turn to cheese. Just never know when or where a lawyer might pop up these days, so it's better to squelch volunteerism altogether than risk some irregularly constructed cream puff shooting across the garden and assaulting some unsuspecting guest. Now really. If health and safety is their concern, wouldn't council officers be better served worrying about the epidemic of litigation paranoia sweeping through every village and town? How healthy can rampant paranoia be for society? More to the point, how will society survive when loony councils have snuffed out the last of Britain's hard-working, generous volunteers?

There are so many examples of health and safety madness in Britain these days it's hard to choose which to share. The following should suffice to make the point....

News Report—*Grieving families have been told not to put plastic flowers in a garden of remembrance because they pose a health and safety risk. A spokeswoman for the cemetery said: "The mementoes make it difficult for staff to carry out maintenance. We also have health and safety reasons to consider. If the flowers get caught up in the lawnmower the bits of plastic flying around could be very dangerous."48*

Just when you think there might be other legitimate reasons for council actions (like normal maintenance issues), suddenly—invariably—out comes the health-and-safety mantra, as if to trump any reasonable objection. Or maybe health and safety is just a guise for other liberal-Left agenda items....

News Report—*Bosses from Leicester's three main hospitals said they were considering moving the Bible from patients' bedsides because it may cause offence and may be responsible for spreading the superbug MRSA. The worry is that the Gideons testaments could offend people from other faith groups, and also that there's an increased risk of spreading MRSA if they become contaminated with body fluids.*

Gideons International commissioned reports from medical consultants about the potential risk which found there was no danger. The Christian organisation has also agreed to the hospitals' request to run its volunteers through criminal records bureau checks before they are allowed to enter wards to distribute the Bibles.

In a statement released today, the NHS trust denied that Christian patients would be refused access to the Bible, but said it was looking to provide religious texts for all faiths.[49]

Criminal background checks for the Gideons? You've got to be kidding. Risk of MRSA? Not a chance. Providing Muslim patients with copies of the Koran? Someone must figure Bibles are far more likely to transmit MRSA. Which leaves only one reasonable conclusion—that health and safety concerns are nothing more than a pretext for chucking out Bibles! Little wonder that hospital officials attempted hasty damage control when news spread that this policy was under consideration.

Time to yell "Fire!", or not

News Report—*The traditional fireman's pole is to be banned because it poses a "health and safety hazard." Bosses overseeing the construction of a new fire station ruled the poles too dangerous. Firemen will now have to run down the stairs of the new Greenbank Fire Station in Plymouth. Said one firefighter, "In more than thirty years in the brigade I have seen one or two accidents on poles compared to tens of accidents with people tripping on stairs while responding to incidents." Another firefighter said: "It seems crazy to say it's too dangerous to have a pole when we make our living from running into burning buildings."*

A spokesperson for the Fire Brigade said there was no general safety policy precluding fireman's poles, and that the Plymouth station decision had been blown out of proportion.[50]

If safety concerns weren't the reason for Greenbank Station's design, why cite such concerns in defense of the decision? And if safety concerns truly were a consideration, then why would you *not* eliminate poles from all new fire stations? Sometimes the absence of a slippery pole is the best way to recognize a slippery slope.

And then there's always the opposite direction to consider....

News Report—*Thanks to health and safety regulations restricting the use of ladders, builders say they are having to turn to expensive scaffolding even for relatively small jobs on private houses. Allan Buchan of the Confederation of Roofing Contractors said: "The health and safety people have gone crazy to the point where our members think it's not worth using a ladder. The HSE carries out spot checks all the time and if you get caught you're in serious trouble. In some cases the scaffolding costs more than the job."*

The Government's Working at Height Regulations (introduced following a European Union directive) state: "Every employer shall ensure that a ladder is used for work at height only if a risk assessment...has demonstrated that the use of more suitable work equipment is not justified...."

The HSE has denied that ladders are all but banned. According to the head of the HSE, "It's probably not a bad thing—a one or two-day training course to become a certified ladder-climber."[51]

There's no question but that serious injuries and deaths are caused by workers falling from ladders. Probably wouldn't be a bad thing to have some industry-wide warnings as reminders of safe ladder use... and scaffolding for that matter. (Why are we never given the accident statistics associated with scaffolding? Gotta be lots of injuries with all those heavy poles and planks flying about!)

As always with health and safety, it's being stupidly over-the-top that causes the harm. (A *two-day* ladder course?) When we get to the point where all common sense is abandoned, it's time for a climb down. And if only it were just workplace issues....

Comment—*Think ahead, say, 10 years from now. Remember the pantomime you once took the kids to, the one that was closed by the health and safety inspector because the local amateur dramatic society simply couldn't afford to do all the things he said were necessary to "abide by the rules"?*

And what about Guy Fawkes night? It was only a small gathering on the green, but every family showed up and who could forget the faces of the children in the light of the bonfire? Been going for years; never so much as a burnt finger. But then in came the regulation that only "qualified" volunteers could set off the rockets and the bangers in a public place. And that was the end of that.

You think this is all a bit far-fetched? Not a bit of it. It has already happened. The annual panto at a church in Welling, Kent, has been canceled because of health and safety issues. The vicar is expected to fork out £700 to "weigh test" the iron beam that carries a light bulb. The health and safety inspector has also banned costumes and scenery to be stored behind or under the stage.

They've got their eye on Christmas, too. Some shops have already decided not to light up the high streets this yuletide because of the latest batch of health and safety diktats. Three shops in my town simply cannot afford to. Before, they got up a ladder and strung the lights out themselves. Now they have been told this simple task must be done by a professional electrician "for the public's safety."

Where I live, every Christmas we have a choral service, at the end of which Santa Claus comes riding down the high street in his motorised sledge. Every year he has thrown sweets out to the children. But not now. Sweets could hit them, perhaps hurt them. So sweets have been banned.

Then there's the police. Some forces have even stopped their constables from riding bicycles unless they have, wait for it, "specialist training" under health and safety regulations.

This comment by veteran war correspondent Michael Nicholson (*Daily Express*, October 25, 2007) has been edited for length. Nicholson's list of haywire health and safety regulations goes on and on. From public services, to holiday celebrations, to everyday village life, no area of activity is left untouched by marauding health and safety inspectors—not even those people who make their living by taking risks....

What a circus!

News Report—*Trapeze artists, jugglers, tightrope walkers and other acrobats with the Moscow State Circus, currently touring Britain, have been instructed to wear safety headwear to comply with new EU safety rules. "It is bureaucracy gone mad, with a lot of help from the current compensation culture," said Paul Archer, general manager of the circus. Archer added: "The hats could be more of a liability than anything else. They could* *slip over the artist's eyes or throw the performer off-balance. "This is just another loony law from Brussels and we are the only country stupid enough to pay any attention."*

Goussein Khamdouleav, who performs somersaults without a safety net as part of the highest indoor tightrope act in Europe, scoffed at the idea that a safety hat would be much use to him if he fell 45 ft to the ring below.[52]

Think that's funny? Those health and safety folks aren't clowning around, you know. Except with clowns....

News Report—*When a clown in the Moscow State Circus fell from a three-metre-high slack wire, injuring his foot, he was told he could no longer wear the size 18 shoes that were part of his costume because they compromised his health and safety. His routine includes dressing himself whilst walking on a wire, dressing himself within a hoop of fire, and playing a drum-kit, trumpet and double-bass all at the same time. Mr. Kashkin, the clown, said: "The shoes are an important part of my costume. The impact might be lost on the audience now."[53]*

Granted, this decision was made by the circus' own health and safety advisor, but that advisor was only following suit from the EU and British control freaks who run the biggest and craziest circus ever. When it comes to attempting a balancing act, health and safety busybodies are performing a socially dangerous high-wire act without a safety net of rhyme or reason.

As for clowning around (complete with painted-on smile), nobody beats the European Union. This is one hilarious act you'd have to see to believe....

News Report—*The famed Oktoberfest (Munich's beer festival) has come under threat from a proposed EU directive that would require buxom barmaids wearing low-cut outfits (known as dirndls) to cover up so as not to receive too much sunlight. The mayor of Munich, Christian Ude, was outraged. "A waitress is no longer allowed to wander round a beer garden* *with a plunging neckline. I would not want to enter a beer garden under these conditions." Mark Hastings, from the British Beer and Pub Association, said: "This is the sort of petty bureaucracy that gives politicians a bad name."*[54]

One suspects that this is one EU directive honored mostly in the breach. You needn't fear a sudden disappearance of traditional dirndls at the Oktoberfest, only the outrageous cover-up of common sense by the folks in Brussels who obviously have taken way too much sun lately.

Ripley's believe it or not

To fully appreciate the breadth of Britain's current madness, one need only look as far as the daily paper. The range of health and safety silliness defies belief....

Letter to Editor—*I sympathise with Mrs. Ashton, who was not allowed, on grounds of health and safety, to take her wisdom tooth home with her after it was taken out.*[55]

News Blurb—*A lollipop man [school crossing guard] has quit after being banned from giving high-fives to children, due to a health and safety risk. John Hunter has been the crossing guide in Edinburgh since 1999. But the city council says his high-fives and chocolate treats must stop over health and safety concerns.*[56]

News Item—*Under government proposals to enforce healthy eating, public sector workers face a future without traditional pies and chips [French fries]. Fizzy drinks, confectionary, and crisps [potato chips] could also be limited in an attempt to make the public sector set a good example.*[57]

News Report—*Police officers are being told that they should take drunks into custody only as a last resort for fear that they might fall ill or die in a cell. Instead of letting drunks sleep it off in a jail cell, police now have to take them to hospital and guard them until they are treated. As a result, there* *is reluctance even to carry out arrests. One long-serving officer said, "They might deny it's official policy, but in practice that's what happens.*[58]

Of all the health-and-safety nonsense floating around Britain these days, this one really takes the biscuit....

News Report—*A recent survey sent out as a joke by Fox Biscuits has revealed that council workers have actually been advised on how to eat biscuits [cookies] safely. The tea and biscuits policies were disclosed in a survey which invented the fictitious British Biscuit Advisory Board as part of a £3 million marketing campaign. A spoof "workplace biscuit risk assessment test", written in bureaucratic language, was sent to 5,849 council workers, of whom 437 took time to complete it. Fox's marketing director said: "We developed the idea of the British Biscuit Advisory Board as a parody of the nation's obsession with health and safety, but we never thought it would be taken so seriously."*[59]

When a spoof survey is taken this seriously by members of the public, it's time to quit kidding ourselves about the seriousness of the problem.

Music hits a sour note

News Report—*Health and Safety officers are demanding that performers in the Proms ease off on extra-loud crescendos during the concert series to protect their hearing. BBC employees will have to measure decibels and put barriers up between musicians to guard the delicate flautists, for instance, against too many trumpet blasts. Extra BBC personnel are required at rehearsals to take volume measurements, and ear plugs are provided backstage for use by staff, crew and musicians.*[60]

And in a related news item we learn that music teachers are being told to wear earplugs or stand behind noise screens. The directive from the Health and Safety Executive comes because beginners tend to play their instruments much louder than professionals. When officials visited a school, they found that noise from a cornet, the worst offending instrument, reached 140 decibels. The HSE sets the safe daily limit for exposure to a prolonged noise at 80 decibels. They warn that a school that allows staff to be exposed to the cornet without protection could be in breach of noise regulations.[61]

What's remarkable about these off-key music directives is that they have little or no potential for generating law suits. Can't shift the spotlight to salivating lawyers or fat-cat insurance companies this time. Which only leaves officious intermeddling by do-gooder bureaucrats operating way above their pay grade. Can't you just see them now, busily pouring over the proposed program, deciding which pieces can be played and which ones can't? Mozart, yes, but definitely not Mahler!

Are we to believe that orchestral musicians and primary school music teachers have a centuries-old history of hearing problems? Not even Beethoven's famed deafness was caused by music, but most likely by lead poisoning. Where was health and safety when they were *really* needed?

When liberal causes collide

The problem with liberals is that their policies—divorced from any higher law or set of cohesive values—tend to wind up in internecine conflict. It's not simply a matter of being counterproductive. (Do away with ladders, and before you know it you'll end up with escalating injuries associated with scaffolding. Eliminate firemen's poles, and soon you'll find firefighters tripping down firehouse stairs in their rush to get going.) The greater embarrassment is that fuzzy thinking about one liberal cause ends up being fuzzy thinking about another liberal cause.

Consider the following textbook example....

News Report—*For years, Andre Wheeler has used his wheelbarrow to take glass, cans, paper and garden waste to a nearby tip. The 10-minute walk helps the 61-year-old teacher keep fit, as well as do his bit for the*

92

environment. But now officials have decided that wheeling the barrow onto the village site is dangerous—and he must take his rubbish by car instead.

An outraged Mr. Wheeler responded: "It's too ridiculous for words.... Telling me to burn petrol to drive to the recycling bins is hardly going to save the planet—it's nonsense....It's not joined-up thinking because what they are rally saying is that if you haven't got a car then you can't recycle."[62]

Mr. Wheeler's observation about liberal thinking that is not "joined-up" is perceptive indeed. In this case, it's all about health and safety fanatics running headlong into environmental fanatics—a collision smack-dab in the middle of Liberal Land. In a moment of health and safety madness, the many millions of British pounds spent by environmentalists to rid the road of gas-guzzling cars is blithely consigned to the rubbish bin of liberal lunacy. And given the climate of trendy government regulation, it so easily could have been the other way round—with cars being banned from the recycle site, forcing villagers to push heavy wheelbarrows in contravention of health and safety load limits.

Or consider another liberal policy collision. Many councils in Britain have begun fortnightly rather than weekly rubbish collection, partly because of budget considerations, but mostly to force homeowners to dispose of less rubbish in their bins. Saving the planet and all that. In the meantime, overstuffed rubbish bins are not just unsightly, smelly, and a general nuisance, they have become a breeding ground for rats. Now there's a major victory for liberalism!

Health and safety is (ruining) child's play

As we have already seen, a nanny state lives up to its name most when children are involved. That's a nanny's job—telling children what they can and cannot do. Of course it all gets a bit bossy when those children grow up to be adult citizens and Nanny is still telling them what they can and cannot do. That's why it's so dangerous to let the government think it can autocratically control children when they *are* children. Once a nanny, always a nanny.

It works in reverse as well. The more autocratic the nanny, the more likely children will blindly submit to nanny-like authority even as they grow older. Once nannied, always nannied. If forbidden to think for yourself as a child, and to assume personal responsibility, and to take reasonable risks—the chances of developing more adult-like traits are reduced in direct proportion to the passivity inculcated early on.

The problem is that there are nannies, and then there are *nannies*! The good nannies warn their charges of dangers and then help them grow into maturity by accepting reasonable risks and learning hard lessons, if necessary. Despite cut fingers, broken arms, and banged heads, it's all part of growing up.

By contrast, overlord nannies think it's their job to eliminate *all* risks for children. Left to them, the children would never get out of the house, or be permitted out of one's sight, or allowed to risk personal injury no matter how slight the danger. As you read the following news items, judge for yourself which kind of nanny state Britain has become...and which kind of nanny state liberal-Left Obamaland promises to be....

News Report—*Children at a primary school have been banned from making daisy chains in case they pick up germs from the flowers. Traditional playground games such as handstands, tag, conkers, yo-yos, and even skipping and running have also been banned as "too dangerous."*[63]

No, this is not to say that every child's game in Britain has been banned forever, only that the health and safety hysteria sweeping the land has been taken to absurd extremes by one local council after another, and by far too many "progressive" school administrators. One is tempted to say it's the pits, but even the pits are fast disappearing....

News Report—*Just 2 percent of all playgrounds now contain a sandpit. Fearing health-and-safety risks, and also citing financial concerns, councils across England, Scotland, and Wales have ripped out so many sand pits that* *fewer than 100 pits remain in the 4,815 playgrounds run by the 70 local authorities.*

One of the districts that has removed sandpits from local parks said that "despite regular and ongoing attempts to clean the area, we remained concerned about the potential health risks to children and other users of the sandpit.[64]

That last line pretty much gives away the game doesn't it? Just when you're tempted to concede the financial angle, suddenly the cat is let out of the bag: there are "potential health risks to children *and other users of the sandpit.*" Just exactly who might all those other *non-child* users be? When the case is so ridiculously overstated, you know there's been a fudge all along.

News Report—*Schools are now adopting clip-on ties for school uniforms, fearing that conventional knots pose an injury risk. There are concerns that children at play might pull other pupil's ties too tight, and also might get them caught in machinery. The Campaign for Real Education condemned the move as "health and safety gone mad."*[65]

Americans will not readily identify with children wearing ties as part of their school uniforms. For the most part, American schoolchildren don't wear uniforms, much less ties. All the more's the pity. For tourists from the States, one of Britain's most endearing scenes is the parade of smartly-dressed schoolchildren walking to and from school. What a refreshing sight. What a great tradition. But health and safety could hardly care less about tradition. In nanny-Britain, traditions count for little these days—even the most time-honored...

News Report—*Despite following a custom dating back to 1680 when the local militia would fire their live muskets over the town's Christmas tree, the Wimborne Militia in Dorset has been told that they can no longer fire their muskets because the noise of the blank shots is too loud for children. Chris Brown, the town crier and member of the Militia said: "At the Christmas event there are usually carols and then* *a countdown to the switch being thrown. We then simultaneously fire a blank shot with our muskets into the air. Prior to this, I go around the crowd giving them a warning and safety advice on how to protect their ears.*[66]

Naturally, some traditions are worth honoring, while other traditions are best soon forgotten. It's an especially sad day when traditions intended to build character in young people are forced out of existence by a combination of cultural chaos and over-regulation....

Comment—*Scouts have been told to be slightly less prepared than usual. Penknives may have formed as much part of the scouting experience as badges and campfires, but according to advice from the Scout Association they must no longer be brought on camping trips, except when there is a "specific" need.*

Scouts were at one point allowed to carry a sheath knife on their belt as part of their uniform, but in another change to the traditions originated by Lord Baden-Powell a century ago the advice also states that knives must not be worn with uniforms, except for reasons of religion. Sheila Burgin, a troop leader for Sevenoaks Scout Group in Kent, criticised the guidance. She said: "The Scout Association doesn't want to be in trouble for encouraging people to carry knives, but I think it is very sad. It's health and safety gone mad."

As highlighted in Lucy Bannerman's comment (*The Times*, September 7, 2009), what's the world coming to when the Scouts find themselves on the cutting edge of liberal madness...without a knife? Would it not have been enough simply to say, "Don't carry your knives in public since carrying knives is now outlawed to minimize the crime problem"? When respected organizations like the Scouts bow to contemporary pressures, what's next?

From the campground to the school ground, the whole of child-dom has been declared a No-Risk Zone....

News Report—*School staff have been subjected to a series of increasingly bizarre guidelines to stop schools being sued in the event of an accident. One school ordered adults and children to wear goggles when using Blu-Tack. Another school banned the use of spray foam when marking out spaces, in case a child slips and "drowns" in it. And at one primary school, a three-legged race was dropped from sports day because it was too dangerous.*

In a survey of almost 600 school staff, almost half of those polled said health and safety rules were now "too restrictive," negatively impacting on pupils' education. More than four-in-ten said school trips had been reduced or can-celled because of safety concerns. A Government-funded report last year said that "perceived health and safety regulations were felt to have systematically undermined communities and the quality of their children's education."

Judith Hackitt, chairman of the Health and Safety Executive, said: "Hardly a week goes by without another health and safety myth appearing. The examples cited in the…article are quite frankly ridiculous."[67]

Is the Chair of the HSE saying that the examples cited are ridiculous because they *never happened*, or ridiculous because they *did happen*? Who wouldn't agree that, if they happened, they are patently ridiculous? And if supposedly they *didn't* happen, how are we to explain all the (quite specific) reports coming in daily from the hinterlands?

HSE points fingers at everybody else

If you pull up the website for the Health and Safety Executive (www. hse.gov.uk) the first thing you notice is a summary of HSE's remit: "Our job is to prevent death, injury and ill health to those at work and those affected by work activities." Who could take issue with that?

Dig more deeply, however, and you'll find a testy, defensive HSE dis-claiming responsibility for Britain's current health and safety mania. In an attempt to dispel widespread public dismay, the website actually features the "Myth of the Month," highlighting popular rumors pointing fingers of blame at the nation's barmy health and safety culture. Read the myths superficially, and HSE looks as innocent as doves. Read between the lines, and all innocence is lost. Consider this brief sampling....

Myth: Pancake races are banned!
Reality: Health and safety requirements were given as the reason that a pancake race couldn't take place last year. A straightforward event like this one only needs a short, simple risk assessment. And when an event has taken place lots of times before, all that's needed is a review of the previous assessment so that the fun can go ahead.

A short, simple risk assessment? No such thing. Whereas for centuries folks assessed risks informally, using common sense, nowadays there has to be an official form (happily provided by HSE) with all the appropriate boxes ticked. Takes time; takes money. Wastes time; wastes money. And what is the risk associated with not filling out a formal risk assessment? Nothing less than the possibility of being penalized by HSE—or worse—being denied insurance in the rare event something did go wrong.

And how do insurance carriers get away with holding hostage every activity known to man? Thanks to the HSE, the basis for denying coverage is simply a failure to do the required assessment. It's HSE's answer to the age-old ploy of "good cop, bad cop." HSE's assessment policy is the "good cop," naturally requiring only what is in your best interest. The "bad cop" is the insurance industry slapping you around for failing to do whatever HSE benevolently has decided is in your best interest.

Myth: New regulations would require trapeze artists to wear hard hats.
Reality: Despite being widely reported and regularly repeated, this story is utter nonsense. There never were any such regulations. Hard hats do an excellent job of protecting building workers from falling debris, but they have no place on a trapeze.

Never *any* such regulations? Maybe not from HSE directly, but certainly from their big brother, the EU, with whom they work hand-in-glove. At least HSE is right about one thing: requiring hard hats for trapeze artists is utter nonsense, whether the idea came from the HSE or the EU.

Myth: *Health and safety bans traditional school ties.*
Reality: *Quite rightly, few parents would see wearing school ties as a safety issue. After all, millions of kids have been wearing ties for years without any real problems. Taking simple precautions during laboratory work or around machinery makes sense. But if the concern is about kids fighting, although clip-on ties may help, the real issue is discipline. So no, we don't ban school ties—it's down to the school to make decisions about uniform, not HSE.*

Okay, so it's local councils and silly school administrators who make all those daft health and safety decision on the front lines. Kind of like the havoc-producing horse that bolted from the barn when the door was left ajar. But who caused the door to be opened? In this case, it was the HSE. Changing the metaphor, the HSE doesn't personally pull the trigger. It only loads the rifle and aims! Want a *really* good example of that process…?

There were those gravestones, of course

News Report—*In an attempt to distance the Health and Safety Executive from spurious rumors, Judith Hackitt, Chair of the HSE said, " There is Health and Safety, you see, and health and safety. People are forever confusing the two. As a rule of thumb, she says, whenever the media is in a lather about health and safety, the Health and Safety Executive has nothing to do with it."*

But that's not always the case. Almost ten years ago, after a couple of deaths from wobbly gravestones, the HSE looked at the problem and circulated guidelines which local councils eagerly took ever so seriously. Now a decade on, many local authorities still employ certified "topple-testers" who apply a predetermined amount of force to suspect gravestones by means of a special

German-built machine (also known as a topple-tester) to see if they wobble. Despite the HSE putting out two more sets of gravestone guidance in an effort to roll back the effects of the first, councils are still topple-testing, to the tune of about £2.5 million. Of the initial set of guidelines, Ms. Hackitt says, "It was a mistake, made with the best intentions at the time."[68]

It's hard to underestimate what a punch Hackitt's admission packs in summarizing the process that unfolds when *regulation-heavy* morphs into *regulation-happy*. Not all the "best intentions" in the world can "roll back" the inevitable effects of heavy-handed bureaucracy. When government becomes even benignly omnipresent (as it has in America under successive governments, but now with a vengeance under the Obama administration), it rarely has sufficient omniscience to avoid widespread abuse of its delegated powers—especially when "the little people" at the bottom of the ladder get a taste of the power wielded by omnipotent policy-makers at the top. Add all those omni-traits together, and it's simply too much like God...without being God. What could be more of a grave error for a free society?

House rules a picture of extremism

In the News Report immediately above, Judith Hackitt claims that Britain has the best health and safety performance in the world—the only other country coming anywhere close being Sweden. Maybe, but at what cost? While the HSE also prides itself on having one of the best safety records in Britain within its own 31 offices (107 injuries per 100,000 workers compared with 150 per 100,000 in education, for example), the house rules at the HSE beg belief.

News Report—*Employees at the HSE have been banned from shifting furniture on the remote chance that they might injure themselves. Signs reading "Do not lift tables or chairs without giving 48 hours notice to HSE management" have been plastered across the walls in several meeting rooms.*

Labour peer Lord Berkeley noticed the signs when he attended a meeting at the London headquarters of the HSE, whose responsibilities include work-

ers at nuclear plants, oil rigs and huge factories. Incensed by what he considered to be "health and safety gone mad," Lord Berkeley spoke of the matter in the House of Lords. "It's ridiculous to mollycoddle people like that. It's taking health-and-safety precautions to a ridiculous level. The HSE is an office like any other, so if it is not required in other offices, why there? It's the epitome of a nanny state."[69]

With due respect, Lord Berkeley has the situation just the opposite way around. What's required today at the HSE offices *will* be required tomorrow at all other offices of any kind. The spawning of progeny begins at home. Of course it's not *furniture* rearranging that is most worrisome, but how regulators of all types are intent on rearranging a once-free society. And, my, how proud they'll be of the results...until society grinds to a screeching halt.

Is there any wonder that an insider at the HSE (according to Arthur Martin's report in *The Daily Mail*, April 2, 2007), described life there as "a nanny state gone absolutely bonkers"?

Shades of nightmares to come

Bans on furniture-moving; bans on children's play-time rituals. Topple-testing for gravestones. Stripping Scouts of their knives and firemen of their poles. In Britain today, no corner is safe from the health and safety gestapo, whether spelled with capital letters at the head office or lower case with all the local busy-bodies constantly dreaming up new ways to nannify the nation. But all of this pales by comparison with the latest Orwellian plans....

Comment—*Health and safety inspectors are to be given unprecedented access to family homes to ensure that parents are protecting their children from household accidents. New guidance drawn up at the request of the Department of Health urges councils and other public sector bodies to "collect data" on properties where children are thought to be at "greatest risk of unintentional injury." Council staff will then be tasked with overseeing the installation of safety devices in homes, including smoke alarms, stair* *gates, hot water temperature restrictions, oven guards and window and door locks.*

The draft guidance by a committee at the National Institute for Health and Clinical Excellence (Nice) has been criticised as intrusive and further evidence of the "creeping nanny state." Nice also recommends the creation of a new government database to allow GPs [doctors], midwives, and other officials who visit homes to log health and safety concerns they spot.

Matthew Elliott, of the TaxPayers' Alliance, said: "It is a huge intervention into family life which will be counter-productive. Good parents will feel the intrusion of the state in their homes, and bad parents will now have someone else to blame if they don't bring up their children in a sensible, safe environment."[70]

So writes Robert Watts in *The Sunday Times*, November 15, 2009, at a time when there are increasing reports of home invasions by hoodlums. Is *good* motive versus *bad* to be the only distinction when one's home is no longer sacrosanct? And which is more to be feared: *lawless* invaders, or invaders *cloaked with the full authority of law*? Whereas one might defend himself and his family against criminals, what defense does any citizen have against a government gone rogue?

In keeping with the purpose of this book—to sound the alarm about a creeping Obama-led nanny state right here at home—check out the following from The Heritage Foundation (July 17, 2009)....

Editorial—*The massive 1,018-page health care bill introduced by House Democrats is full of bad policy ideas, and they're not all even about health care. One troublesome provision calls for a home visitation program that would bring state workers into the homes of young families to improve "the well-being, health, and development of children."*

Lawmakers have essentially inserted the "Education Begins at Home Act"—which was introduced in 2008 and again this year by Rep. Danny Davis (D-IL) and Sen. Kit Bond (R-MO)—into the health care bill under the home visitation section. Despite the fact that as a stand-alone bill the Education Begins at Home Act failed to gain traction last year, lawmakers intent on increasing the federal role in education into the preschool years have inserted the language into the mammoth health care bill.

If ever there were any doubt, America is following bureaucratic Obama-ites blindly down the path of our leftist liberal British cousins, from health and safety madness outside the home to government intrusion within the home. Once you unleash the State, you can never limit how vicious it becomes.

As almost an aside in his *American Spectator* editorial on the old sailors march in Scarborough cited earlier, Hal G.P. Colebatch astutely observes that "The constant stream of incidents reported in the press probably every day (most ominously, many of them no longer make the big national papers—there is no news in them) can be seen as part of the same pseudo-Gramscian culture war, and directed at the same targets."

Colebatch is right—that what once was shocking and newsworthy has now become so commonplace it no longer merits a headline. Still, not a day goes by that national papers in Britain don't have at least one article reporting the further advance of health and safety lunacy of a type which already is taking a firm hold in America, the land of the free and the home of the brave...new world. Which is anything but *brave.*

The roots of being risk-averse

What engine is pulling this train? Why is it so important for a nanny state to be fanatical about health and safety? It can't all be about control freaks in government, or greedy lawyers just waiting for accidents to happen, or insurance moguls conspiring with the state to squeeze out every penny possible. Or even about average citizens who complain to high heaven about regulations and insurance premiums, but are only too happy to join the compensation club when they stand to profit from the system.

Apart from the obvious tie between big government and hyper-regulation, it is the very nature of a parent substitute—the nanny—to look after the health and safety of her charges. It's the mothering instinct raised to a statist level.

Yet there's more to the nanny state than merely benign protectionism. As long as a nation regards even her adult citizens as wards incapable of making good decisions, it will always be about rules rather than about more mature personal responsibility. Rules are for those who can't be trusted. A sign of good parenting (and even good nannying) is when children are gradually given more and more responsibility, and with it given commensurate freedom. By contrast, the parent who refuses to relinquish control over maturing children is quite rightly seen to be a tyrant. As with parents, so with governments. Big government is not just annoying, but a tyrannical, distrusting, controlling monster—a despotic wolf clothed with wooly thinking.

Dig even deeper and it becomes clear that health and safety madness ultimately has to do with a nation becoming more and more risk-averse. It doesn't take a rocket scientist to appreciate how obsessed both the Brits and Americans are with avoiding risk. Know many people in the current economic climate who are eager to risk their retirement nest-egg in high-risk stocks? And with one epidemic after another sweeping the globe, who dares risk getting the latest strand of virus? About the only people seemingly oblivious to risk are the countless teenagers having unprotected sex despite mammoth campaigns for "safe sex." Otherwise, it would be hard to think of a generation more risk-averse than ours. And that includes even rocket scientists.

Critics of America's space program cite the excessive caution of NASA in the wake of the Apollo 13, Columbia, and Challenger incidents. In the words of Apollo 13 director Gene Kranz (as immortalized by the title of his autobiography), "Failure is not an option." NASA has spent billions attempting to make things "safe" as America has sought to open new frontiers in space. Right idea, of course, although perhaps over-cautious for the task at hand. Putting it somewhat harshly, aerospace pioneer Burt Rutan is famous for having said that if we're not killing people, we're not pushing hard enough. Even a lot of explorers killed in the pursuit of new frontiers likely would agree. By its very nature, frontier-breaking invariably involves high risk. The question is: Just how many exciting frontiers will a risk-averse generation cross?

It's not just about space frontiers. A little-noticed phenomenon of corporate life is how increasingly fearful corporations become the higher you climb the corporate ladder. At the lower levels, it's about pure entrepreneurial risk-taking. "What works?" "What doesn't?" "How can life be improved through innovation?" But move from the "leaves" to the "branches" (as the model has been described), and suddenly you find an escalation of corporate angst. "What if the product flops and we blow the budget?" "Will we run afoul of regulations?" "Is there any chance we might get sued?" The notorious banking industry aside, it would be mind-boggling to know what technological progress has been stifled simply because of corporate risk-aversion.

As a variation on theme, check out this intriguing article....

News Report—*Four of the six projects nominated for the Stirling prize— the most prestigious awards for architecture—are for buildings overseas, prompting attacks on the conservative attitudes of British clients. David Chipperfield, who has been nominated for two projects—one in Germany and one in Spain—says, "In Britain no one wants to take any risks, and good architecture often comes out of risk."*[71]

As is often said, "ideas have consequences." Sometimes that is true in the most unlikely places, such as in architecture and far beyond. Witness Ulrich Beck's 1992 book, *Risk Society*, wherein he highlights the increasing risks in industry, chemicals, pollution, nuclear accidents, global warming and terrorism. Where do we expect the rise of greater *risk-awareness* to lead if not to greater *risk-aversion*? Today, we are obsessed with risk—locally and globally, politically and personally. Merely observe the portrayal of victimization in the media, and you will appreciate how viewers react to those who took risks and were scarred for life by whatever misfortune befell them. The lesson? Avoid risk at all cost! Even when it comes to nothing more serious than sports (as seen in this October 17, 2009 editorial in *The Independent*)....

Comment—*If the youngsters are any guide, football is increasingly becoming a game in which the avoidance of risk is paramount, the consequence of which is a growing emphasis on speed, of thought and movement. That is one of the key conclusions from Uefa's technical report on the European Under-21 championship.*

Uefa notes that every team played a back four with the central defenders rigidly holding their position—there were no budding Franz Beckenbauer's gliding forward from the back. Moreover, they tended to pass square, with the full-backs playing the ball forward. Protection was provided by at least one, often two, screening midfielders.[72]

Merely a coincidental trend in soccer strategy, you say? Maybe. But inquiring minds want to know just what risks a younger generation will be willing to take, whether in the workplace, or on the sports field, or—far more important—on the battlefield.

Risk-aversion a losing war

On March 26, 2003, Mick Hume, editor-in-chief of British-based "spiked-online" wrote a piece regarding the start of the Iraq war which in retrospect seems all the more lucid, prophetic, and even (given the website's usual proclivities) surprisingly conservative....

Blog—*What's going on? The short answer is that this is what happens when our risk-averse Western societies try to go to war in the twenty-first century.... President George W. Bush and Prime Minister Tony Blair have been propelled into this "pre-emptive" attack on Iraq primarily by the contemporary Western obsession with precaution and risk aversion. If, as Clausewitz suggested, war is* *the continuation of politics by other means, then this war is the projection of our fearful domestic political culture on the world stage.*

The notion of a pre-emptive war of this kind applies to international affairs what conservative scientists would call the precautionary principle, or what your grandmother might call the doctrine of "better safe than sorry."

So began the world's first big risk-averse war. The trouble is, the risk-averse outlook driving them to war also inevitably distorts their military strategy. The same anxieties propelling them into the conflict tend to hold them back from seeing it through decisively. What is now being called the Rumsfeld Strategy... seems to have been designed to achieve victory with the minimum risk.

So the US-UK military planners sit with official lawyers at their shoulders, warning them against bombing targets that, though strategic, could lay them open to the risk of future prosecutions for crimes against humanity. Risk-averse warfare turns out to be a mortal danger to us all.

So there we have it in a nutshell: To avoid the risk of further terrorism after 9/11, Britain and America struck out at Iraq, but with only the kind of "shock and awe" that could be inflicted with the minimum of risk, further increasing the risk of terrorism by those who are willing to risk everything for a cause in which they believe.

Fast-forward now to the war in Afghanistan. This time, it's Frank Furedi's turn to focus "spike's" spotlight (September 7, 2009) on waging war in a risk-averse culture....

Blog—*A major international conflict has been treated as a banal health-and-safety issue.... Since there are no guarantees that a military venture will be risk-free...the current criticisms of the engagement in Afghanistan really apply to all wars. Of course, the loss of a soldier's life is always a terrible tragedy for his or her family, friends and comrades—but unless a community is prepared to countenance such terrible losses, or willing to experience some uncertainty and risk, then it implicitly invites others to trample on its freedom and liberties.*

The attempt to abolish risk and uncertainty in military operations resonates with today's powerful risk-averse culture. Risk aversion in the domain of childhood and everyday life is bad enough, but when it is extended to the battlefield, its consequences are potentially lethal.

Unlike some institutions in society, the military cannot survive without taking risks. And yet the military values associated with the warrior ethos are continually challenged by today's potent cultural hostility to risk-taking behaviour. Despite the many Hollywood action-packed movies that cele-brate heroism and bravery, there is little cultural validation of risky mili-tary behaviour these days. The military is not immune to the influence of the predominant precautionary culture. A culture that has a low threshold for coping with losses in everyday life is unlikely to be able to celebrate risk-taking behaviour with military institutions.

Disturbing reading? It ought to be. We're no longer talking simply about inane health-and-safety edicts requiring teachers to check "the weather, currents, weeds, rip tides, river or sea beds and breakwaters before allowing school children into the water for recreational swim-ming."[73] We're talking about those same mollycoddled young people growing up to be the nation's defenders in hostile environments that are anything but healthy and safe. And about public support for a war being dependent on little more than the latest media-highlighted body count. And about politicians (once those same mollycoddled children) who are more fearful of election risks than mustering the courage to do the right thing regardless of the political fallout.

Assessing the risks of health and safety

Listen to Britain's health and safety overlords, and you'd be right to conclude that hardly a breath can be drawn without a formal risk assessment. So in the spirit of risk assessments, perhaps it's time that the Health and Safety Executive itself was assessed (using its own model template).

What are the hazards?
- Heavy-handed bureaucrats micro-managing the lives of individuals and businesses
- Contributing to a litigious, compensation-culture mentality
- Being a shill for insurance companies wishing to minimize their risks by refusing to cover perfectly proper activities without prohibitive premiums
- Inculcating a pervasive risk-averse mentality, stifling innovation, entrepreneurial initiative, and creativity
- Creating a dangerous precautionary culture on the part of police and other emergency services personnel
- Reducing a nation's ability to respond to threats from external enemies

Who might be harmed, and how?
- A whole generation of young people, robbed of normal childhood experiences
- A nation of people, devoid of personal responsibility
- Charities and community activities, forced to survive without generous volunteers
- Local government autonomy, having to kowtow to big government

What are you already doing?
- The "little people" are grumbling, but the politicians aren't listening
- The newspapers are reporting the daily madness, but the bureaucrats aren't bothered

What further action is necessary?
- For Britain, pull the plug on EU health and safety guidelines
- For America as well, slash budgets, personnel, and power of health-and-safety bodies, top to bottom
- Withhold tax money from regulation-crazy local councils
- Make excessive regulation as shameful as hyper-regulation has been made respectable
- Restore the primacy of common sense over regulatory nonsense

Action by whom?
- By politicians at the top, shutting down rogue bureaucrats, regulatory agencies, and EU diktats
- By bureaucrats, exercising self-restraint in the larger interest of society
- By local government officials, sharply paring down the number of rules and regulations
- By individual citizens raising the alarm through letters, articles, voting, and generally speaking out against the madness

Action by when?
- Sooner rather than later
- As of the next election
- Before it's too late

We Americans may not have the imperious Health and Safety Executive breathing down our necks, nor the autocratic European Union, but even within our own multi-layered government and complex maze of federal, state, and local regulatory agencies, the same hazards and societal implications are already threatening. All the more reason, then, for constant vigilance and a renewed determination to stop any further advance of bureaucratic tyranny.

Health and safety gone mad is not just good government gone bad. Excessive risk avoidance has a corrupting influence on individuals and institutions at all levels, undermining fundamental character, prudence, duty and courage. Of all the risks we might wish to avoid, the greatest possible risk is a culture obsessed with risk.

The risk we ought to be obsessing over is the risk of our inheriting the no-risk culture of our cousins across the Pond. President Obama may have been publicly cool to those distant cousins, but there's hardly any denying their shared liberal-Left, regulation-driven DNA. If this chapter has done nothing else, hopefully it has highlighted the greatest risk you face the next time you step foot into a voting booth....

5

Sure You Want British-style Healthcare?

America's health care system is neither healthy,
caring, nor a system.

—WALTER CRONKITE

While Britain's Government is obsessed with "health and safety," the grand irony is that there is neither *health* nor *safety* in great abundance these days. Especially public health. For all of its admirable aims in providing universal coverage for citizens of every economic level, the National Health Service (NHS) is an inefficient, bureaucratic, debt-ridden shambles. If perhaps there are other models of socialized medicine which might be alluring, Britain's system is not one to be envied.

Anyone wondering about the sweeping implications of President Obama's massive "Affordable Care Act" would do well to read this chapter with eyes wide open. In fact, it would be hard to read this chapter without having your eyes bulging! Certainly, there are significant differences between "Obamacare" and Britain's full-out nationalized health system, but if you want to get some sense of the dangers lurking behind any "Big Brother" approach to national health care, all you have to do is double-click on the NHS icon. You won't believe what comes up on the screen.

By the time you read this chapter, the U.S. Supreme Court may well have rendered its decision on the legal viability of the ACA. Maybe it's still standing, maybe not. Or maybe *parts* of it are plowing ahead, while other parts aren't. Whatever the case, any future consideration of how we in the United States should proceed regarding health care reform ought to be informed by a close-up look at the British health system. It is not a system to be envied or followed.

Unlike in the previous chapters, the articles below speak eloquently for themselves with little need for additional commentary. A good starting point is Britain's dismal ranking among other socialized health care systems....

Headline—British healthcare ranked 14th out of 33. *The Euro Health Consumer Index has ranked Britain's NHS 14th out of 33 European health-care systems, just ahead of Slovenia and the Czech Republic. National healthcare systems are evaluated using 38 factors, including patients' rights and information, waiting times, access to medicines and treatment outcomes.*

The top countries were: Netherlands with 875 points followed by Denmark, Iceland, Austria, Switzerland, Germany, France, Sweden, Luxembourg, and Norway. The bottom countries were; Bulgaria, which scored 448 points, followed by Romania, Latvia, Albania, Lithuania, Slovakia, Malta, Poland, Portugal and FYR Macedonia. With a score of 682, Britain ranked above Italy and below Ireland.

Dr. Arne Björnberg, Director of the Euro Health Consumer Index, said: "The UK…has showed surprisingly negative feedback from patient organisations on the waiting time situation, particularly after government spending on the NHS has been increasing heavily. It seems that management of the behemoth NHS organisation is difficult to do under a centralised paradigm."

The report ranked the NHS 23rd out of the 33 countries on 'bang-for-buck', a calculation that tries to take into account the different amounts spent on healthcare in each of the countries.

A spokesman for Britain's Department of Health said: "Once again, the European Consumer Health Index report is based on flawed methodology and old data. The NHS is treating more people and saving more lives than at any time in its history with waiting times at their lowest levels since records began."[74]

What do you expect to hear from the Department of Health? If the NHS is treating more people than ever, and the waiting times are at their lowest levels in years, it's only testimony as to how appalling the system has been in prior decades. In today's NHS, there is little reason to be proud.

Headline—Health inequality worsens. *Under the Labour Government, health inequality (measured by life expectancy and infant mortality) has gotten worse. While life expectancy for all social groups is improving, and infant mortality figures are going down, the health gap between rich and poor has widened. Babies born to poor families now have a 17 percent higher than average chance of dying, compared to a 13 percent higher than average chance 10 years ago. And the life expectancy of people living in poverty has fallen further behind than it was when Tony Blair was elected. The figures are embarrassing for the government because cutting health inequalities has been one of its priorities.[75]*

Headline—NHS cancer care a disgrace. *Despite the tripling of investment in cancer care in Britain over the past decade, there has been no striking improvement in cancer survival in a system "riddled with bureaucracy," says cancer specialist Professor Karol Sikora. Five-year survival rates for most common cancers have improved in England, but England came 15th in a league of five-year rates among 22 European countries.*

Professor Sikora lamented that "Cancer patients' notes have become riddled with shabby stamps warning of targets about to be breached. Armies of administrators were recruited to operate the system, adding massively to the cost of care. The ridiculously poor performance of information technology in

British hospitals dramatically increased the cost of trying to improve cancer care."

Access to new cancer drugs is poor in the NHS, with the use of six cancer drugs approved in the past three years, equivalent to just a fifth of the average across the EU. "The postcode lottery abounds, with those that shout loudest getting better services" he added.[76]

Delay, delay, and more delay

If there is any single complaint most often heard anecdotally from Britain's citizens, it is the diabolical delays they experience before benefitting from the health care system they have paid over a lifetime to enjoy. Have a heart attack or some other real emergency, and the NHS is all over it. Few complaints there. But if you need a knee or hip replacement, you're likely to wait months while the NHS is attending to all of the heart attacks. However, it's not just the hospitals that are slow. The long lines begin even at the local GP (General Practitioner)....

Headline—Patients lose patience waiting for doctors. *Nine years after the Government pledged that all patients should be seen by their doctors within 48 hours, patients often can't see their GP within that time. Millions of people are still struggling to get appointments when they need them. Just 53 percent of Primary Care Trusts achieve that mandated target.*[77]

Headline—Disabled children wait for wheelchairs. *A recent survey showed that 58 percent of disabled children in England had to wait at least three months for an electric wheelchair and 14 percent waited more than six months. The NHS has been told to stop relying on charities to fill funding gaps after figures revealed many trusts would not pay the full cost of wheelchairs for disabled children.*[78]

Headline—Scots wait for cancer treatment. *In Scotland, waiting times for cancer treatment have fallen short of the target of 62 days from* *urgent referral by a doctor to starting of treatment. Cancer experts said that patients elsewhere in Europe would be outraged at having to wait two months to start treatment. Most Europeans are seen within two weeks.*[79]

NHS-style health care would never work in the States, if for no other reason that Americans would never put up with the delays typically tolerated by British citizens accustomed to queuing for everything. If all you've ever known is endless delay, then you expect nothing better. But even with a system that has its own minor delays, Americans are spoiled silly with generally expeditious health care. And the wonderful irony of it all? "Obamacare's" most vocal supporters (including, above all, the legislators who passed it!) have such gold-standard private healthcare service that they will never, ever get close to experiencing the NHS delay syndrome or what will soon be America's equivalent. Delay? What delay!

Where have all the beds gone?

Why all this maddening delay? Seems that in Britain there's a never-ending game of "musical beds" being played. Not that the NHS is so broke it couldn't actually buy more beds. The problem, of course, is that more beds mean more hospital space to house them, and more doctors, nurses, and staff to attend them. Stories abound of patients arriving at the hospital for a scheduled surgery, only to be told, "Sorry, but there aren't any beds available. We'll have to reschedule." Depending on what surgery is needed, just how frightening can that be...?

Headline—Bed shortage postpones surgeries. *A three-year-old girl awaiting heart surgery has had her operation cancelled three times this month because of a shortage of beds. Ella Cotterell was due to have aorta-widening surgery on Monday at the Children's Hospital, Bristol. But the crucial operation was cancelled 48 hours beforehand—for the third time—as all 15 beds in the intensive care unit were occupied.*

Last year, more than 57,000 surgeries were postponed for non-clinical reasons, including a lack of beds.[80]

Headline—Elderly patients refused intensive care. *A six-year survey of four million operations found that 85 percent of the most vulnerable patients do not get the intensive care that could save their lives. It is estimated that up to 5,000 frail and elderly patients die each year because they are not put in intensive care beds for monitoring after their operations.*

Research by the Intensive Care Society has shown that only 2.5 percent of hospital beds are allocated for critical care in the Britain, compared with 3.5 percent in France and Germany and 4 percent in Denmark.[81]

Headline—Expectant mothers turned away from hospitals. *The NHS has admitted that women in labor are being refused entry to overstretched maternity units and told to give birth elsewhere. Birthing centers may not be all they were cracked up to be. Tory health spokesman Andrew Lansley found they were more likely to refuse entry to mothers in labor because all the beds were full.*[82]

While we're on the subject of beds, Americans visiting many NHS hospitals in England can be forgiven for thinking that they are in a time machine, visiting war-time Britain. Few Americans have ever *seen* multiple-bed wards, much less endured their indignity. Yet, still today, wards are a common feature of the NHS. And not just wards, but *mixed-sex* wards....

Comment—Hospitals still putting patients in mixed-sex wards. *Ministers have finally admitted that hospital patients are still suffering the indignity of being cared for on mixed-sex wards after years of insisting the problem was under control. A decade after promising to phase out mixed-sex wards, one in six hospital trusts are flouting government rules designed to stamp out the practice.*

The Daily Mail has been campaigning to scrap mixed-sex wards since first highlighting the problem 12 years ago. Labour pledged in both 1997 and 2001 to phase out mixed-sex wards. Indeed, a year before Mr. Blair became prime minister, he said it was not "beyond the wit of government and health administrators" to get rid of them.

A Patients Association spokesman said: "We've been promised an end to mixed-sex wards so many times in the past but we know that they are still very much in existence. Women particularly feel very vulnerable. Having to share bathroom and toilet facilities in the 21st century is unacceptable.[83]

Suffocating from bureaucracy

Ever wonder why an onion stinks? Might it have anything to do with its many layers? Probably not, but that's certainly the case with bureaucracy, whether in government generally or state-sponsored medical care in particular. The more the layers, the more it stinks.

A corollary is that the more targets one sets, the more targets one misses....

Editorial—Target culture prevents nurses from caring for patients. *I started as a nursing cadet before there was an NHS. As someone on the bottom rung of the ladder I spent most of my time cleaning and scrubbing to make sure no bacteria could ever get near patients. That was a big worry for everybody because infections in those days could not be treated with antibiotics. It was right after the war and antibiotics were reserved for the use of people in the armed forces.*

The main difference between then and now is that we were not expected to rush patients through anything. Whatever they needed they had, and the emphasis was always on them. But then in the 80's Mrs. Thatcher, strongly influenced by US advice, decided to run the NHS like a business and see if she could cut corners and cut costs. So the target culture was born and hospital managers increased in large numbers. They created rules which were often impossible to follow.

For example, patients could only wait in Accident and Emergency for up to four hours—impossible if there has been a major incident that has filled the A&E department to the brim. This target, like all targets, in time led to all sort of cheating and trickery. Ambulances were told that unless their patients were desperately ill they would have to wait outside A&E until other patients close to the time limit had been moved on. That's because the time the patient was spending in the ambulance didn't count as time spent waiting in A&E.

The target culture has, from the start, led to a dreadful waste of professional time and extra layers of management. Nurses have been estimated to spend as much as 40 percent of their time writing and "capturing data" to help the managers upstairs appear to reach their targets. If nurses are busy "capturing data," to fit this week's targets, how can they possibly give enough care to their patients?

We need an NHS management that will get off the backs of doctors and nurses and instead allow them to care for patients properly. [84]

Headline—Waiting-list target achieved by eliminating patients. *Liberal Democrat leader Nicol Stephen reported the "shocking and scandalous situation" of a Lothian woman who was told she was being taken off a consultant's waiting list so the target 18-week waiting time for treatment could be met. The patient had been told by the doctor: "I am afraid I am writing to inform you of some bad news. I have been instructed by hospital management to remove your name from my waiting list. The prime reason for this decision relates to the 18-week target for patient treatment which is now in enforcement. I currently have a significant number of patients in breach of this and the simple solution by management is to reduce my waiting lists by removing patients' names."*[85]

Headline—Private managers brought in to save NHS. *Alan Johnson, the Health Secretary, is to announce that private managers could be brought in to run failing hospitals under measures to tackle poor performance in the health service. Doctors, politicians and unions gave warning last night that the measures risked undermining the fundamental principles of the NHS. Labour MP Ian Gibson said: "The privatisation of the NHS is becoming less than subtle. This is a blatant snub to the health service."*[86]

NHS hospitals flunk health and safety standards

We've already spoken about the irony. When it comes to that arm of the government most directly concerned with health and safety—the National Health Service—suddenly health gets second billing. When one of the unhealthiest places to be in Britain is in a hospital ward, one would think Health and Safety would shut them down in a heartbeat. As it happens, Health and Safety does indeed "shut down" hospitals, but for all the usual wrong reasons....

Comment—Safety regulations create health crisis. *Strangely, while the government has promoted evidence-based medicine within the NHS, whereby treatments and procedures are supported by clear, tangible, robust research, health and safety policies seem exempt from such scrutiny. Stories abound of trusts imposing daft regulations in order to avoid possible lawsuits, despite little or no evidence of the actual level of risk involved. But health and safety regulations can also impact on the way that clinicians work to the detriment of the patients, as well as common sense.*

Guidelines that were intended to ensure safe practice become monolithic and immoveable. This has led to the situation, for example, where a surgeon friend of mine was forced to wheel patients down to the imaging department to have scans because none of the porters on duty had done the course in how to push someone in a wheelchair, so for health and safety reasons they were not allowed to. This situation was, of course, ridiculous—surely it is more of a risk to health and safety to have a surgeon leave a ward of sick people to push someone down to X-ray? And exactly how does this compare to the risk pushing someone in a wheel chair poses when you haven't done a certificate in it?[287]

Headline—Patients dying of accidents in NHS care. *Parliament's Public Accounts Committee has reported that 1 in 10 patients admitted to NHS hospitals is accidentally harmed and almost a million safety incidents, more than 2,000 of which were fatal, were recorded last year. As if those figures weren't "terrifying enough," the report said that the reality might be worse because of what it called "substantial under-*

reporting." "The NHS simply has no idea how many people die each year from patient-safety incidents," said Edward Leigh, the committee's chairman.[88]

Headline—Problems with out-of-hours doctor care. *A report by the Care Quality Commission, the health care regulator, says that patients' lives are being put at risk by "widespread problems" in out-of-hours GP care, particularly where foreign doctors may not be able to speak good English, and staff may be overworked.*[89]

It's all about the money

Certainly, Britain is not alone when it comes to the financial aspects of public health care. No nation is spared the challenge of getting the best bang for the buck. But Britain's experience can be a sober warning about trying to solve the American dilemma by simply throwing untold billions at the problem.

If private health care does its own fair share of rationing, public health care is under even more pressure to trim vital services in order to meet budgets overburdened by both genuine health services and the typical bureaucracy that comes with government involvement. At the level of the individual, these cuts take on a far more personal perspective....

Headline—Heart procedure denied by budget. *Dorothy Simpson, 61, was refused a routine heart operation recommended by her specialist, because of budgetary concerns. The Primary Care Trust is said to have cited her age as one of the reasons for refusal. "I can't believe that at 61 I'm too old for this operation," she said. "A friend has had exactly the same thing done and it has changed his life. I feel as though I've been put out to grass and surely deserve better than this."*[90]

Comment—Doctors slam NHS drug rationing. *Britain's top cancer consultants have accused the government's drugs rationing body of ignoring the plight of patients forced to sell their cars and remortgage their houses to pay for cancer treatments freely available in Europe.*

Twenty-six professors blame the severe restrictions imposed by the National Institute of Health and Clinical Excellence (Nice) on its failure to "get its sums right." Nice refuses, on grounds of cost, to recommend some drugs for patients with advanced kidney cancer.

Their letter to The Sunday Times states: "We now spend similar amounts to Europe on health generally and cancer care in particular, but less than two thirds of the European average on cancer drugs. It just can't be that everybody else around the world is wrong about access to innovative cancer care and the NHS right in rationing it so severely." They say: "The time has come for a radical change in how the NHS makes rationing decisions for cancer."

This weekend Andrew Dillon, the chief executive of Nice, and Sir Michael Rawlins, the chairman, challenged the cancer experts to explain which acutely ill patients should be sacrificed to free resources for cancer sufferers.[91]

Comment—NHS tells patients to treat themselves. *Millions of people with arthritis, asthma and even heart failure will be urged to treat themselves as part of a Government plan to save billions of pounds from the NHS budget. Instead of going to hospital or consulting a doctor, patients will be encouraged to carry out "self care" as the Department of Health (DoH) tries to meet Treasury targets to curb spending.*[92]

Dental care like pulling teeth

The old saying, "Don't look a gift horse in the mouth," might be apropos for this section on socialized dentistry. No offense intended, but if ever you wanted to pick American and British citizens out of a lineup, just look in their mouths. While Americans have a national obsession with beautiful, smiley teeth, the Brits have a long history of backwater dental practices still in need of catching up. Even apart from cosmetic dentistry, the most basic dental services are still problematic for large sections of the British population....

Headline—NHS dentists complain of 'drill and fill' targets. *Since the Labour Government introduced a new contract for dentists in 2006,*

121

more than 1,000 practices have stopped providing NHS care and 500,000 fewer patients see NHS dentists. Dentists complain that the new system forces them to provide "conveyor belt care" and to "drill and fill" to meet meaningless targets.

A great-grandmother from Scarborough has told how she pulled a tooth with a pair of pliers from her husband's toolbox after drinking beer as an anaesthetic. A survey of patients and dentists has exposed a case in Lancashire in which a man had to remove 14 teeth using pliers.[93]

Headline—Villagers left toothless. *1,000 people in the village of Tadley, population 11,500 ended up on a waiting list for a dentist after only a single NHS practice opened in the Hampshire village. The only alternatives for villagers were paying privately for dental care, or travelling miles to another NHS dentist, or simply going without treatment.*

With much fanfare, then-Prime Minister Tony Blair promised that within two years everyone would have access to an NHS dentist. Eight years later he admitted failure. The new contract introduced three years ago to increase numbers of NHS dentists has made the situation all the worse, with 1,000 dentists fleeing the NHS.[94]

It's worth pausing here to note that, as go the dentists, so go the doctors. Why are there so many foreign doctors in the NHS? Because British doctors have fled the NHS in droves. Here's a prophecy for you: Give any conceivable form of "Obamacare" a decade, and what you'll see is "doctor flight" in dramatic numbers not unlike "white flight" from the inner cities. There will then be a Balkanization of medical care, with middle and upper class Americans getting local doctors, and everybody else having to settle for physicians with whom they can barely communicate. And Obama wants to avoid class distinctions…?

Using health care as fitness sledge hammer

When budgets get tight in national health care, it's not long before some begin to question why all taxpayers should foot the bill for those whose medical problems stem from personal lifestyle choices...or what are *believed to be* lifestyle choices. Aye, there's the rub...

Headline—NHS assaults smokers and the obese. *Health Secretary Patricia Hewitt has defended NHS hospitals that have imposed a ban on smokers and the obese from receiving particular treatments, including joint replacements for the obese and orthopaedic surgery for smokers. A survey last year found that two in five hospital doctors believed that smokers should pay for bypass operations.*[95]

Headline—Doctors call for chocolate tax. *Dr. David Walker, a family GP who is also a trained food scientist and nutritionist, has told a medical conference: "Obesity is a mushrooming problem. We are heading the same way as the United States. There is an explosion of obesity and the related medical conditions, like type-two diabetes. I see chocolate as a major player in this, and I think a tax on products containing chocolate could make a real difference."*

A motion calling for the introduction of a chocolate tax was defeated by only two votes by doctors at the British Medical Association (BMA) conference.[96]

If you haven't already noticed, this same Diet Diktat mentality is hitting the streets back home in the Good Ole USA. You say you want chocolate, sodas and potato chips, fatty? Just wait till "Obamacare" fully kicks in....

NHS—a Trojan horse for liberal causes

"With money goes the power of the purse strings," the saying goes. Whoever pays can decide how the money will be spent. So if the government is paying for national health care, you can rest assured that, as the government thinks, so goes the health care system.

Have a liberal government? Your health care system will be liberal. Have a government giving full approval to abortion? Your health care system will provide for abortion. Have a government obsessed with sex? Your health care system will be obsessed with sex....

Headline—NHS tells students sex is good for health. *An NHS leaflet titled "Pleasure" is telling school children they have a "right" to an enjoyable sex life and that it is good for their health. The leaflet says experts concentrate too much on the need for safe sex and loving relationships, and not enough on the pleasure it can bring.*

Under the heading "An orgasm a day keeps the doctor away," the leaflet says: "Health promotion experts advocate five portions of fruit and veg a day and 30 minutes physical activity three times a week. What about sex or masturbation twice a week?"[97]

And you think "Obamacare" won't do the same? Once the camel's nose is under the tent, America's young people will be barraged with mixed messages: Practice safe sex. Guard yourself against STDs. Teen pregnancy is to be avoided at all cost. But, oh by the way, sex is great for your health!

NHS—an ethics nightmare

When faith and morality have been kicked out of the public square, difficult ethical conundrums are made all the more difficult, especially at the margins of life—whether at the beginning or the end. Even where medical guidance seems to be reasonable and prudent, one begins to sense that there's a backstory in the fine print. Look carefully for the operative line in the following incident....

Headline—Guidelines declared baby too early to save. *Sarah Capewell, who had suffered five previous miscarriages, pleaded in vain for doctors to save her son, born two days too early under mandated guidelines. Ms. Capewell says her increasingly desperate pleas to assist her baby were met with a brusque response from doctors, who said she should consider the labor as a miscarriage, rather than a birth. After asking doctors to consider his human right to life, she says she was told: "He hasn't got a human right, he is a foetus."*[98]

Did you catch that last operative line? (If true, shouldn't the word have been "it" rather than "he"?) Dangerous assumptions drive deadly results!

Never is that more true than in a society's attitude toward the elderly and frail. If corners are to be cut in national healthcare, no one should be surprised when the cuts involve senior citizens who are so easily marginalized....

Headline—Doctors warn about patients 'sentenced to death' by NHS. *In a letter to The Daily Telegraph, a group of experts who care for the terminally ill claim that some patients are being wrongly judged as close to death. Under NHS guidance to help medical staff deal with dying patients, patients can have fluid and drugs withdrawn and many are put on continuous sedation until they pass away. But the experts warn that this very approach can also mask signs that the patient's condition is improving.*

The warning comes just a week after a report by the Patients Association estimated that up to one million patients had received poor or cruel care on the NHS.

One of the experts said: "I have been practising palliative medicine for more than 20 years and I am getting more concerned about this "death pathway" that is coming in. He said that he had personally taken patients off the pathway who went on to live for "significant" amounts of time and warned that many doctors were not checking the progress of patients enough to notice improvement in their condition.[99]

Headline—Pensioner dies after wrongly being put on 'death pathway.' *A pensioner died from pneumonia after being put on a "death pathway" when doctors wrongly thought he had cancer. His widow repeatedly told medical staff at the Marie Curie hospice that she thought her husband was suffering from pneumonia, but medical staff put him on a palliative care programme called the Liverpool Care Pathway. A post mortem examination found no evidence of cancer.*[100]

Health care for the sick, or Wish List for everyone?

If you so choose, you can buy a basic, no-frills car pretty cheap. But who would think of driving just a stripped-down model when you can have all the luxury add-ons? That's a no-brainer! When it comes to an already-over-priced health care system, the only thing that's a no-brainer is assuring that taxpayer dollars are being spent on *health* care, not on every medical procedure known to man that might make one's life just a bit happier.

Headline—Welsh NHS to fund more sex-swap operations. *Public funds from the Health Commission Wales will now provide for gender reassignment therapy for treatment of gender dysphoria, a condition in which individuals feel trapped in the body of the wrong sex. Surgery to treat gender reassignment from male to female can cost between £8,000 and £15,000. Surgery from female to male is more expensive.*[101]

The following piece contends that it's all about choices and what we're willing to pay for....

Editorial—Why should IVF be available on the NHS? *I feel sorry for childless couples—who wouldn't?—but listening to the radio this morning about the postcode lottery of IVF treatment I wondered why no one raised the obvious point: Sorry, that's sad, but it's not the taxpayer's responsibility.*

In most cases this treatment has to be undertaken because people have left it too late....But even if the couples have other fertility problems, the NHS is not made of money, or as Melanie Phillips put it, "It's the National Health Service, not the National Happiness Service." When this incredible organisation, a rightful source of national pride, was conceived (so to speak) it was intended to help the sick, not to provide liposuction for people who could easily lose weight themselves, sex-change operations and reverse-sex-change operations, pills for men who can't get erections, boob jobs and fertility treatment, not to mention a staggering 180,000 abortions a year, each costing around £500 (the other 20,000 are paid for privately).[102]

Comment [responding to the article above]— *I couldn't care less about every other person's wish to have a child and should not be forced to fund their attempts, anymore than they would ever feel the responsibility to fund me to have plastic surgery to make myself look like a character for Star Trek (Maybe some pointy ears?).*

It is the natural creep of socialism in which the same arguments about "greater good" are used in ever-expanding contexts. What was once a system to help cure, becomes preventive, becomes psychological, becomes optional.

My own conscience prevents me from stealing like this from others, but indeed the selfish are more than happy to rip from your hands whatever they can for IVF treatment, breast implants and Viagra, all of which have been, and will continue to be, supplied on the NHS in the name of psychological happiness and the NHS addiction with "sexual liberty."

However, even if we could get around the argument that these are not really health measures, I only have to look to Sweden to see that sexual liberty is just a system of appeasing the removal of real liberty, and I'd rather be frigid and free. [James]

Great line, that, from James. It bears repeating that "What was once a system to help *cure*, becomes *preventive*, becomes *psychological*, becomes *optional*. Words to seriously consider as our leaders continue to debate "Obamacare." Under The Affordable Care Act or anything remotely like it, happiness healthcare isn't just a slippery slope. It's a philosophical certainty.

Click on NHS to pull up larger social planning issue

Revisiting the sad state of British dentistry under the NHS, the following editorial by Llewellyn H. Rockwell, Jr. puts into pointed, painful perspective the whole matter of socialized medicine—whether in Britain or in the United States. Indeed, it highlights the dubious wisdom behind all grand, ideological social planning....

Only 49 percent of adults and 63 percent of children are registered with a dentist in England and Wales, according to the New York Times. You have to be registered to get service, but there is still no guarantee. You wait months, even years, if you get in at all.

This experiment in British socialism was concocted by a class of intellectuals who imagined that their scheme would provide equal access to all of life's wonderful things. The result has been a tragedy. And this tragedy has, in many ways, ended in a terrible farce: people yanking out their own teeth in the land that gave us the most conspicuous example of the industrial revolution.

Someone may claim that he has an idea for providing universal access to dentistry, if only you give him the power to do what he wants. But there are a number of questions you should ask. Will he or you be the one to suffer if something goes wrong? Who is going to be held to account if the plan results in deprivation rather than plenty? What is the exit strategy for abolishing the system if it doesn't work? Where is the guarantee that this exit plan will be followed?

Free enterprise can't make the reality of tooth pain disappear. It can't alter the makeup of the universe. It can't change human nature. It can't abolish mortality. It can't take away the need for parents to train their children on the difference between right and wrong. It must accept the structure of reality as a given. Neither, however, can the state do these things.

If you try to improve on freedom by means of the state, you not only create a worse situation but you end up slowing the pace of progress and actually bring about retrogression in advances made through the capitalistic era. The socialization of dentistry has plunged Britain back more than a century in tooth care. Abolish capitalism altogether and you can find yourself back in the Stone Age. Even the metal drill will seem like a welcome tool.[103]

It's not as if liberals, even Leftist liberals, never have any good ideas. Serving the needs of the poor and oppressed through universal health care is a righteous cause. It's just that the means most typically chosen by liberals to provide the greatest good for the greatest number tends so often to produce the opposite effect. Compassion is not the question. Competence is. And rarely is any grand government policy as competent as private benevolence and enterprise.

A last-chance warning

British public healthcare is so fraught with systemic problems that frustrated Brits are increasingly turning back to free enterprise to save the day. More and more Brits who can afford private health insurance are paying heavy premiums so that if forced to have a hospital stay, at least they will be in the "luxury wing" of the exact same building, where there are tolerable creature comforts and guaranteed good medical care. Either that, or they're taking the first low-cost flight to Poland or other European countries where (apart from equally-dismal local public healthcare) *private, free-enterprise medical care* is available, efficient, affordable, and of high-standard. Call it "medical tourism." Whatever it takes, the British people have resorted to gaming their broken system any way they can. It's not a *heart* bypass the Brits are wanting but an *NHS* bypass!

Is this what we in America are hoping for from a government-heavy, nanny-nurse overhaul of our approach to healthcare? Will it make us feel any better thinking that we've achieved equal access to healthcare if the only thing we achieve is equal access to an intolerable health system that desperate folks will start gaming any way they can? For anyone looking for a good investment, maybe you should consider buying stock in LOT, the Polish airline....

If Britain's creaking National Health Service is anything to go by, Americans would be well advised to quarantine anything that looks remotely similar to it. Even if our current system is ailing, the last thing we want as a nation of health providers and consumers is to end up in intensive care.

6

Sleepwalking Into a Police State

No tyranny is so irksome as petty tyranny: the officious demands of policemen, government clerks, and electromechanical gadgets.

—Edward Abbey

News Report—*It has become commonplace to call Britain a "surveillance society," a place where security cameras lurk at every corner, giant databases keep track of intimate personal details and the government has extraordinary powers to intrude into citizens' lives. But the intrusions visited on Jenny Paton, a 40-year-old mother of three, were startling just the same. Suspecting Ms. Paton of falsifying her address to get her daughter into the neighborhood school, local officials here began a covert surveillance operation. For more than three weeks, an officer from the Poole education department secretly followed her....*

It turned out that Ms. Paton had broken no rules. Her case has become emblematic of the struggle between personal privacy and the ever more powerful state here.

The Poole Borough Council says it has done nothing wrong. In a way, that is true: Under a law enacted in 2000 to regulate surveillance powers, it is legal for localities to follow residents secretly. Local governments regularly use these surveillance powers—which they "self-authorize," without oversight from judges or law enforcement officers—to investigate malfeasance like illegally dumping industrial waste, loan-sharking and falsely claiming welfare benefits.

But they also use them to investigate reports of noise pollution and people who do not clean up their dogs' waste. Local governments use them to catch people who fail to recycle, people who put their trash out too early, and people whose dogs bark too loudly.[104]

Sarah Lyall's report for *The New York Times* (October 24, 2009) is striking for at least two reasons—first, because it focuses the spotlight on Britain's reputation for being a "surveillance society" with all that power-packed phrase entails; and second, because it is written by a correspondent for an American newspaper, suggesting a significant contrast between Britain and the States in the arena of intrusive, governmental snooping. Given the already-high level of government-sponsored surveillance in the United States, that's some statement!

The case of Jenny Paton and her three children being tailed as if they were hardened criminals on the prowl ought to be a warning shot across the bow of any nation headed down the road of saturation surveillance. Without public protest beginning *now*, it won't be long before targets of surreptitious surveillance here in the States will include, not just potential terrorists and bank robbers, but anyone not toeing the line on garbage collections, accepted noise levels, and pet poop. Britain's surveillance experience is the best possible window into mission creep—from CCTV security cameras to GPS tracking, from private records checks to gum-shoe detectives hired by the local town hall following you home.

If you don't think it can happen here in the States, who ever would have thought it could have happened in any civilized democratic society, much less in Britain—once the bastion of civil liberties? Rubbish, you say…?

News Report—*Garbage men are being issued computers to build a "rubbish profile" of households across Britain, only slightly masquerading the* *ultimate purpose: paving the way for a pay-as-you-throw bin tax. GPS technology allows councils to store information about individual rubbish collections, including whether householders fail to recycle properly.*[105]

Editorial—*The Telegraph reports today that two million households now have microchips in their bins, planted by local councils to see how much rubbish we throw away. Last time, we were told that councils needed to know how much rubbish everyone was chucking out so they could charge us fairly. But the "Big Brother bin tax," and the microchips they even admitted didn't work, soon bit the dust...or so we thought. This time around, councils are telling us they need to check our rubbish to see if we're recycling properly.*[106]

All of which brings this rollicking response from one frustrated citizen....

Anonymous Blog—*First they came for the rubbish bins. Then they came for me!*

Brilliant! But who will be laughing when it actually comes true? What's next, GPS microchips implanted under the skin? For any skeptics out there, it's already happening in Britain to some of man's best friends....

News Report—*Under plans supported by the Tories and Labour, dogs in Britain will have to be fitted with microchips that carry details including the pet's name, breed, age and health record along with the owner's address and phone number, all of which would then be stored on a national database that local councils could access. In theory, the scheme is designed to curb the trade in stolen dogs, prevent the use of animals in anti-social or violent incidents, and reduce the number of stray dogs being found on British streets. Owners in noncompliance would face the possibility of their dog being confiscated.*[107]

Predictably, the "benign" puppy microchip scheme is supported by Britain's animal charities, who are so micro-focused on animal welfare that they completely miss the implications for pet *owners*. We're talking yet another *national database*, containing *names, addresses, and phone numbers* of the millions of pet owners throughout the land. If it were just lost animals at issue, a local registry of serial numbers without owner ID surely would suffice. If a dog went AWOL, it would be simple enough for their owners to find them in the local pound. Of course, if it's bad guys we're after, the bad guys will simply figure out ways to evade the whole scheme.

Under any number of scenarios, a seemingly innocuous "pet" microchip program is more about humans than pets. Merely consider that dogs often travel with their masters. So trace the dog and you've traced the owners! Which, by close analogy, is what Britain's proposed National Identity Card scheme is all about....

Editorial—*We start the year in Britain with a challenge to our essential nature, for 2008 might turn out to be the year when we decide to rip up the Magna Carta. Among the basic civil rights in this country, there has always been, at least in theory, an inclination towards liberal democracy, which includes a tolerance of an individual's right to privacy....Surveillance cameras and lost data will prove minuscule problems next to ID cards, which will obliterate the fundamental right to walk around in society as an unknown.*

The compulsory ID card scheme is a sickness born of too much suspicion and too little regard for the meaning of tolerance and privacy in modern life. Though we don't pay much attention to moral philosophy in the mass media now...it may be worth remembering that Britain has a tradition of excellence when it comes to distinguishing and upholding basic rights and laws in the face of excessive power.[108]

Andrew O'Hagan, who wrote that piece in 2008, might be breathing slightly more easily now. Owing to a combination of budgetary concerns and political pragmatism leading up to elections, the Labour Government temporarily mothballed the proposed identity card scheme in December, 2009, and the Conservative party pledged to prevent such a scheme under a Tory government.

We'll see. But never doubt that if there is ever sufficient national fear over terrorism or any other catastrophic social upheaval, compulsory ID cards will always be on the table. On both sides of the Atlantic....

Smile, you're on candid camera

News Report—*Under Conservative Party plans, the Government would refuse to pay for the installation of any new speed cameras, and onerous restrictions would be put on councils to stop their introduction. The idea is to force councils to enforce speed restrictions using other means. Over the past decade, the number of speed cameras has tripled. The cameras are a lucrative source of income for the Government.*[109]

They seemed like a good idea at the time, speed cameras. Eliminated the need for roving police vehicles to check for speeders. In an odd way, they are to be preferred over American-style cops with their pesky radars hiding just over the crest of the hill. With speed cameras, at least all the locals knew exactly when to slow down... and when to speed back up again! Even non-locals have to be awfully distracted to get caught these days, what with warning signs as you approach and reflective yellow paint all over every camera. Road maps and GPS devises even tell you when to hit the brakes! No surprise, then, when the Brits began to notice roving speed-camera vans sitting in laybys—not to mention those nasty "average-speed cameras," which means you daren't speed up over an extended distance, sometimes for several miles.

Somehow you just knew it wouldn't be long before America would discover Britain's traffic cameras—and the money they generate. Ever so gradually now in the States, we're beginning to see intersection cameras, lying in wait for all those dangerous red-light runners. Again, this seems like a good idea for the rest of us drivers who stubbornly believe that red lights actually mean *stop*. But wouldn't you know, all we've managed to do is watch as intersection accidents have skyrocketed. Sure, red-light offenses have decreased by 24 percent, but rear-enders have shot up by 40 percent as drivers slam on their brakes to avoid getting caught on camera in the middle of the intersection.

As inevitable with government regulation generally, there are unintended consequences to surveillance cameras of all types, not the least of which is the "familiarity-breeds-contempt syndrome." The more cameras there are out there, and the more visible they are, the less bothered we seem to be. Over time, we become surveillance-numb. Get slapped often enough, and you hardly seem to notice the next slap. Lose enough privacy, and one day privacy is no longer important. We just roll over and play dead. "It *is* what it is!" "Whatever!" Might as well just forget about it, go to your local pub and have a quiet drink away from all the madness...or not....

News Blurb—*Composer Michael Nyman (who wrote the soundtrack for "The Piano") has railed against the Government's "growing surveillance" culture after learning that his local pub is installing CCTV cameras. Nyman said he was "ashamed that Britain is the most visually and information-controlled country in the world." Under its license agreement, his local, like all other pubs, will be required to share CCTV images with police.*[110]

So much for the pub idea! Maybe the toilet. Is it possible we can escape police surveillance in the toilet?

At least there is sweet irony back at the police station itself....

News Report—*Police have installed a CCTV camera above the kitchen sink in their own canteen after complaints from tidier officers that some officers aren't cleaning up dirty plates and litter. Many of the officers who use the kitchen have furiously called the scheme "grimewatch." One unnamed officer lamented that the move was "a waste of public money. Tough on crime, tougher on causers of grime." Brian Stockham, chairman of Sussex Police Federation, said: "The mind boggles as to what abuses of facilities could be monitored by the service in future."*[111]

Better check out the toilet, Brian. It's just gotta be next! Toilet paper on the floor? Seats left down while officers are taking a leak? Guys going out the door without first washing their hands? Yikes! Now we've even got health-and-safety issues! Yep, it's got to be the toilet next. Watch for it. Wait for it.

So let's hear it for the Cambridge City Council—not the one in Cambridgeshire, but the one in Massachusetts....

American News Report—*The Cambridge City Council has pressed the "Stop" button on a project that would have activated eight surveillance cameras in the community, citing concerns about invasion of privacy.*

According to the American Civil Liberties Union of Massachusetts, this is the first time a community in the state has rejected the cameras. Following the Sept. 11, 2001 terrorist attacks, the U.S. Department of Homeland Security has funded the installation of hundreds of surveillance cameras in communities across the country, but not without debate over "Big Brother-style intrusion into everyday life.[112]

War on terrorism? The terrorists have already won! How they must gloat when they see the shrunken world of freedom they have managed to achieve in the once "Free World"! But Muslim extremists are not the only terrorists on the loose. Which is to be greater feared: known, declared enemies of the state, or states whose own citizens—moment to moment—are treated like enemies? What say you, George Orwell?

And then there's the flip-side. While the state feels empowered to take pictures of *you*, it's *you* who can no longer take pictures....

Want a picture of Britain? Watch out!

Editorial—*At a Downing Street news conference earlier this year, Gordon Brown found himself flummoxed by a question from a foreign journalist. He was asked what impression the rest of the world was getting of civil liberties in Britain now that tourists could be arrested for taking a photograph of a building. Mr Brown responded: "I don't accept that is the true* *picture of Britain at all." He then moved on, having dismissed the question as beneath contempt.*

But actually, it is a true picture of Britain; and it is threatening to cause this country great harm in the eyes of the world. Last week, Jeff Overs, a BBC photographer, was stopped under counter-terrorist laws for taking pictures not of a secret military establishment, or a nuclear power station, but of St. Paul's Cathedral at sunset.

Wren's masterpiece must be one of the most photographed buildings in the world. A million snaps are pasted into picture albums around the globe. So what had Mr. Overs done wrong? Well, nothing. But even though he did not fit the likely profile for a terrorist, he was required to account for who he was by police using powers granted to them in order to make the country safe.

The community support officer (PCSO) who stopped Mr. Overs was taken aback by his indignation. She told him she had stopped lots of people taking pictures that same afternoon "and nobody complained."

Alex Turner, another amateur photographer, was arrested after he took pictures of Mick's Plaice, a fish and chip shop in Chatham, Kent, evidently a building of great strategic importance to the jihadi godfathers in Waziristan. A few days ago, Jerome Taylor was stopped while taking pictures of the House of Commons from the South Bank of the Thames. "For 10 minutes," he recalled, "I was questioned about my evening and asked to give my height, name, address and ethnicity—all of which were recorded in a form that will now be held at the nearest police station for the next year." The reason he had been stopped was also noted: "Using a camera and tripod next to Westminster Bridge."

The message is that the police are using the "stop-and-account" powers contained in Section 44 of the Terrorism Act 2000 to question anyone they want, often for no obvious reason at all. If people take umbrage, they can be threatened with arrest, either for breaching the peace or for impeding the public highway. In February, further powers were introduced that made it an offence to elicit information "likely to be useful to a person committing or preparing an act of terrorism," a catch-all provision now used to stop people taking photographs of police officers.[113]

Bizarre, isn't it? Just when everyone and their housecat has both a digital camera and a cellphone with a built-in camera collectively taking billions of photos every day, Britain—in all its imperial wisdom—has determined that it will decide when, where, and how many photographs the average Joe or Jane can take. Of course, it's not really about the photos, but about the government having a pretext to detain you and force you, at the risk of arrest, to give an account of yourself. For virtually any reason. Or no reason at all.

Some of us have experienced that very civil liberties nightmare behind the Iron Curtain during the Cold War era. Detained for no reason other than a curious camera. Film confiscated. Questions. Just the kind of thing you'd expect from a totalitarian government....

Endemic surveillance—O what a tangled web

News Report—*In just one week, the average person living in Britain has 3,254 pieces of personal information being recorded with every phone call, click of the mouse, and use of a credit card. Most of this information is kept in databases for years, sometimes even indefinitely.*

Internet service providers (ISPs) compile information about their customers when they go online, including name, address, the unique identification number for the connection, known as an IP address, any browser used and location. They also keep details of emails, such as whom they were sent to, together with the date and time they were sent.

A national automatic license plate recognition system is maintained by the Association of Chief Police Officers along roads and highways. Every number plate picked up by the system is stored in a database for two years. Travel passes such as the Oyster Card (used in London) and the Key card (used in

Oxford) can also reveal remarkable amounts of information about an individual's journey history, dates, times and fares.[114]

In case you missed it back home in the States, a recent network broadcast featured a special news report coming out of Seattle, where thousands of workers in the Mecca of coffee and computers were being given ORCA cards to travel to and from work—whether on buses, trains, boats, streetcars or vans. What workers probably don't realize is that their bosses have the ability to trace their every move. Think it might be fun to call in sick and catch a ride to the beach instead? Better remember not to use your ORCA card, because your boss will be kicking you out the door before you can say "invasion of privacy" ten times fast![115]

Got your attention yet? The Snoopy State has certainly got the attention of Britain's own information commissioner....

News Broadcast—*Fears that the UK would "sleep-walk into a surveillance society" have become a reality, the government's own information commissioner has said. Richard Thomas spoke after research found people's actions were increasingly being monitored. There are up to 4.2 million CCTV cameras in Britain—about one for every 14 people.*

The Report on the Surveillance Society says that surveillance ranges from US security agencies monitoring telecommunications traffic passing through Britain, to key-stroke information used to gauge work rates, to GPS tracking of company vehicles.

The report's co-writer Dr. David Murakami-Wood told BBC News that, compared to other industrialised Western states, the UK was "the most surveilled country." "We have more CCTV cameras and we have looser laws on privacy and data protection," he said. "We really do have a society which is premised both on state secrecy and the state not giving up its supposed right to keep information under control while, at the same time, wanting to know as much as it can about us."

Privacy International also reports that Britain is the worst Western democracy when it comes to protecting individual privacy. Britain is cited along with Malaysia and China for "endemic surveillance." [116]

"Endemic surveillance" is an interesting term, begging comparison with yet another interesting term. In 1999, the Macpherson Report (prompted by the killing of Stephen Lawrence, a young black man) concluded that British police were "institutionally racist." What does that phrase mean? According to the Commission for Racial Equality, it means that, "If racist consequences accrue to institutional laws, customs or practices, that institution is racist whether or not the individuals maintaining those practices have racial intentions." In the words of Ambalavaner Sivanandan, Director of the Institute of Race Relations, "Institutional racism is that which, covertly or overtly, resides in the policies, procedures, operations and culture of public or private institutions—reinforcing individual prejudices and being reinforced by them in turn." [117]

By those two definitions, it sounds very much as if "endemic surveillance" is a first cousin to "institutionally racist." Given that similarity, the evidence of "endemic surveillance" in Britain seems particularly overwhelming....

News Report—*Telecom companies and internet service providers will be required by law to keep a record of every customer's personal communications, including who they are contacting, when, where and which websites they are visiting. 653 public bodies will be given access to the confidential information, and will not be required to seek permission of a magistrate to access the information.*

State bodies, including local town halls, made 519,260 requests last year— one every minute—to spy on the phone records and email accounts of members of the public. Shami Chakrabarti, director of the civil liberties organization Liberty, said: "The Big Brother ambitions of a group of senior Whitehall technocrats are delayed but not diminished." [118]

So there we have it: covert surveillance residing in the policies, procedures, operations and culture of public and private institutions. Wasn't that the test of "institutionally racist"? How could anyone possibly deny that Britain today is "institutionally surveillant"? Or claim that surveillance is not endemic? Funny you should ask....

The Government Reply presented to Parliament by the Secretary of State for the Home Department *(The Fifth Report From the Home Affairs Committee, 2007-08, "A Surveillance Society?")*, says: "*We reject crude characterisations of our society as a surveillance society in which all collections and means of collecting information about citizens are networked and centralised in the service of the state.*"

Indeed. And there really are good fairies sprinkling stardust on sleepy children's eyes. What do you expect a police state to say when accused of being a police state? No less a person than Dame Stella Rimington, the former head of MI5 (Britain's top-secret Security Service), argued in a Spanish newspaper interview against the growth of surveillance powers. She said: "It would be better that the Government recognised that there are risks, rather than frightening people in order to be able to pass laws which restrict civil liberties, precisely one of the objects of terrorism: that we live in fear under a police state."[119]

America headed there fast

Did you catch that line in one of the earlier news reports about "US security agencies monitoring telecommunications traffic passing through Britain?" The "special relationship" between Britain and the U.S. means, first and foremost, that matters of domestic and international security are shared between our two countries perhaps more intimately than between any other two independent nations on the globe. "Have your people call my people, and we'll do lunch" is a regular occurrence in British-American security circles. Indeed, "lunch" is a sumptuous feast of mutually-shared intelligence without which neither nation could long survive in the current crisis. No surprise, then—at least on one level—that the U.S. falls into the same category as Britain when it comes to "endemic surveillance."

News Report—*Privacy International, a UK privacy group, and the U.S.-based Electronic Privacy Information Center have put together a world map of surveillance societies, rating various countries for their civil liberties records. Along with Thailand, Taiwan, Singapore, Russia, and Malaysia, the U.S. and Britain are colored black for "endemic surveillance."*

Concerned with immigration issues, countries have implemented identity and fingerprinting systems, often without regard to the privacy implication for even their own citizens, leading to the conclusion that all citizens are under suspicion. The privacy trends have been fueled by the emergence of a profitable surveillance industry dominated by global IT companies and the creation of numerous international treaties that frequently operate outside judicial or democratic processes.

In terms of statutory protections and privacy enforcement, the US is the worst ranking country in the democratic world. [120]

Given the particular focus of the interest group providing the evaluations, it's hard to know whether this ranking of nations has any particular spin to it. Maybe the rankings are biased. Maybe the process used was skewed in some way. There's no doubt, however, that all of us— especially those of us in the U.S.—are bombarded daily with privacy threats from every direction, public and private. While the U.S. can't hold a candle to Britain's CCTV "surveillance society" (what nation can!), American business interests along with the rise of computer, internet, and cellphone technology have joined together in an unholy alliance ripping privacy rights to shreds and lusting for even more opportunities.

Want some examples? Buy your wife a Christmas frock from any major retailer and you needn't worry that you've forgotten her size. The computer has it right there for you, along with all of her prior purchases so you don't end up duplicating some cute little item she's already got in the closet. The only missing information is that the husband is handsome, suave, and debonair!

Grocery stores also know you pretty well. From your past purchases, they know what you're likely to buy, right down to your preferred brands. And doesn't your VISA or Mastercard account send you a year-end summary of all your credit card purchases—by *category*? Forget your *carbon* footprint. Who all do you suppose is looking at your *customer* footprint? And just how long can it be before they're looking specifically at your *carbon footprint*...and dictating the minutia of your everyday life?

Naturally, there's always Amazon.com. "Hello F. LaGard Smith. We have recommendations for you." And they're usually not far off! Then, too, have you ever wondered how the Google ads on the side of your computer screen magically match that email you're writing or that Web page you're reading? They *know*, you know!

The most alarming part of this scary business is how all these spying eyes are getting so intimate with us. Moment by cyberspace moment, we're handing over our most personal details to them on a silver platter! Every click of the mouse, every Google search, every phone call, every downloaded iPhone app, every gas purchase, every meal out, every doctor's appointment fairly shouts: "Would anybody care to know everything there is to know about my life? Anybody at all?" And that doesn't even begin to touch what the government knows about us....

Ask Americans how important their privacy is, and you'll quickly learn that it comes right at the top the social-needs shopping list. There's the famously-entrenched "right of privacy" for abortion, of course. And then there's all those maddening security questions and passwords supposedly guaranteeing our privacy when we call any utility company, or open up our computers, or withdraw cash from the ATMs, and on and on.

If you're having trouble breathing, don't go to your doctor. You can't get past the receptionist without being suffocated by all the stupefying legalese required by the Health Insurance Portability and Accountability Act (HIPAA) which was passed by Congress in 1996 to set a national standard for electronic transfers of health data. In the world of health care these days, things are so private that you can hardly visit a friend in the hospital without an engraved invitation, nor certainly inquire as to their condition unless you're a certified family member. For government regulated entities, the answer to the old television program, "Who Do You Trust?", is…*no one*.

In the case of HIPAA itself, that's still the right question and still the right answer. If you get the idea that what you do there (in the doctor's office) stays there, you'd be wrong. It's hardly Las Vegas. Your medical history can be siphoned off for marketing purposes, and your doctor may disclose your health information to business associates who process medical bills, or to lawyers, accountants, data processors, software vendors and so on with hardly any restrictions. But don't we all feel so much better having signed a long sheet of unreadable (and thus unread) mumbo-jumbo supposedly guaranteeing our privacy?

Sure, but we're a funny bunch of folks, aren't we? Gotta have our privacy at all cost! Yet the minute we've got that point settled we're off to the computer to expose ourselves to the entire world on Facebook or Twitter. Social networking, we call it. And just who are your "friends"? You really think it's only those you invite to be your "friends"? Unknown to you, there are countless eyes pouring over every keystroke you use in order to share those inmost thoughts and intimate family photos. Eyes that, if you only knew, you'd "de-friend" in a heartbeat.

Here's an interesting question: How often do you think you'd use your favorite social network to communicate with your friends if you lived in, say, China or Iran? Naturally, that question is moot since those governments have blocked all potentially seditious websites. Only raising the far more interesting question: How, exactly, *does* a government block entire websites and social networks? Or more curious yet, what technology allows a government to tell from the *contents* of your emails that you're a political activist, or a revolutionary...or a Christian...so that they can come knocking at your door? And if China and Iran can do this, what apart from self-restraint prevents our own government from doing it?

Brave new world

News Broadcast—*The US and UK governments are developing increasingly sophisticated gadgets to keep individuals under their surveillance.*

> *"Five nine, five ten," said the research student, pushing down a laptop button to seal the measurement. "That's your height."*
> *"Spot on," I said.*
> *"OK, we're freezing you now," interjected another student, studying his computer screen. "So we have height and tracking and your gait DNA."*
> *"Gait DNA?" I interrupted, raising my head, so inadvertently my full face was caught on a video camera.*
> *"Have we got that?" asked their teacher, Professor Rama Chellappa. "We rely on just 30 frames—about one second—to get a picture we can work with," he explained.*

I was at the University of Maryland just outside Washington DC, where Professor Chellappa and his team are inventing the next generation of citizen surveillance. Gait DNA, for example, is creating an individual code for the way I walk. Their goal is to invent a system whereby a facial image can be matched to your gait, your height, your weight and other elements, so a computer will be able to identify instantly who you are.

Opinion polls, both in the US and Britain, say that about 75 percent of us want more, not less, surveillance. Some American cities like New York and Chicago are thinking of taking a lead from Britain where our movements are monitored round the clock by four million CCTV cameras.[121]

If "gait DNA" and similar cutting-edge technology doesn't keep you awake at night, the thought that 75 percent of both Brits and Americans want *even more* surveillance certainly ought to! If that figure is anywhere near correct, it's probably because Americans don't have a clue what they're asking for in reality, and the Brits are already so addicted to having security cameras on every corner that they just can't get enough of them.

Democracy's great challenge

Whether Americans live in a surveillance society is no longer the question. Surveillance is everywhere, growing, and never to disappear. The only question is whether by some yet-to-be-seen political courage we can halt the persistent advance of "Big Brother" in America—especially in an era of international terrorism. Can we, in short, avoid having a "democratic police state" (the ultimate oxymoron) such as already exists in Britain? Do we have the public will to resist the inexorable slide into an irreversibly sinister infrastructure of data banks, commercial dataveillance, and systematic visual intrusion into every aspect of our lives?

In assessing the risks of a surveillance society, David Murakami-Wood and his team at the Surveillance Studies Network, caution that "we do not have to imagine some wicked tyrant getting access keys to social security or medical databases to see the problem. The corruptions of power include leaders who appeal to some supposed greater good (like victory in war) to justify unusual or extraordinary tactics."[122] Wolves in sheep's clothing are always a danger. Even "wolves" with the best of motives, who forget about the doctrine of unintended consequences, and mission creep, and the always lurking possibility that one day there just might be that wicked tyrant walking into frame. A tyrant wolf with no pretense of sheep's clothing, who is both willing and eager to utilize the full resources of an entrenched surveillance infrastructure for his own twisted purposes.

Even without any doomsday scenario, the subtle and profound effects of surveillance are deeply submerged within society's collective psyche. "Today's surveillance processes and practices bespeak a world where we know we're not really trusted. Surveillance fosters suspicion. The employer who installs keystroke monitors at workstations, or GPS devices in service vehicles is saying that they do not trust their employees. And when parents start to use webcams and GPS systems to check on their teenagers' activities, they are saying they don't trust them either. Some of this, you object, may seem like simple prudence. But how far can this go? Social relationships depend on trust and permitting ourselves to undermine it in this way seems like slow social suicide."[123]

These cautions are coming from folks who ought to know—Brits who live each moment in the eye of snooping cameras. Before it's too late, America must wake up to the inescapable reality that surveillance risks invariably increase in direct proportion to the rise in socialist-style governance. Any President and Congress intent on widening the involvement and control over the lives of ordinary citizens (as in "Obamacare") will wittingly or unwittingly beg for greater and greater surveillance. "Cradle-to-grave health-and-welfare, once the proud promise of social-democratic governments, has been whittled down to risk management and—here's where the surveillance society comes in—such risk management demands full knowledge of the situation. So personal data is sought in order to know where to direct resources."[124]

We mustn't kid ourselves. The ever-burgeoning health-and-welfare state being birthed under our current government (not alone by the Democrats) is a socialist state in waiting—an unfolding risk-management nightmare and a surveillance time-bomb already ticking away from the hallowed halls of Washington to your local town hall.

Nor can we afford to overlook the knock-on danger. Once a complex, multi-layered surveillance infrastructure of this magnitude is in place, how possibly can any single individual challenge the system? Or know what personal data is being kept? Or trace where that information has flown in the darkness of cyber night?

Which brings us full circle: *First they came for the rubbish bins. Then they came for me!* At which point there will be nothing any of us can do about it.

A more personal perspective

Of all the omnipresent eyes watching us, only one truly matters. It is the eye of the Almighty who sees all and knows all, cradle-to-grave and beyond. Who alone can discern which of earth's rulers govern with honesty, truth, and wisdom.

Are you one of thousands of out-and-proud secularists in positions of political power who thinks such talk is just a bunch of religious hoo-ha? Care to risk that there really is an Almighty who knows you inside-out? Maybe you're right in thinking that this world has no divine overseer judging your actions and cynical disbelief. So do as you wish. Proceed as planned. Assume in your role of governance the omniscience and omnipotence you would deny any higher power.

Of course if you're wrong, have you ever considered how the divine database one day will be brought to bear in the Court of Last Resort? If every personal movement, key-stroke, phone call, Website, purchase, and health-care decision is under your strict scrutiny in this life, how much more will your own hyper-intrusive, oppressive actions be judged in the life to come? For those who would deign to be society's all-wise seers, there may be much more to "saturation surveillance" than meets the eye. It's certainly worth considering: Might there be Someone watching the watchers…?

7

Faith Under Fire

We must respect the other fellow's religion,
but only in the sense and to the extent that we respect his theory
that his wife is beautiful and his children smart.

—H. L. MENCKEN

News Report—*Helen Slatter, a practicing Catholic, is facing the possibility of having to choose between her faith and her job as a phlebologist for the NHS. Her employers are demanding that she remove the one-inch crucifix which she wears beneath her uniform. "They have told me that for health and safety reasons and for infection control I must take it off or I will be sent home," said Ms. Slatter. "They have told me I can carry it in my pocket but that simply isn't the same. Nuns who visit patients in the hospital openly wear a crucifix, and many patients wear a cross or crucifix."*

A spokesman for the Gloucestershire Hospitals said "The issue is not one of religion. Necklaces and chains present two problems—firstly, they can provide a surface that can harbor and spread infections and secondly they present a health and safety issue whereby a patient could grab a necklace or chain and cause harm to the member of staff."

Canon Massey, who is the Catholic chaplain at the hospital where Ms. Slatter works, said: "There seems to be an inconsistency in the trust's approach. When I visit patients in the hospital I wear a cross myself. It could be interpreted by some people that the problem is not "that" she is wearing it, but "what" she is wearing."

In 2006, British Airways employee Nadia Eweida lost her fight to wear a cross necklace while working at Heathrow Airport, but was reinstated after the company changed its uniform policy.

BBC's high-profile anchor Fiona Bruce has also come under fire from BBC managers for wearing a cross while presenting the news.[125]

Helen Slatter's experience is typical of faith in the public square in Britain these days. Nothing quite stirs the blood of secularists like the sight of the cross. (No surprise, given the power of its moving imagery and sublime message.) But in this case the cross was being worn *under* a uniform. Hardly in your face. Not the least bit confrontational. But they *knew* it was there, didn't they, and that was enough to send the hospital management into liberal apoplexy.

Of course, there are those health concerns. Might not even hidden jewelry spread infections? Yet, if that was the objection, why allow Slatter to carry the cross in her pocket? Or permit priests and nuns— even patients—to wear *their* crosses in the hospital? (And you can bet they're the next target.)

No, this was not a "uniform" problem, but a *religious discrimination* problem. Indeed, a *Christian* discrimination problem. Can you imagine the furor had a "uniform policy" banned any traditional Muslim garb?

As it happens, unfortunately, there is one sense in which Slatter's problem *is* a "uniform problem," since everywhere you turn in Britain, the cross *uniformly* is raising concerns. Just ask British Airways' Nadia Eweida, or popular television presenter Fiona Bruce. In neither of their cases was health and safety at risk, only a shining symbol of faith which Britain's secularists detest. (The *faith*, that is, not just the symbol.) And the *Christian* faith specifically, since those same secularists are all too willing to cut incredible slack for Muslims (who, ironically, castigate morally-vacuous secularism far more than their mostly-secularist "Christian" neighbors).

It was in much the same spirit that the Privy Council of Trinidad and Tobago recently ruled that the Trinity Cross of the Order of Trinity—established by the Queen in 1969—is discriminatory and illegal. The case arose when a group of Muslim and Hindu islanders objected to both terms of the "Trinity Cross" on the ground that they discriminated against non-Christians.

If they stopped to think about it, the islanders probably would do better to change the name of the island itself. "Trinidad" was the name given by Christopher Columbus in honor of the Trinity.

As *The Times* points out, "If this cross is illegal, where does that leave the Victoria Cross and the George Cross, the only decorations that take precedence over the Trinity Cross? Moreover, the whole menu of the honours system is stiff with crosses and grand crosses, saints and the British Empire, and other relics of the age of chivalry. The Union Flag is blazoned with no fewer than three crosses.[126]

Think there's no way any cross in Britain itself could ever run afoul of the law? Think again....

News Report—*Chris Bryant, Labour's Foreign Office minister, has raised hackles by urging that an alternative symbol, such as the "red crystal," is needed for the Red Cross because of the logo's supposed links to the Crusades. "The religious connotation of the cross undermines the work of the humanitarian organization," Bryant insists.*

Philip Davies, a Tory backbencher, said: "At face value to the layman it seems at best a solution looking for a problem and at worst another example of extreme political correctness. No one has ever suggested to me that the Red Cross refers to the Crusades."

In 1863, the Founding Conference of the Red Cross Movement adopted a red cross on a white background—the reverse of the Swiss flag—as the emblem of the voluntary medical personnel who assisted the wounded on the battlefield. It was never intended to have any religious meaning and is believed to have been a tribute to traditionally neutral Switzerland, which hosted the conference.[127]

In whatever way all the various implications fall out, it should be acknowledged frankly by all concerned that the cross symbolic of the Red Cross organization does indeed have Christian roots. Being a reversal of the Swiss national flag (adopted to honor Swiss native and Red Cross founder Henry Dunant), it's hard to deny the obvious Christian connection. The cross depicted on one of the original versions of the Swiss flag even included the body of Jesus hanging on it.

Certainly no one denies that the crescent of the Red Crescent organization is distinctly Muslim, having been used first in the war between the Ottoman Empire and Russia in 1877-78 and officially adopted in 1929. The Red Crescent organization is active in 33 Islamic states today.

The new "red crystal" may not appear to have religious connotations (except, perhaps, for anyone who knows anything about the New Age Movement and its fixation on crystals), but its adoption certainly has a religious history. The crystal is part of a wider compromise worked out to accommodate Israel's emergency relief agency, the Magen David Adom (MDA), literally meaning "Red Shield of David," though usually translated as "Red Star of David." You just knew that was a non-starter! Hence the compromise crystal...and the eventual demise (watch for it, wait for it) of both the Christian cross and the Muslim crescent.

Don't miss what's happening here. It's not the replacement of religion by non-religion. It's the replacement of three major world religions by no lesser a religion than militant secularism. Secularism too has it tenets, doctrines, priests, and fervent disciples who are as unrelenting and destructive in their own secularist crusades as any religious Crusaders ever were. Is the danger now *crystal* clear?

When faith can get you fired

Question: How do you stamp out a faith as deeply entrenched as an established national religion? Not by reasoned argument, not by persuasion, not even by popular vote. When you have the unabashed hubris of the liberal-Left you do it by *intimidation*, pure and simple....

News Report—*Anand Rao, a male nurse with 40 years' experience, was taking part in a role-playing training session to see how he would advise a woman with a serious heart condition about how to reduce stress. When he told the "patient" that she might consider going to church to ease her stress (and that, if God wished, she might live longer), Rao was fired for breaching the Nursing and Midwifery Council's code of conduct on respecting a patient's dignity.*

A spokesman for the NHS hospital said: "Since joining us Mr Rao had continuously shown a disregard for the nursing council's code of conduct, which he had breached on more than one occasion."[128]

Ah, "on more than one occasion." Looks like we have a real troublemaker on our hands. Or is it just the opposite—that, on more than one occasion, the NHS has interfered with Mr. Rao's religious freedom? This was, after all, a *training* session. So why not some sensitivity training rather than a heavy-handed axe at the base of the head?

If this were a single, isolated case where a nurse gets the axe for daring to interject a faith-based suggestion (which just happens to have been beneficial to millions throughout the centuries), maybe we could all agree that he's just a "one-off" nut case. But what if there are other similar cases? *Lots* of other cases...?

News Report—*Council worker, Duke Amachree, a homelessness prevention officer, was suspended for encouraging a terminally-ill woman to turn* *to God. The woman was hoping to find accommodation near a hospital, where she could be treated for what he says she described as an "incurable bowel condition." Amachree told the woman to put her faith in God, saying that "sometimes the doctors don't have all of the answers."*

Council officials claim that the woman was subjected to a half-hour barrage of faith. Mr. Amachree says he was told that he could not raise the issue of religion at work and that talking about God with a client—even saying "God bless"—was inappropriate.[129]

Whether the incident was a "half-hour barrage" or a sensitive attempt to treat the woman holistically—body and soul—is a case of "he said, she said." At the very least, the conversation about the health benefits of faith, and about the doctors not always having all the answers, echoes what many doctors themselves would say.

Don't get hung up over the details of this one case. Maybe Mr. Amachree crossed the line. Maybe he went *way over* the line. Who knows? But even if Mr. Amachree's tone and presentation had been unquestionably faultless, the crucial fact remains that—by official employment policy—God has been banned officially from the workplace. To the liberal mind, any mention of God whatsoever in the workplace is a "religious rant" which won't be tolerated.

To *forbid* faith, all the Government need do is to *privatize* faith. Sure, you can have your faith, as long as you check it at the door on the way into work.

The only thing worse than the Government forcing Christians to keep their faith private is for Christians themselves to beat the Government to the punch and decide on their own never to mention their faith while on the job. When enough believers compartmentalize their faith like that, the secularist Faith Patrol can take off early. Job done!

As is refreshingly obvious from the foregoing news articles, not all believers are willing to hide their faith while in the workplace. The following article provides yet another great example of standing up for one's faith...and being knocked over for it. This time, not in Britain but in New York....

American News Report— *Alliance Defense Fund attorneys have filed suit against Mount Sinai Hospital on behalf of a Catholic nurse who was forced to participate in a late-term abortion under the threat of possible termination and loss of her license. The hospital has known of her religious objections to abortion since 2004.*

Hospital administrators told the nurse that the scheduled abortion was an "emergency," and insisted moments before the procedure to dismember a child in the 22nd week of gestation that she assist doctors despite her repeated objections. Federal law prohibits federally-funded hospitals from forcing employees to participate in abortion procedures.[130]

What's a believer to do when not even the protection of the law protects her? Even in the States today, liberals still don't get it. Witness the insensitive slam which contributed to the stunning Senate defeat of Democrat Martha Coakley in Massachusetts. When asked in an interview about health workers' religious freedom in the emergency room, Coakley replied, "The law says that people are allowed to have that. And so if you can have religious freedom, you probably shouldn't work in the emergency room."

Coakley couldn't have put it more starkly: Either forego your Constitutionally-guaranteed religious freedom or quit your job! Surprisingly (or not!), even one of America's most liberal states saw right through that one. Would that America's illiberal liberals could be seen so transparently all the time.

More than one way to lose your job over faith

Of course, not all employment discrimination takes place in an office or hospital. Sometimes religious discrimination, like charity, begins at home....

News Report—A woman who has fostered over 80 children has been banned from being a foster mother after a Muslim girl in her care converted to Christianity, choosing to be baptized at the age of 16. The girl, now 17, who was taken into foster care after being assaulted by a family member, saw baptism "as a washing away of the horrible things she had been through and a symbol of a new start," the woman said. "I offered her alternatives. I offered to find her places to practise her own religion. I offered to take her to friends or family. But she said to me from the word go: 'I am interested and I want to come to church'."

Social services personnel were aware that the girl was attending the woman's evangelical church, and council officials objected only when they found out the girl had been baptized. Officials advised the teenager to reconsider her decision and stop attending Christian meetings, and the struck the carer off their register.[131]

In assessments before the baptism, authorities had said the girl's emotional needs were being met and that the foster mother was showing understanding and respect for the girl's culture. In the end, that respect was far more than what the Government itself was willing to show her. Ironic, isn't it? The teenager was old enough to have sexual relations with the Government's blessing (complete with contraceptives, morning-after pills, and even abortion if necessary), but she could not decide to be baptized of her own accord without the Government forcing her to take a kind of religious "morning-after faith reversal."

This case is irreligious Britain in a nutshell: You can toy around with Christianity all you want. Acknowledge your particular faith allegiance, make guest appearances at church, have a Christian burial when you die. Just don't make a personal, life-changing "watershed" commitment that you take so seriously it might risk alienating your family. Even hard-core secularists—themselves totally immersed in cynical disbelief—understand the profound significance of a personally-chosen baptism re-enacting the Lord's own foretelling burial and resurrection in the waters of the Jordan.

Crosses? Baptisms? What's next, pray tell? *Prayers...?*

News Report—*Caroline Petrie, a community nurse employed to make home visits to sick and elderly patients, was suspended for offering to pray with one of her patients. "It was around lunchtime," said Ms. Petrie, "and I had spent about 20 to 25 minutes with her. I had applied dressings to her legs and shortly before I left I said to her: 'Would you like me to pray for you?' She said 'No, thank you.' And I said: 'OK.' I only offered to pray for her because I was concerned about her welfare and wanted her to get better."*[132]

Is the mere offer of prayer now so offensive as to raise eyebrows, or even hackles? Has the mere mention of prayer actually become insensitive, illiberal, diversity-denying hate speech worthy of dismissal from one's job? Apparently so. As prayerful as Caroline Petrie is, when faced with the militant secularism that is now *de rigueur* in Britain these days, she didn't have a prayer!

When private prayers turn public

If prayers in the privacy of a home are threatened, it goes without saying that traditional *public* prayers will be high on the secularist hit-list....

News Item—*A councillor has threatened to take legal action against Kendal Town Council's traditional prayer reading before meetings. He called for prayers to be scrapped or to be held in a different room, citing equality concerns. "This council has to be seen to be acceptant of all people regardless of creed, colour or race," he told councilors. A fellow councillor argued that the council was a "Christian council" and he could see nothing wrong with the tradition.*[133]

Ouch! A "Christian council"? Probably not. But in a move to be accommodative, the Kendal Town Council voted to read the prayers five minutes prior to their meetings.[134]

There's no suggestion here that the matter of prayer in public places is always an easy call—especially in a multicultural society. How would Christians feel with the roles reversed—say, in a predominately Muslim community where prayers to Allah were being said? What does seem to be an easy call is that people of faith have far more in common with each other than with radical extremists of any faith or, certainly, with the radical secularists intent on trampling roughshod over religious expression of any kind.

Hypocrisy, always hypocrisy

If only the liberal "progressives" could see themselves as others see them. Do they really *not* see? Are they so morally blind as not to recognize their breathtaking hypocrisy? Even young children have an innate sense of unfairness. ("That's not fair!") So whatever happened to rid progressives of that innate moral trait...?

News Report—*Jacalyn Oghan, who helps out at St. Mary's Church in Brighton, went to the city's library to put up a poster inviting children to "come along and have fun" at the craft, singing, and drama day at her church. Library staff denied permission, saying the poster would promote religion. Oghan noted that the library shop offers products which appear to mock Christianity, including "Messiah Mints" sold in a container featuring a picture of Jesus and claiming to provide "Holy fresh breath." The ad line says: "He can't feed the 5,000 with this cute little tin of peppermints, but you'll feel a whole lot better after your hearty banquet of fish and loaves!"*

A spokeswoman for the council said: "In the interests of fairness, we have very clear and strict guidelines for displaying information in the library and we do not accept any material promoting a particular religious view point. With regards to the mints, these are one of a series of tinned mints sold in the shop. The labelling is not meant to offend and this is the first time we have received negative comments about them."[135]

Under Britain's new Equality Bill, it doesn't matter whether or not the "Jesus mints" were *intended* to cause offense. If Mrs. Oghan had not been so gracious, she could have brought suit against the library for religious offense, though—given the British courts' track record—she likely would have lost. One can safely bet that none of the mint tins carried a picture of Mohammed with the caption: "Surely Mohammed wouldn't mind if you sucked on one of these little peppermints during your Ramadan fast!"

And the following hypocrisy must really put liberal activists in a stew....

News Report—A *Catholic group has been denied permission to post flyers in libraries and community centres advertising a presentation: "Climate Change is a Christian Issue" because it would be in conflict with policy against the promotion of religious ideas.*

Jo Siedlecka, who organized the climate change meetings for the Our Lady parish, said: "I went to the local library with the posters and a lady in a yashmak, a Muslim lady, told me that they could not advocate religions or promote religious ideas. Then I spoke to officials at the Campden town hall who told me again that they could not promote a religion. They said they would be very happy if it was green, but it could not be Christian."[136]

Little wonder that Ms. Siedlecka instantly turned from green to red! It's yet another instance where liberal causes collide—this time between environmental activism and open antipathy towards religion. (Well at least the *Christian* religion.) No surprise that liberalism's anti-religious bias is so strong that it even ends up kicking environmental concerns right off the bulletin board. Cutting off noxious religious nose to spite environmentalist face, it would seem. Given the high priority of environmentalism, the liberals must *really* hate God talk!

As always behind the scenes is the continuing double-standard in the treatment between anything Christian and all things Muslim. Although Campden borough officials insisted they could not lend a hand to a Christian group, the borough continually provides for inquirers details of no fewer than 13 mosques, Muslim study groups, and Islamic social groups. When it comes to religion, the Equality Bill loves to play selective "peek-a-boo." Now you see it; now you don't. But for Muslims (and the secularist liberals who invariable cave into their every demand), the following case isn't just innocent peek-a-boo....

News Item—*Librarians have been told to move the Bible to top shelves, along with copies of the Koran, so as not to offend the Islamic community who believe the Koran must always be placed above" commonplace things." The city's librarians consulted the Federation of Muslim Organisations and were advised that all religious texts should be kept on the top shelf to ensure equality.*

However, Inayat Bunglawala, of the Engage think tank, which encourages Muslims to play a greater role in public life, said that there should not be a "one size fits all" rule. "If Muslims wish to see the Koran placed on a higher shelf, and library rules say it should be there, then that is a welcome and considerate gesture. But one size does not fit all. If Christians do not want to see the Bible treated in the same way, I do not see why it has to be dealt with the same."[137]

That's ever so reasonable, suggesting that one size doesn't fit all. But wouldn't that run counter to the Equality Bill? Funny how putting the Bible on the top shelf in this case actually lowers the level. On the top shelf, the Bible is no longer easily accessible to those who might be looking for it. Didn't the Reformation already fight that war—to the benefit of Protestants and Catholics alike? And what is "equal" about the physical location of the Bible unilaterally being dictated by adherents of a competing religion without the slightest input from those who would have particular interest in reading the Bible?

More intriguing...why should liberal secularists inevitably and always come down on the side of Muslims? Does it have anything to do with current Muslim issues giving them a great excuse to destroy every minor vestige of the Christianity they so loathe? If so, what will they do when the day comes that—with the demise of Christianity—the Koran on the top shelf comes crashing down on their secularist heads in the form of Sharia law...both harsh and unmitigated in its total eradication of all things secular?

First they came for the Christians....

"Rejoice that you participate..."

It's crucial to remember that there needn't be specific laws for ethnic riots like the anti-Jewish pogroms of Nazi Germany to occur. Religious and ethnic persecutions (even those historically instigated by Christians) can come in the form of almost any pretense. So it is that no specific anti-Christian legislation is necessary for Christians to be persecuted for their faith, even in "Christian" Britain....

News Report—*Hotel owners Ben and Sharon Vogelenzang were arrested after a Muslim woman, a guest at their hotel, complained to police that she had been offended by their comments. The couple has been charged under public order laws with using "threatening, abusive or insulting words" that were "religiously aggravated." Although the facts are disputed, it is said that the couple suggested that Mohammed was a warlord and that traditional Muslim dress for women was a form of bondage.*

Neil Addison, a prominent criminal barrister and expert in religious law, said: 'The purpose of the Public Order Act is to prevent disorder, but I'm very concerned that the police are using it merely because someone is offended. It should never be used where there has been a personal conversation or debate with views firmly expressed. If someone is in a discussion and they don't like what they are hearing, they can walk away. He added that the police had a legal duty under the Human Rights Act to defend free speech "and I think they are forgetting that."[138]

"Never talk about religion or politics in polite company," so goes the adage. But who ever would have guessed that even a heated table discussion (if it was) would have been cause for criminal arrest? Because it was a private conversation within the premises owned by the accused, even at face value this simply can't be a *"public* order" offense. And what likely would have been the police response had Christians been offended by some slur against Christ by a person of another faith? Need we ask?

The rise of militant humanism

What's so amazing is that all this religious persecution of Christians is happening in a nation where the Church of England is the established church. Where the Queen is the titular head of the Church, and where—by history, heritage, and the (unwritten) British Constitution—the Christian faith is the official religion of the land. A land that gave the world The King James Bible, Handel's *Messiah*, and C.S. Lewis. Hard to believe. Which, if given the right emphasis, is precisely why all this chaos is happening in Britain. For an increasing number of Brits these days, it's simply hard to *believe*.

In a later chapter, there's much more to say about the decline of faith in Britain. For now, it's important to get at least a glimpse of the rise of militant humanism (atheism) in Britain and the effect it's having from top to bottom in British culture. It would be hard to think of many targets more strategic for militant secularists than that quintessential British institution, the venerable BBC....

News Report—*Secularists are claiming a huge breakthrough at the BBC, as a new committee that the corporation will consult on religious broadcasting is to include a humanist. This move is a significant shift for the BBC, and follows a series of recent victories for secularists in public life, including a legal ruling in favour of the so-called "atheist bus," the addition of humanism to a GCSE religious studies syllabus, and the launch of the first major national student secular society.*

Humanist Andrew Copson suggested his appointment will provide him opportunity to challenge the long fought-over Radio 4 religious slot, "Thought for the Day." The philosopher A C Grayling praised the appointment, saying the news was "incredible," and signified the culmination of a series of successes for secularists.[139]

Just so we get this straight...the BBC is now taking advice from atheists as to the content of its only regularly-scheduled "God slot"? It could be argued that the BBC has no business having a "God slot" at all, but as long as it does, what possible purpose is served by looking to atheists for advice on matters of faith? Has even the once-highly-respected BBC gone loony? Has it, too, sold out to the liberal-Left?

Grayling is right, of course. "Incredible" is certainly the right word to describe the secularist invasion of what little sacred space remains at the BBC. Already halved in time from its original five-minute slot, "Thought for the Day" has been targeted repeatedly by secular humanists for not including non-religious viewpoints...on a program designed to offer "reflections from a faith perspective on issues and people in the news." Go figure. As a concession to the secularists, celebrated atheist Richard Dawkins was given a one-time 2 ½ minute segment in a different time slot to offer a reflection from an atheist perspective. That was all it took to establish a beachhold for the subsequent invasion.

These are the same secularists whose British Humanist Association (BHA) has been allocated £25,000 out of a Government fund set aside principally for "building faith communities."[140] By contrast, the Government department responsible for the fund is headed by Communities Secretary Hazel Blears, who has said faith groups should be funded only if they promise not to proselytize. Blears seems not to realize that humanists also proselytize....

News Report— *Atheist adverts declaring that "There's probably no God" have been placed on 800 buses around Britain after an unprecedented fundraising campaign. This is being done in response to Christian adverts warning of "eternal damnation" for unbelievers. The campaign is heavily financed by Richard Dawkins and the British Humanist Association. It is the first-ever atheist advertising campaign to take place in Britain. Similar campaigns are underway in America and Spain.*

Prof. Dawkins, the renowned evolutionary biologist and author of "The God Delusion," said: "I wanted something stronger but with hindsight I think it's probably a good thing because it makes people think. It's just food for thought—people will have conversations in pubs when they see these buses."[141]

Bring it on! Let's have the debate. It's high time we got the fundamental issue of God out into the open. Christians, certainly, have nothing to fear from that conversation—a conversation that lies at the very core of the Leftist loony madness speeding our way across the Pond. Maybe we could start by discussing why atheists feel they need to respond to Christian adverts "threatening eternal damnation." Since they're firmly convinced beyond all doubt that there really and truly is no God, why worry...?

The Scouts, always the Scouts!

If anyone needs more proof of the militancy of secular humanism both at home and abroad, you need look no further than the liberals' favorite punching bag—that seemingly innocent but insidiously dangerous organization, the Scouts! Never can be too wary of those uniformed young people who disguise their religious radicalism by helping old age pensioners cross the road....

News Item—*The Scout Association is the latest target of the British Humanist Association, which has complained to the Equality and Human Rights Commission about discriminating against atheists by making them swear an oath to God. Ever since Lord Baden-Powell founded the 100-year-old organization, scouts have promised to "do their best to do their duty to God and the Queen." To accommodate the movement's 28 million members around the world, the words can be modified to encompass non-Christian faiths, but Scouting leaders said that they had no intention of changing the oath drawn up by Lord Baden-Powell, a "muscular Christian" who believed that faith was an essential element in the development of young people.[142]*

Really now. Is society to be a case of the lowest common denominator— where the touchiest segment of society sets the standards for all others?

And playing on Groucho Marx's line about not wanting to belong to any club that would have him as a member, why would secular humanists even wish to be part of any organization that historically believes in a Higher Power (by whatever name), contrary to the adamant disbelief of atheists? Or is that precisely the idea—to reduce all beliefs to the lowest common denominator so that there are no higher standards with which to compete intellectually or—dare we say it—spiritually?

So will the Secular Humanists get a fair hearing? You bet, they will. And if the ACLU could have its way back here at home, the Boy Scouts would be banished altogether. Every time you turn around, there's yet another lawsuit being filed against the Scouts. It seems that, for the unofficial legal arm of the liberal-Left in the States, the Scouts are simply too American, too apple pie, and...maddeningly too religious! You still think Britain's secular looniness is not speeding our way? To employ the Scouts' own motto: "Be prepared." It's already here!

In the States, of course, no organization is more virulently anti-religious than the American Civil Liberties Union—once a staunch libertarian defender of religious liberties, but now committed to a liberal-Left political agenda trampling on those very freedoms. Given its unrelenting assault on public expressions of faith, prayers in the classroom, public displays of the Ten Commandments, Christmas creches, crosses, and, of course, always the nefarious Boy Scouts, the ACLU's anti-religious credentials are impeccable.

Naturally, no single organization can have such a devastating impact without complicity from fellow liberals and secularists in education, the press, the media, Hollywood, Congress, and certainly the courts—all the way to the Supreme Court, several of whose members over the years have arisen from among the same liberal ranks. What they have in common is not just liberal politics, but the secularist mindset that drives liberal politics.

As bizarre at it appears, that ideological coalition includes many who, like Barack Obama, openly profess religious faith, and many who are staunch members of "mainline" (liberal) Christian churches. Yet, the disconnect is stupefying; the schizophrenia, palpable; and the lack of religious tolerance (all in the name of Christian tolerance), simply dumbfounding.

Liberal do-gooders "doing God"

It's not surprising, of course, that there should be political differences among those who profess Christian faith. In the strictest sense, Christianity is apolitical. Christianity is about the Kingdom of heaven, not the kingdoms of earth. "Render to Caesar what is Caesar's and to God what is God's."

Yet it's not as if Jefferson's famous "wall of separation" prevents all interplay between matters of faith and matters of government. Indeed, there is an intimacy between the two not unlike the unity of a man and a woman in marriage—the blending of the two into one. The sacred without the secular is a denial of the Incarnation. The secular without the sacred is a denial of the Divine. To understand the one, you must understand the other.

To be spiritually or religiously ignorant is to be politically naive. The secularist politician who looks with disdain on those who are religious, or dismisses faith as an unwelcome hindrance to political governance is a politician with his head in the sand, understanding nothing. One politician who says he has come to appreciate more fully the interaction between religion and politics is former British Prime Minster Tony Blair....

News Report—*Specifically countering his former head of communications, Alastair Campbell, who once famously said, "We don't do God," former Prime Minister Tony Blair has said recently that politicians must "do God," even if they have no personal religious faith. Since leaving Downing Street, Mr. Blair has converted to Roman Catholicism and become increasingly open about the importance of religion.*

Mr. Blair said: "As the years of my premiership passed, one fact struck me with increasing force: that failure to understand the power of religion meant failure to understand the modern world. Religious faith and how it develops could be of the same significance to the 21st century as political ideology was to the 20th.[143]

For Blair, "doing God" in this particular context is only understanding how people of religious faith think and operate, not necessarily personally joining in their enthusiasm for God. Even here, Blair evidences a lack of understanding about the intimacy between faith and politics—sharply contrasting political ideology from religious faith as if they existed on separate planets.

In truth, communism and fascism, and to a lesser extent political liberalism and socialism, reflect corresponding attitudes towards faith, running the gamut from atheism to agnosticism to liberal Christian thinking to secularism of all stripes. To understand communism, one absolutely must understand atheism. To understand classic political liberalism, one must understand classic Christian liberalism. To understand socialism, one typically must understand secularism.

So Tony Blair is definitely onto something here, even if still fuzzy on the details. And yet it would be hard to think of a better example of religious God-talk combined with wooly-headed liberalism than Blair himself. More than any Prime Minister in recent history it was Tony Blair who pressed the Leftist agenda that produced the liberal looniness reported in this book—including the marginalization of Christians which Blair insists he laments. In a piece for *The Spectator*, journalist and author Melanie Phillips has responded insightfully to Blair's glaring inconsistency....

Editorial—*Tony Blair has said that Christianity is at risk of being sidelined in Britain's "aggressively secularist" society....A few days after his wife Cherie told a Channel Four documentary of her dismay at the apparent "terminal decline" of Christianity, Blair told the Church of England Newspaper:*

I hope and believe that stories of people not being allowed to express their Christianity are exceptional or the result of individual ludicrous decisions. My view is that people should be proud of their Christianity and able to express it as they wish.

But one of the things which has hammered Christianity in Britain in recent years is "human rights" law, which has effectively handed every minority a judicial weapon to upend majority or Christian values. And it was Tony Blair who, as soon as he took office in 1997, made human rights law the key element of his radical and reforming agenda; and it was Cherie who, as a prominent human rights lawyer, put that Christianity-busting legal doctrine into practice.

Mr. Blair disclosed…that while prime minister he believed equality and diversity were more important than religion in the case of the Catholic adoption agencies, who failed in their bid to be exempted from laws requiring them to consider homosexual couples as potential parents.

> *"I happen to take the gay rights position," he said. "But at the time of the Catholic adopting society dispute I was also concerned that these people who were doing a fantastic job were not put out of business. You have got to try to work your way through these issues."*

Well, when that issue was "worked through"…concern stopped being a Catholic one.…When it came to adoption, Catholics could not express their values as they wished, as a direct result of the doctrine Blair promoted to such effect.[144]

Tough words for Mr. Blair, but bang on. When someone wants to affirm the certainty of some statement, you often hear the expression, "Is the Pope Catholic?" With a different slant in this instance, one is entitled to ask: "Is Tony Blair really Catholic?" Can he be a practicing Catholic while calling for "human rights" that inevitably trump Catholic beliefs? Only in a postmodern world!

Liberals who speak of the importance of religious faith while simultaneously pressing so-called "human rights" provisions that deny the open expression of that self-same religious faith are living in la-la land. For all the grim-faced "concern" of politicians like Blair, Cameron, and our own Barack Obama, who shower us with sanctimonious God-talk, the fact remains that religious speech is as religion does, and secular thinking is as secularism does. In the Jekyll-and-Hyde world of Leftist liberalism, religion may be welcomed with open arms at the front door, but it is quickly and unceremoniously ushered out the back door.

Forked-tongued liberals like Tony Blair may bemoan that faith is seen increasingly to be nothing more than, as Blair put it, "a personal eccentricity." Yet, it's their own secularist liberal policies which promote that very attitude! There was a time when schizophrenia was considered psychotic....

A cold, cold climate for faith

At least one Labour Member of the European Parliament makes no apologies for consigning religion to the privacy of one's own mind. Left to Mary Honeyball, faith would never be more than "a personal eccentricity." It certainly wouldn't have a place in the public square or at the table of government.

News Item—*Irish MEP Gay Mitchell says the EU is seen as a "cold place for Christianity." Speaking in the European Parliament, Mitchell said there are "people here who see themselves as fair minded and liberal but who are anything but that when it comes to trying to see things from the point of view of people who have religious belief."*

Responding to comments made by Tony Blair who said: "In general terms in British society there is a risk that people see faith as a personal eccentricity," Mrs. Honeyball said faith "is and should remain exactly that—a personal eccentricity."[145]

There you have it in a nutshell. What Tony Blair *says* he opposes, but really doesn't, Mrs. Honeyball *says exactly* what she opposes, and really does—as do many, if not most, of her colleagues in the European Union's Parliament. And some folks wonder where all the loony EU legislation comes from!

In America, we regard cautiously anything which might have a "chilling effect" on free speech. In both Britain and the European Union today, the kind of anti-religious rhetoric such as expressed by the Labour MEP has such widespread support throughout the halls of government at every level that a "chilling effect" is slowly but surely freezing out anything to do with religious belief.

Does this not also go a long way towards explaining where America's own loony legislation is coming from? With liberals in Washington together with the ideologically-aligned ACLU constantly chipping away at religious expression in the public square, we can hardly be surprised that we are experiencing early signs of our own "chilling effect." Fortunately, praise God, the high percentage of Americans who still maintain a genuine and vocal faith are sufficient salt and light to hold back the secularist tide...at least for now. At least for a time. At least today....

Sometimes it takes an outsider

Do you find it fascinating that it takes a moderate Muslim to call attention to the Government's assault on faith in Britain? Just listen to this stinging rebuke of Britain's Government from Baroness Warsi, speaking at the Conservative Party Conference....

Conference Speech—"*Under Labour, the State has become increasingly sceptical of an individual's religious belief. We've all seen the stories. How appalling that in Labour's Britain a community nurse can be suspended for offering to pray for a patient's recovery. Or a school receptionist could face disciplinary action for sending an email to friends asking them to pray* *for her daughter. At the heart of these cases lies a growing intolerance and illiberal attitude towards those who believe in God.*

"This skepticism against faith communities, and in some cases outright hostility, is both wrong and dangerous. Strong societies are built on cherishing their heritage. So when some misguided liberal tries to downgrade Christmas, or a school tries to ban the nativity play, or a child is not taught about the British Empire in case it offends, it's no wonder we lose track of who we are.

"I am not for one minute suggesting that faith communities should get a special deal, but I do believe they should get a fair deal. One that doesn't discriminate. One that isn't intolerant. And one that truly understands and appreciates religious communities... and their contribution.[146]

Hear, hear! And it's even from the mouth of a British Muslim! When any "Christian" culture begins to experience the persecution of Christians in the workplace, and the outlawing of Christian traditions, and the free expression of Christian faith, the nation itself is at risk. You can only knock out so many of the fundamental props under a culture before it comes crashing down around everyone's head—including those who are bashing away at the props. Privatized faith may still serve well for eternity (God knows each heart), but it is disaster for society. Britain's society, Europe's, and especially our own.

Be alert, America! Faith matters. Faith makes a difference. A public square devoid of faith is not just a lonely place. It's a loony place.

8

The Deadly Path of Political Correctness

Political correctness does not legislate tolerance;
it only organizes hatred.

—Jacques Barzun

News Report—*A 140-page "diversity handbook" instructing police how to deal with minority groups has landed the Association of Police Chiefs in Scotland in hot water. The controversial guide covers age, disability, gender, faith and religion, race, and sexual orientation in aid of engaging diverse communities. After all the time and public money spent on the guidelines, police now know that they should not shout at the deaf nor certainly lean on a wheelchair. According to the manual, "It may move."*

Laura Midgley, co-founder of the Campaign Against Political Correctness, said: "This booklet would be better named as the Stating the Obvious handbook. Most people would rather the police got on with policing effectively. They can use their own common sense in sensitive situations, instead of worrying about this sort of politically correct nonsense."

Tory justice spokesman Bill Aitken said: "Clearly no one wishes to cause offence, but who are these self-appointed champions of PC who tell us you cannot 'man' a police station? Everyone knows what this means, and 99.99 percent of people could not give a damn about this sort of thing."[147]

After several decades of what its detractors call the bane of "political correctness," the beat goes on. First it was the feminists and people of color who began to use words as weapons and strategies in the raging cultural wars. Then it was the homosexuals, and it's anybody's guess who's next.

In fact, that last sentence just broke the Scottish police rules by mere mention of the word "homosexuals." In a section on "lesbian, gay, bisexual and transgender (LGBT) awareness," officers are told not to use the term "homosexual," which some LGBT people find offensive. Seems they prefer "gay" instead. But then, wasn't the word "gay" itself hijacked for political purposes in the first place? Hard to keep up these day.

The Scottish correctness guide is protective of "transgenders" as well (if that's a word...and an *acceptable* word), stating "A transgender person is not breaking the law by using the opposite gender toilet facilities from the gender they were labelled at birth." One wonders if all the other folks in those toilets would be protected by law if they protested their privacy being invaded.

The directive also makes it a no-no to "touch a buddhist monk on the head." (No word on whether not capitalizing "buddhist" is a slap in the face while you're not touching his head.)

Noticeably absent from this latest outrage of diversity protection are all normal people who the police summarily have arrested for spanking their children, or taking photos of children in a public place, or daring to speak openly about their faith. Seems there's nothing sufficiently diverse about normal folks to warrant their protection, even though they comprise the bulk of the population, pay the lion's share of the taxes, and cause the least trouble to society.

As for the terminology wars, the old-fashioned "Miss" has pretty much been replaced by the more up-to-date "Ms.," much to the dismay of many married women who far prefer the genteel "Mrs." to the crassly-truncated "Ms." But it seems the battle to blur gender lines continues unabated. Not even "Ms." seems to satisfy....

News Report—*In an effort to create gender-neutral language, the Secretary of the European Parliament has produced a booklet warning European politicians that they must avoid referring to a woman's marital status. This means that Miss and Mrs, Madame and Mademoiselle, Frau and Fraulein, and Senora and Senorita are banned. Instead of using the standard titles, Members of the European Parliament are being directed to address women by their names.*

The new rules also ban MEPs saying 'sportsmen' and 'statesmen.' The terms 'athletes' and 'political leaders' should be used instead. 'Man-made' is also taboo—it should be 'artificial' or 'synthetic.' 'Firemen' is disallowed and 'air hostesses' should be called 'flight attendants.' Headmasters and headmistresses must be 'heads' or 'head teachers,' layman becomes layperson, and manageress or mayoress should be manager or mayor. 'Police officers' must be used instead of policeman and policewoman unless the officer's sex is relevant.[148]

The public's reaction is best described in words like laughable, ludicrous, and loony. Most members of the public agree with P.D. James, who (as a woman author often wrongly assumed to be a man) opined, "I believe that political correctness can be a form of linguistic fascism, and it sends shivers down the spine of my generation who went to war against fascism." And also with Charlton Heston (not a man ever wrongly assumed to be a woman!) when he said, famously, "Political correctness is tyranny with a happy face."

The good news—if there is any—is that "the man on the Clapham omnibus" (as the Brits say) hasn't yet succumbed fully to PC madness. Just listen as ordinary Brits (and even the French) weigh in on the EU directive....

Blog Responses—

• *Now that we cannot call our leaders 'Sir' or 'Madam' should we use 'Mein Fuhrer'?*

• *You have not gone the full way towards total stupidity yet, but you are getting there. May I suggest the next step be to ban all references to male and female and to replace this gender specific description with the word CITIZEN? There you go, job done, sieg heil!*

• *When I read of yet another example of EU lunacy, I wonder anew at the mentality of the people responsible. I mean, it's not normal behaviour, is it? Imagine spending your working day as an unaccountable cog in the Brussels machine, your sole purpose in life being to generate ever more trivial, meaningless edicts carefully designed to blight the lives of millions. What job satisfaction, what an ego trip for a sadistic mindless moron! If it wasn't so tragic, it would be comical. What can be done about it? Can we ever be free of Brussels again? Can we ever be BRITISH again? So many questions, so much frustration, so much anger....*

• *"Komrad" should just about cover it.*

• *Monsieur/Madame:*
We live in France; I do not believe for one moment that the French will take the slightest notice of this latest stupidity. Britain should do the same.

• *I was born to be polite and I will continue to be polite, so to hell with the EU and all those creepy lefty ignorant fools.*

There is no end to the public outcry aimed at the EU's latest lunacy. What's needed is some thoughtful articulation of the cultural, historic, and linguistic rationale pushing an agenda that seems so out of touch. In his editorial response, Gerald Warner makes a good start....

Editorial—*It has long been a complaint of purists that the English language, so superlative in many ways, is defective in just one respect. It does* *not contain equivalents of those delicately nuanced courtesies in which other European languages abound: monsieur, madame, mademoiselle; signora and signorina; and so on.*

The forms of personal address such as "madame" are redolent of the courtesies of a more civilised age. When a Frenchman met a woman in the street he would traditionally address her as "madame" and remove his hat, keeping it in his hand until his lady interlocutor graciously said "Couvrez-vous, monsieur." In Poland, the most courteous society of all, even under communism a dustman would greet a woman by kissing her hand.

These are the remnants of Christendom, of an ancient Thomist civilisation in which every individual had an assured place and certain recognition. It is because of the memory of Christian civility enshrined in these salutations, along with the marital and familial status they imply, that the dictators of the New Order at Brussels seek to excise them, as their predecessors tried to impose such synthetic styles as "citizen" or "comrade" on the totalitarian societies they tried to create and dominate. They should be ignored, derided and dismissed. Are we agreed, ladies and gentlemen?[149]

Equality campaigners miss the mark when, in an attempt to achieve more civility, they show utter disdain for the intricate, time-worn, beauty of civilization which *invented* civility and *maintains* it. Civility doesn't exist in a vacuum. It has to be cultivated in a proper environment. To the great chagrin of secularist social engineers, it is marriage, family, and religion—the very institutions they're trying so desperately to dismantle—that are the bedrock of social civility. Already, the decline in those three institutions explains much of the decline in public social graces.

Not all PC was frivolous or loony

Yet, one has to admit that what these days is said to be "political correctness" might never have bubbled to the surface had it not been for legitimate underlying causes. In the same way that extreme religious doctrines arise to counter other extreme doctrines, and extreme political movements react to equally extreme political movements on the opposite end of the spectrum, wars over words tend to be declared only when the first person uses some particularly offensive (s)word to assault others. Should we be surprised, then, that those on the receiving end suddenly draw their own (s)words to fight back?

Speaking on BBC Radio 4, comedian Stewart Lee (co-writer and director of the controversial stage show *Jerry Springer - The Opera*) reminds us of how far we *needed* to come on the matter of racially-tinged terminology....

Radio Interview—*I'm of an age that I can see what a difference political correctness has made. When I was four years old, my grandfather drove me around Birmingham, where the Tories had just fought an election campaign saying, "If you want a nigger for a neighbour, vote Labour," and he drove me around saying, "This is where all the niggers and the coons and the jungle bunnies live."*

And I remember being at school in the early 80s and my teacher, when he read the register, instead of saying the name of the one asian boy in the class, he would say, "Is the black spot in," right? And all these things have gradually been eroded by political correctness, which seems to me to be about an institutionalised politeness at its worst.

And if there is some fallout from this, which means that someone in an office might get in trouble one day for saying something that someone was a bit unsure about because they couldn't decide whether it was sexist or homophobic or racist, it's a small price to pay for the massive benefits and improvements in the quality of life for millions of people that political correctness has made.[150]

Good point...up to a point! The good point is: Do we really want to turn back the clock to the day when blacks and other people of color were castigated by terminology aimed at making them less than human? Sticks and stones may break my bones, but words can...*hurt far more deeply, and for generations.* Apart from those who will always be inveterate racists (for whom no laws could ever change their attitude), few today would fault the giant strides taken through changes in terminology brought kicking and screaming into social vogue by determined activists.

Yet from the dizzy heights of that hallowed moral high ground, what we've witnessed more lately is a gradual slide into petty, hyper-sensitive victim-chic not to be confused with any meritorious social cause. The lessons learned about legitimate political expediency have been put to twisted use, not unlike little children who quickly realize that the same instinctive crying and screaming that gets their parents' undivided attention in those early days can also be used in the "terrible twos" toward strictly selfish ends. If "political correctness" worked for a noble cause, so it seems, why not for ignoble ones?

It's crucial to remember that the movement for racial justice was not principally about prickly sensitivity to ethnic slurs. The epithets "niggers" and "jungle bunnies" were nowhere near being in the same category as "polocks," "paddies," or "spicks." (Nor certainly Brits being called "limeys," or the French, "frogs.") For socially-oppressed blacks, ethnic slurs played but a supporting role to the real villain: widespread, officially-sanctioned, deeply-entrenched, institutionalized prejudice.

Name even one cause today where offensive slurs are symptomatic of endemic social abuse on anything like that scale! Are women in sports, or female flight attendants, cops, mayors, entrepreneurs, married women or—least of all—women MEPs so victimized throughout society that they need curative, protective terminology?

And what about homosexuals? Are homosexuals forced to sit in the back of the bus, or to use separate drinking fountains and toilets, or forbidden to eat in heterosexual-only restaurants? Are they *today* the victims of widespread, systematic job discrimination? Apart from marriage, do they not have virtually every civil right afforded heterosexuals? (Even the "don't ask, don't tell" policy in the military is yesterday's news.) Why, then, the continuing battering ram of "politically-correct" terminology?

And what in the world has prompted men who have sexual relations with other men (if we can still put it that way) to insist that we call them "gays" and not "homosexuals"? After all this time of being out and proud, is there still something shameful about being a "homosexual"? And why the sudden reversal in which the word "queer"—socially taboo for decades—is now being reintroduced along with lesbians, gays, bisexuals, and the transgendered (as in LGBTQ)? Is it just the Rolling Stones syndrome—that, no matter how compliant society becomes, "I can't get no satisfaction"?

Deep down in their souls, most people (if perhaps reluctantly for some) recognized the rightness of political correctness in aid of racial equality. In the same "deep down" of their souls, most people today all too easily recognize the utter phoniness of the petty causes pushing the current strain of political correctness. No wonder people loathe it. How, then, can political correctness in aid of unworthy substitutes not end up being counterproductive? If it's respect that's being sought, it's only disrespect that's being achieved. If promoting a good cause is the object of the game, that good cause is being set back, not advanced. By Newton's law, illegitimate political force will always be countered by an equal and opposite social force.

If *equality* is the concern, look who's now so pitifully "unequal" that they're in a commanding position to impose heavy-handed political correctness from the highest offices in the EU, Britain, and the United States! And if it's *civility* that one is trying to force on everyone, does cramming petty-minded legislation down people's throats fit neatly within the definition of civility?

Even more irritating is the shrill tone persistently used by those who are demanding that the rest of us speak civilly to everyone so that we not risk even "indirectly offending" anybody (the scary new subjective, victim-determined standard laid down by Britain's Equality Bill). Equality campaigners miss the mark when, in an attempt to achieve increased civility, they themselves demonstrate so little of it. Secularists as well as religious folks are honor-bound to "practice what they preach." This runs the gamut from thoughtful word-choice and tone to respecting fellow citizens sufficiently so as not to shake a governmental fist in everyone's faces just because your office cubicle happens to be in Brussels, Westminster, or Washington.

Yes, you say, but of course. Isn't that obvious? What's obvious is that sometimes that which is obvious to the whole world is not obvious to the very ones for whom it ought be the most obvious! They're like the maddeningly-oblivious neighbors whose constantly-barking dogs are disrupting the peace and enjoyment of a quiet neighborhood. If you *have* to tell some folks the obvious, then you can *never* tell them. Might just as well try to teach pigs to sing.

Not just *correct* speech, but *no* speech

If you have your ear to the ground, even in America these days you'll hear lots of talk about "hate speech" and "hate crimes" (as if premeditated murder wasn't always a crime of hate). In Britain, the regulation of "hate speech" has become an art form....

Editorial—*On Thursday, a British diplomat was fined for "racially aggravated harassment" because he fulminated at the television screen when he was exercising in the gym. Rowan Laxton, head of the South Asia desk of the Foreign Office, was watching a report about the death of a farmer killed by Israeli bombs when he exclaimed: "_____ Israelis, _____ Jews!"*

Two other members of the gym were on the floor below and heard Laxton's imprecation. They complained to the staff, who told the police, who arrested Laxton. He was fined £350, ordered to pay £500 prosecution costs and a £15 victim surcharge (to whom?). He might now lose his job.

He was threatening nobody. He was unaware that there was anyone within earshot. Had he said the same thing in his sitting room, and been overheard through an open window by someone walking past, should he then be arrested and prosecuted? What is really worrying is that there are people who think the answer to that question is yes.[151]

183

Rather undiplomatic language for a diplomat, to be sure, but worthy of arrest and criminal prosecution? (Just wondering, ACLU, which side would you be on in a court of law—free speech or political correctness?)

Consistent with the trickle-down theory (but hardly Reaganomics), "hate speech" is one of the targets even at the office Christmas party (as long as we're still permitted to call it that)....

Employment Law Memo—*An employer has a duty towards all its employees while they are in the "course of employment." Tribunals have decided that this includes the traditional Christmas party even if it is in the evening and not at the office. So if one of your employees suffers any form of harassment or discrimination connected with the party, you will be responsible. This goes beyond unwelcome alcohol fuelled advances to whether the entertainer tells sexist or racist jokes....[152]*

Merry Christmas to all, and to all a...sober warning about Santa not bringing you free speech next year.

Brainwashing the young

While the Government is intent on curtailing any and all speech deemed politically rude to others, it seems to have no concern whatsoever about the other kind of "rude" talk which in Britain can also mean *filthy* talk. Imagine your own children or grandchildren getting this classroom assignment...at a *faith-based* school, no less....

News Report—*Parents have been shocked to find foul and abusive words in the schoolbooks of 10-year-olds, including variations on the F-word, crude slang for sex acts, female and male genitalia, and racist and derogatory name-calling. As part of an anti-bullying campaign at their Church of England school, the children were asked to compile a list of hurtful words leveled at victims and categorize them in four sections: really upsetting, upsetting, not nice, and harmless.*

The lesson at the center of the controversy was part of the widely-used Social and Emotional Aspect of Learning (Seal) classroom programme, which addresses issues dealing with bullying and family matters.

One mother said in disgust: "Some of the words used were so bad I'd never heard them before. Certainly, many of the kids came home with a new vocabulary of filth. The whole episode begs belief."[153]

What a creative object lesson—teaching children how language can be *really upsetting* by making their parents apoplectic! And don't forget that this was not the lone stunt of some wild-eyed teacher doing her own weird thing. Where did the idea for such a socially-conscious assignment come from? From material used by schools all over Britain!

Are you sufficiently outraged yet? That last article was penny-ante compared with the next one. To give some context to anyone who might have missed it (how could you?), Britain's "9/11" came on July 7, 2005—a day when terrorist bombs on London's public transport system during the early morning rush hour killed fifty-six people, including the bombers, and injured around 700. A terrible nightmare by any calculation. Now read the shocking aftermath....

News Report—*As part of the Government's strategy to combat violent extremism, an exercise has been floated, requiring schoolchildren to imagine they are suicide bombers plotting the July 7 attacks. They are asked to summarise the reasons why they thought the bombers wanted to carry out their attacks, and even to suggest some more.*

Jacqui Putnam, who survived the Edgware Road bomb on July 7, said: "I can't see why anyone would think it is a valuable exercise to encourage children to put themselves in the position of men who treated people in such an inhuman way. To encourage children to see the world in that way is a dangerous thing. Surely there must be a better way of achieving their objective?"

185

Labour MP Khalid Mahmood said the exercise risked "encouraging the sort of belief we're trying to work against. They should be looking at it from the victims' view," he said. Whoever thought this up has no understanding of the communities where we are fighting against extremist beliefs." Patrick Mercer, the chairman of the Commons terrorism sub-committee, said: "Imagine the uproar if we suggested that children play-acted the role of Hitler."

In response to public criticism, the education department has now withdrawn the exercise from the teachernet website. A spokesman said: "While the resource in no way looks to justify or excuse the terrible events of 7/7, and is designed to educate against extremist beliefs, we appreciate that it may not be appropriate for use in schools."[154]

Inappropriate, indeed. There seems to be no limit to fuzzy-mindedness in Britain's educational system. No one doubts the good intentions of mainstream educators, only their abysmal collective judgment, borne out of a liberal mentality that seems rarely to touch base with common sense.

Groveling multicultural appeasement

When does even potentially-helpful political correctness cease being protective and become mere appeasement? If ever there were a good example, you'll see it in the following report....

New Item—*More than 1,000 British men are believed to have multiple wives. Bigamy is illegal in Britain, but those who have immigrated after marrying more than one woman in Islamic countries are allowed to remain in polygamous partnerships—and can even claim benefits for their additional spouses.*

Politicians fear discussing the issue of multiple marriage lest they offend Muslims. But no less than Baroness Warsi, the Muslim peer, blamed "cultural sensitivity" for the failure to tackle the problem of polygamy. She urges the Government to consider ordering that all religious marriages must be registered, as civil ceremonies are, in order to stop men marrying more than one wife.[155]

It's another one of those instances where liberal causes collide. Want to be liberal enough to tolerate the polygamy honored by a religion other than the narrow-minded Christianity you so despise? After all, if "gay marriage" is to be sanctioned, why not polygamy? The problem is that the self-same Muslim faith just happens to condemn unequivocally all homosexual conduct. The Muslim faith also tends to wink at the denigration of women—best seen in the objectification of women as multiple wives, especially when they are brought into the country specifically to obtain greater state benefits.

So why this open-ended acceptance of a religion far more narrow-minded than British Christianity ever dreamed of being? According to Baroness Warsi, herself a Muslim, it's because politicians dare not offend their Muslim constituency. It's not a case of political correctness, but of political expediency and pragmatism. Need all the votes we can get, don't we? In one fell swoop, we can assure our reelection and show ourselves to be blissfully tolerant.

While chipping away at all things Christian, the British Government knows no length to which it will not go in promoting tolerance for Muslims. Merely consider this latest example....

News Report—*A Government-funded charity has published a controversial cartoon strip in which a boy wearing a large cross around his neck is shown telling a friend that a smiling Muslim girl in a veil looks like a terrorist. He later confronts her and shouts: 'Hey, whatever your name is, what are you hiding under your turban?' She replies that the garment is called a hijab and it is part of her religion, 'like that cross you wear.' The girl is then shown standing up for another boy, who is being bullied, and her behaviour is contrasted with that of the boy wearing the cross.*

Mike Judge, of the Christian Institute, said: "It is a clumsy caricature, symptomatic of a culture which says it is okay to bully Christians in the name of diversity." Philip Hollobone, the Tory MP for Kettering, said: "I think it is very unfortunate that the lad who is pointing the finger is wearing a cross. You can hardly imagine anyone producing a magazine in which the roles were reversed and it was the Muslim girl who was behaving badly."

The charity's chief executive, Natasha Finlayson, said she had no intention of withdrawing the cartoon, describing the cross as 'bling' rather than a religious symbol.[156]

Excuse me? How possibly could anyone dismiss the cross as nothing more than "bling" jewelry when the Muslim girl herself describes her hijab as *part of her religion, "like that cross you wear"*? If not *civility*, how about at least some *honesty*?

The plain truth is that no one in power these days in Britain seems to worry in the least about offending Christians, but it's another story altogether when it comes to offending Muslims. Remember the "biscuit wars" in the chapter on health and safety? Here's another far more serious permutation on theme....

News Report—*In an article for Personnel Today, members of the Employers Forum on Belief have advised employers to honor the Muslim festival of Ramadan by keeping biscuits out of meetings and rearranging working hours for Muslim employees. The EFB says public bodies in particular should be studying religious practices in preparation for the Equality Bill, which will "promote equality" among religions.*

Jo Barclay of the Co-operative Group said: "Productivity may drop during the month of Ramadan as participating Muslims are not getting any fuel. Our managers may therefore encourage those workers not to organise meetings past 3 pm, or to leave earlier where possible."

Graham White, Human Resources Director at Westminster City Council, said the Council had developed special spaces in their building for "meditation, prayer and religious observance" in preparation for Ramadan.[157]

No suggestions, of course, that government offices and private businesses honor Christian holidays such as Christmas...er..."the winter holidays." Nor any mention of the many Christians employed in the public sector who have been fired or disciplined for expressing their faith at work. And can you imagine the uproar if a city council set aside a special room for Christian worship? So much for the *Equality* Bill!

Which brings us back to the counterproductive boomerang-effect of all misdirected political correctness, a principle better understood by many Muslims than by wooly-headed liberals....

News Report—*Home Office staff have been officially warned in a five-page information sheet not to eat in front of their fasting Muslim colleagues during Ramadan. "In practical terms, please be sensitive when eating lunch near a Muslim colleague who is fasting. This can make an individual feel hungrier and make it more challenging to observe the fast."*

The guide is now at the center of a row among Islamic groups. The Muslim Public Affairs Committee has attacked the document, saying: "It is designed to create more hatred in the hearts of non-Muslims. We don't care how much non-Muslims eat in front of us. It's never been an issue and never will be. We have never asked for any special treatment or sensitivity from non-Muslims whilst fasting."[158]

Just how politically incorrect can some particular action be when not even the "victims" it's meant to protect feel the need for such protection? Which raises an interesting dilemma for political correctness campaigners when the target group itself has different opinions about what is offensive....

News Report—*The Dundee police force has apologised to Islamic leaders for an "offensive" postcard advertising a new non-emergency telephone number. The card shows a six-month-old trainee police dog named Rebel, a German shepherd puppy who has proved hugely popular with the public. Hundreds have gone online to read Rebel's training diary.*

But some Muslims have been upset by the image because they consider dogs to be "ritually unclean." Muslim shopkeepers have refused to display the advert card.

A spokesman for Tayside Police said: "We did not seek advice from the force's diversity adviser prior to publishing and distributing the postcards. That was an oversight and we apologise for any offence caused. If we had seen it was going to cause upset, we would not have done it."[159]

Giving new meaning to James Dean's...er...Rebel without a cause, who in their right mind ever would have thought it necessary to consult diversity officers over the use of a bouncing cute puppy for a promotion campaign? And suppose the police diversity officers had consulted with the Scottish-Islamic Foundation, only to be told that the puppy photo was not offensive, when other Muslims angrily disagreed? Must there be a referendum on every issue even remotely touching on touchy minorities? (And might that include dog owners upset over puppy discrimination?)

As the case of the sinister "Police Puppy Ploy" illustrates, one of the most alarming aspects of the Equality Bill is how anyone can know with any certainty who, or when, they are offending. Under the bill's subjective standard, the excuse given by the police ("If we had seen it was going to cause upset, we would not have done it") would not prevent the police themselves from arresting someone charged with innocently upsetting, say, a gay man by using the term "homosexual" in his presence.

The question of the hour is: Why all the pandering to the Muslim community in Britain? When the police begin groveling and apologizing over something as innocent as puppy pictures, we're no longer talking about your typical "political correctness" but about a minority so powerful that they've got everyone else running scared. Extremist tail wagging ritually-unclean dog. Co-dependent majority feeding the selfishness of an abusive minority.

Take, for example, the noise ban curtailing amplified music and sermons at the Immanuel International Christian Centre in Waltham Forest following a complaint from a Muslim neighbor. Council officials explained to church leaders that "this is a Muslim borough, so you have to tread carefully."[160] Everybody on tippy-toes, please! And don't even think about mentioning the amplified sounds of the Muslim call to prayer five times a day....

All the while, there is precious little reciprocity from the "protected minority." In fact, in some quarters, there is nothing in return but open hostility, like guests in one's home despising everything about their hosts except the protective roof over their heads. If this sounds a bit harsh, judge for yourself after reading Denis MacEoin's comment....

Editorial—*Music, chess and cricket are just three things banned in some Muslim schools in the UK. Others are drama, dance, sport, Shakespeare, and, in some cases, any aspect of Western culture whatever. According to the management committee of London's Madani Secondary Girls' School, this is because "our children are exposed to a culture that is in opposition with almost everything Islam stands for."*

Some Muslim schools teach social cohesion, others regard it as a deadly sin. Some schools impart the skills necessary for a fulfilling life alongside non-Muslim friends and co-workers, others try to recreate a Pakistani or Bangladeshi lifestyle and to make it exclusive.

Not infrequently, Ofsted inspectors give glowing reports to schools that require much closer examination. Al-Mu'min Primary School in Bradford is linked to the al-Mu'min journal, which carries material from schoolchildren. Its website teaches that Western culture is "evil," that photographs are "an evil practice of the unbelievers," and that "the person who plays chess is like one who dips his hand in the blood of a swine."

But here's a sample of the Ofsted report: "Al-Mumin Primary School provides a good education for its pupils and ensures that they have good attitudes and a very good work ethic....The provision made for the spiritual, moral, social and cultural development of pupils is outstanding."

Many commentators have spoken of the long-term consequences to society of an over-lenient policy of multiculturalism. In the Islamic case, the growth of exclusive communities in major cities carries the added risk that young men and women may be more easily lured into violence. If Muslim children are to be left to the tender mercies of religious extremists, we all face an uncertain future. The Government has the power to stop this. It is time it did.[161]

The Muslim advocacy group www.Islamophobia-watch.com cited MacEoin's report as an example of Islamophobic propaganda, but without countering the facts reported. Given the many concessions constantly being made to appease British Muslims, one would think it an uphill battle to convince anyone outside the Muslim community that Britain is cursed by Islamophobia. Certainly, no one will ever accuse the Government's education watchdog *Ofsted* of being overly critical of radicalized Muslim schools. "Liberal coverup" comes to mind.

If MacEoin's facts are right, the greater problem among hard-line Muslims, surely, is Britophobia. Since when did a game of chess become evil? Cricket maybe, but *chess*? Oh, but of course. There's all those kings, queens, Crusader knights, and Christian bishops. Hard to believe any conscientious Muslim would have immigrated to a country with all that Western evil lurking on every corner.

And funny how that works out for radical Muslims planning suicide attacks against the Great Satan. They don't seem to mind sacrificing *pawns....*

When political correctness turns deadly

Is MacEoin just blowing right-wing, Islamophobic smoke, or is there actually something to his fears about Britain's appeasement of hate mongering among more-radical pockets of the Muslim community? If the proof is in the pudding, the "pudding" is found in the continuing embarrassment that Britain's terrorist are mostly home-grown, well-educated Muslims coming out of Britain's own universities. Douglas Murray, director of the Centre for Social Cohesion, gives us this chilling insight to consider....

Editorial—*The fact that the latest suspected terrorist threat involves students should come as no surprise. It is the predictable result of three things: an insatiably violent Islamist ideology; the politically-correct refusal of our political class to admit reality; and the comprehensive neglectfulness of our university authorities. This country has already produced a number of students who have gone on to become jihadist murderers.*

Muslim students who don't care about foreign conflicts are made to feel un-Islamic unless they endlessly whip themselves up into a fury against Israel and America. Just as, internationally, the Islamists give us the offer "say my religion is peaceful or I will kill you," so domestically we are told "say there's no radicalism or we'll be radical."

There are many messages that we should be giving out. But one in particular should go straight away to our political class: political correctness may be something that they are willing to fight for, but it is not something that most of us are willing to die for.[162]

That was Douglas Murray writing in April, 2009. Britain had just dodged another terrorist bullet at the hands of British-born and British-educated Muslim extremists. Fast-forward to December 25, 2009 and the attempted bombing of Detroit-bound Northwest Flight 253 by Umar Farouk Abdulmutallab. Care to venture a guess where he was educated...?

Editorial—*Friday's attempt to blow up a transatlantic airliner by a British-educated Islamist was foiled by the bravery of its passengers and crew. We cannot assume that we will be lucky next time. And the indications are that there will be a next time. According to police sources, 25 British-born Muslims are currently in Yemen being trained in the art of bombing planes. But most of these terrorists did not acquire their crazed beliefs in the Islamic world: they were indoctrinated in Britain. Indeed, thousands of young British Muslims support the use of violence to further the Islamist cause—and this despite millions of pounds poured by the Government into projects designed to prevent Islamic extremism.*

Radical Islamist leaders are not stupid: they know how to play this system. The indoctrination of students carries on under the noses of public servants who are terrified of being labelled Islamophobic or racist. Therefore they fail to do their duty, which is to protect Muslims and non-Muslims alike from a terrorist ideology. If providing that protection requires fewer "consultations" with "community leaders" and more arrests, then so be it.[163]

So writes the editors of *The Daily Telegraph* (characterized by www.Islamophobia-watch.com as "The Torygraph"). Are the editors wrong? Is there not a war going on here? Are we not in a whole new ballpark from the usual "culture wars" over abortion, gay rights, and the rights of women? In this all-too-real, body-count war between competing cultures, 3,000 people died on 9/11. Thousands more brave soldiers have died in Iraq and Afghanistan, the Yemeni port of Aden, and Fort Hood. And this doesn't begin to include the countless thousands of innocent civilians—both Muslim and non-Muslim—who have died in the crossfire. In the current political climate, any and every attempt at petty political correctness ought to be summarily banned. But wouldn't you know, Britain's liberal elites still don't get it.

Commenting on Britain's Equality Bill, columnist Charles Moore reminds us that there are none so liberal as liberals who are still blindedly liberal when all the world around them is at war....

Commentary—*In the "Impact Assessments" which the Bill prescribes, "intersectional multiple discrimination" must be rooted out. That is when your nasty prejudice links two or more characteristics of the person discriminated against.*

This is the official example given: "A bus driver does not allow a Muslim man on her bus, claiming he could be a 'terrorist'.... A multiple-discrimination claim will allow him to show that the reason for his treatment was the specific combination of being a man and a Muslim, which resulted in him being stereotyped as a potential terrorist."

Think about this bus driver in real life. She (as, inevitably, the official document designates her, though most bus drivers remain male) sees a Muslim man getting on her bus, perhaps young, carrying a rucksack, looking nervous. If she has watched any news programme in the 21st century, she will have noticed that more than 95 percent of terrorist acts in Britain or Spain or Israel or the United States have been carried out by people with that "specific combination" of being Muslim and male. Many have been suicide bombers and have detonated their bombs on public transport. In Israel, in particular, many lives have been saved by drivers who have spotted something suspicious in time.

So what does the driver do? Does she impede the Muslim man whose demeanour alarms her? Or does she consider that, if she were accused of "intersectional multiple discrimination," she might be out of her job? Is this a real-life dilemma which any government should put a bus driver in?[164]

Any liberals out there who want to answer that question? Anyone who still wants to defend the Obama Administration's on-again, off-again decisions to provide terrorists with trials in America's courts rather than treat them as enemy combatants intent on destroying the very system under which they are now being given a forum for spewing out their hatred for all the world to see? It doesn't matter which side of the Atlantic they're on, loony liberals are always on the wrong side of common sense.

The American version of dangerous tolerance

Britain is not the only nation enamored with barmy political correctness. Egged on by a liberal coalition of feminists, gays, neo-Marxist educators, and the ACLU, radical political correctness is on a decades-long roll. As noted by Lance Morrow in his thoughtful *Time* article on "The Roots of America's Cultural War," right here at home we see political correctness in "hate crimes," gender equality legislation, in forced corporate "sensitivity" training, and in the menace of coerced "right thinking" in the universities. And who could have missed the spectacle of Al Gore's failed presidential bid only barely floundering on a platform of class warfare and identity politics?[165]

Despite historically being blessed as an ethnic melting pot, America does not have the same lethal ethnic cocktail to contend with as does Britain. Which is not to say that individuals on the home front haven't been radicalized as instruments of Islamic jihadists. Merely consider Major Nidal Hasan's killing of 13 people at Fort Hood. Hasan might have been a lone, unstable gunman, but all evidence points to his act of terrorism directly stemming from his radical Muslim beliefs.

The crucial question of this chapter is the extent to which America's own penchant for political correctness played a role in allowing that act of terror to occur. With each additional inquiry, the picture is becoming more and more clear. As reported by The Washington Post, "Fear of offending Muslims or being insensitive to religion was likely a key factor to why Army supervisors missed signs that the suspect in the deadly Fort Hood shooting rampage was a Muslim extremist, according to national security experts."

Counterterrorism experts quoted in the report speak of an "atmosphere of intimidation" ensuring that everyone gave Maj. Hasan a pass, despite both his poor performance record and indications of his extremist religious views. When those who led the Pentagon review were asked whether political correctness had contributed to the oversight, the terse response was that radicalization of any kind was the concern, without singling out the Islamic religion.[166]

Astounding, isn't it? You know that political correctness has become fully entrenched when the U.S. military feels compelled to give only politically-correct answers to obvious and important questions directly related to national security. "Our concern is not with any particular religion, only radicalization of any sort," comes the disingenuous party line, despite President Obama's firm (if belated) assertion that "America is at war."

And with whom might we be at war? Radicalized Nazis? Radicalized Communists? Radicalized Hindus, Buddhists, or Baptists? In this ideological war aimed at destroying our very civilization, pray tell what radicalization other than Islamist radicalization is causing the deaths of thousands of Americans? If we can't even identify the enemy (or have the courage to state the obvious), how possibly can we win the war? It's one thing to tippy-toe when Muslims complain about puppy pictures and loud music emanating from a church. But it's sheer madness to tippy-toe when Muslim extremists are on a deadly, culture-exterminating jihadist rampage.

This must certainly be a huge dilemma for President Obama, whose liberal credentials are impeccably tied to the usual issues of political correctness. What the President has to decide is whether, as Chief Executive, he will continue to follow his liberal instincts and maintain political correctness at all cost; or whether, as Commander-in-Chief, he will wake up and realize that with each passing day the inflated cost of political correctness is nothing less than the nation's very survival.

When the next in-bound plane explodes because of a terrorist even remotely aided by the liberal-Left's political correctness of indiscriminate tolerance, it will hardly matter whether the Member of the European Parliament seated in 23E on her way to the Gay and Lesbian Diversity Conference is listed as Kate Simpson or *Mrs.* Kate Simpson.

9

Warning: This Chapter on Gays Could Be Arresting

I don't know why gays want to be in the armed forces.
They seem to look for something they're denied and then
insist on having it.

—Quentin Crisp
Gay activist and author

News *Report—Shakespeare's Romeo and Juliet has been given a modern twist by 14-to-16-year-old students in a mixed school in east London to coincide with Lesbian, Gay, Bisexual and Transgendered (LGBT) History Month. The updated adaptation, called Romeo and Julian, is a reworking of the original text to incorporate a gay theme.*

Much public debate has ensued, even in the halls of Westminster, where Commons leader Harriet Harman said: "I seem to remember that in Shakespearean times, boys would play girls and girls would play boys and the whole point was trying work out which was which."[167]

If there is any single piece of the political-correctness puzzle that is absolutely definitive, it must surely be the carefully-orchestrated movement towards the advancement of homosexuals in every aspect of society.

Already, great strides have been taken in aid of all manner of sexual freedoms, both homosexual and heterosexual. Today, whether in

Britain or in the United States, there are no police running around invading the intimacies of anyone's bedroom seeking proof of illicit sexual activities. Laws once criminalizing homosexual conduct, adultery, and fornication have been wiped mostly from the books. Generally speaking—apart from churches and religious organizations maintaining conscientious objections against hiring those who might actively be engaged in a sexually-immoral lifestyle—employers no longer care whether their employees are heterosexual or homosexual. Voters seem not to care whether a candidate is "gay or straight;" and "out and proud" Hollywood and British entertainers are not penalized either at the box office or in television ratings. Indeed, "civil unions" are solemnized in Britain and "gay marriage" is now legal in several American states and fast headed toward full legalization in the UK.

So the question is: What more do homosexual activists want? And the short answer is: *Approval*. Which is to say validation, and affirmation, and the quieting of all objection to their conduct and lifestyle. And, by gum, they're going to get it, or else....no matter whose consciences they run over, no matter what the cost to social cohesion, no matter what moral standards are undermined, and—hypocrisy of hypocrisies—no matter how intolerant they and their heterosexual friends are of anyone who happens to disagree with their personal agenda....

News Report—*In Waltham Forest, lessons to teach primary school children about homosexual relationships as part of Lesbian, Gay, Bisexual, and Transgender History Month used books such as "King and King." Parents, both Christian and Muslim, who withdrew their children from the controversial lessons are now facing legal action. The Waltham Forest Council website says that parents of truant children can be asked to sign a contract, be fined on the spot, or taken to court.*

A spokesman for the Council explained that, "As part of the borough's policy of promoting tolerance in our schools, children are taught that everyone in our society is of equal value."[168]

Everyone, of course, except conscientious parents. And people of faith. And those who dare swim against the liberal-Left tide of political correctness. You mean, tolerance only for those who agree with you? Maybe there's some confusion here, but isn't that the very opposite of what tolerance requires...?

Tolerance for all but conscientious objectors

News Report—*When Martyn Hall and his civil partner Steven Preddy arrived at the Chymorvah Private Hotel in Cornwall, they were told by owners Peter and Hazelmary Bull that only married heterosexual couples could stay in the same room. The men are now suing the couple for discrimination on the grounds of sexual orientation. Under the Equality Act, it is unlawful to refuse a person goods or facilities on the grounds of their sexuality.*

Mr. and Mrs. Bull have defended their policy, which bans all unmarried couples—both heterosexual and homosexual—from sharing a bed. The policy has been in place since they took over the business in 1986. On the booking page of their website is a "special note" which reads: "Here at Chymorvah we have few rules, but please note that as Christians we have a deep regard for marriage (being the union of one man to one woman for life to the exclusion of all others). Therefore, although we extend to all a warm welcome to our home, our double-bedded accommodation is not available to unmarried couples — Thank you."

Mrs. Bull said that even her brother and his girlfriend had to stay in separate rooms when they visited the hotel. "I have had people clearly involved in affairs and under-age people who have tried to book in here for sex, and I have refused them the same as I refused these gentlemen because I won't be a party to anything which is an affront to my faith under my roof," she added.

The Bulls were sent a letter from Stonewall, a homosexual activist organization, warning them that they were breaking the law. Shortly after, Mr. Preddy rang to book a double room for two nights.

The Bulls' solicitor argues that the Equality Act infringes on the Bull's human rights as Christians. "Under the European Convention on Human Rights, people are able to hold a religious belief and manifest it in the way they act."[169]

Two things jump out of that article. First, the Bull's faith-based policy did not target homosexuals anymore than heterosexuals. Everyone was treated equally—including Mrs. Bull's own brother! Second, it's clearly a Stonewall setup from start to finish. A test case. An intentional bullying of the Bulls to force them to either violate their conscience or close their hotel. Of this you can be sure: Had the Bulls not advertised their morality policy, Hall and Preddy never would have shown up at their doorstep. If it had been a legitimate booking, there were plenty of other accommodations available to them.

If it's tolerance homosexual activists want, you would think they would take the lead in demonstrating tolerance towards others. But, no. Despite all their lofty talk about tolerance, for gay activists tolerance is a one-way street. Maybe it's a reaction to playground bullying where some of them might have been taunted by their schoolmates as sissies. If so, the bullied have become the bullies...and with a vengeance.

Yet it's not just gay activists. Bullies are everywhere in the liberal-Left establishment, from the highest offices in the land to local government councils to the hallowed halls of justice. Merely consider with what disdain anyone bucking that establishment is treated in the workplace....

News Report—*A registrar threatened with losing her job is taking her employer to a tribunal to determine whether she can refuse to officiate at homosexual "weddings" because of her conscientious objections. "I feel strongly about maintaining my Christian beliefs and conscience," said Miss Lillian Ladele. "I can't go against what it says in the Bible. I don't understand why the council can't use other people who have no problem with the ceremonies."*

Ben Summerskill, of the homosexual rights group, Stonewall, said: "Doctors and nurses can't choose who they treat, and nor should a registrar be allowed to discriminate."[170]

The Employment Appeal Tribunal accepted that Islington had acted in an improper, unreasonable and extraordinary manner but ruled it did not amount to religious discrimination. The Court of Appeal agreed, prompting this telling response from the National Secular Society....

Web Blog—*This is an extremely important decision for the protection of the rights of gay people in this country—and the right one. It establishes—we hope definitively—that because a person has strong religious views, it does not give them the right to discriminate against and deny services to others of whom they disapprove.*

Parliament has decided that gay people are entitled to civil partnerships and that their right to such a service be protected in law, so there should be no-opt outs on any grounds, religious or otherwise for public servants from performing these ceremonies. Christian conscience should not be a blanket licence to discriminate against others."[171]

In case you missed the advert: "Coming Soon to Your Local Theater... Gay Rights Trump Religious Conscience." Meanwhile back in Islington, a second Christian registrar, Theresa Davies, has now been disciplined and threatened with dismissal after asking to be exempted from registering same-sex unions. And the response from the homosexual lobby...?

News Blurb—*Revd. Sharon Ferguson, chief executive of Britain's Lesbian and Gay Christian Movement, compared Miss Davies's views to those of a white supremacist. She said: "It is fine for people to hold opinions but you can't use views to discriminate against other people."*[172]

One might think a person of the cloth—even though homosexual—would appreciate, value, and honor the huge leap between *mere opinion* and *religious conscience*. But again, no. There is no tolerance for those who conscientiously object.

If only it were merely work-specific, job-related situations where (if you insist) "opinions" mattered. But just check out this alarming development....

News Report—*Charity worker David Booker has been suspended from his job as a hostel support worker on the grounds of "gross misconduct" after a discussion with a colleague about religion and homosexuality. Mr. Booker said: "I was working nights with a colleague of mine and somehow we got on to the subject of Christianity—and then our discussion moved on to homosexuality in the church....I did say that I didn't agree with same-sex marriages, I didn't believe pastors or vicars should marry same-sex partners and I didn't agree with practising homosexuals being a pastor or a vicar."*

The suspension letter from his employer said that Booker had breached the applicable code of conduct by "promoting your religious views which contained discriminatory comments regarding a person's sexual orientation."[173]

How do you feel about homosexuals being married? Or practicing homosexuals serving as church pastors? If you happen to be opposed to either of those, the time could well be coming when, even here in America, it's better to keep it to yourself—at the risk of losing your job if you don't!

Back in Britain—surprise of surprises—Mr. Booker's situation has been defended by none other than homosexual Mathew Hywel, writing in the *Pink News*, a homosexual publication....

Editorial—*So it seems the battle between gay rights and religious rights continues. It appears that a religious man cannot express his personal views on gay marriage and the ordination of gay clergy even when chatting to a co-worker without being reported. Of course, this depends on what exactly he said, who he said it to, the amount of offence taken and what job he does. Or does it?*

Society's increasing disregard for religious beliefs, whether held personally or collectively, should be a matter of concern for LGBT people. With the Daily Mail brigade's constant rants on the dominant genes of secularism and political correctness, it would be easy to forget that many gay people also regard themselves as religious.

Many non-religious gay people still aren't comfortable with gay marriage. Would the charity worker therefore be suspended if he was a gay man objecting to the 'broad cause' of pushing for same-sex marriage? Almost certainly not.

We've been here before. Only a few months ago Lilian Ladele, a registrar from Islington who refused to perform civil partnerships for same-sex couples because it conflicted with her Christian beliefs, had her case overturned after originally winning a tribunal case on the grounds of religious discrimination. This highlighted the clear division between the rights of gay people and those of faith as almost competing entities.

With this in mind, is the case of the charity worker a case of religious bigotry on his part or religious discrimination by his employer? Whatever the outcome of this case, it seems increasingly apparent that people have more of a right to be gay than to be religious.[174]

Wow, what an admission! At least you can be assured that not every objection to the homosexual rights movement is dreamt up by right-wing religious fanatics obsessing over nothing.

At the heart of Hywel's concern, of course, is maintaining the right of religious free speech for those who are so motivated. Exhibiting a perception rarely observed among the liberal-Left, Hywel understands that shutting down religious free speech threatens to shut down all free speech, including that of homosexuals. Not a good idea. Just as a rising tide floats all boats, and an ebbing tide lowers them, so too the ebb of any free speech lowers the security of all free speech. Hence the recent debate in Britain over the no-small-matter of prohibiting or permitting free speech related to equality and hate crimes legislation....

Free speech has near-death experience

For well over a year, a debate raged back and forth through the halls of Westminster over whether the Government should succeed in its attempt to delete a free speech protection from a "homophobic hatred" offense. Opposition forces were a curious blend of faith-based organizations, civil libertarians, actors, and even homosexuals.

If you've never watched the immensely popular "Blackadder" and "Mr. Bean" series coming out of the UK, you've missed two icons of British comedy. The leading actor in both series, Rowan Atkinson, urged the House of Lords to vote against the Government's attempt to delete the free speech section, saying, "Do I think that I would risk prosecution because of jokes or drama about sexual orientation with which I might be involved if we don't have the free speech clause? Not really, but I dread something almost as bad—a culture of censoriousness, a questioning, negative and leaden attitude that is encouraged by legislation of this nature but is considerably and meaningfully alleviated by the free speech clause."

Atkinson went on to criticize "hate speech legislation" in general, saying, "The last thing that any academic, or cleric, or practitioner in creative writing wants to hear is of police officers walking round with a tool box bulging with sanctions against speech and expression that 'could be useful one day.' I do not believe that legislation of such a censorious nature as that of Hate Speech, carrying as it does the risk of a seven year jail sentence for saying the wrong thing in the wrong way, can ever be justified merely by the desire to 'send the right message.'"[175]

A humorless comedy of errors

Joining in the chorus of dissent against removal of the free speech clause was Christopher Biggins, a homosexual comedian whose brilliant commentary on the raging debate is as insightful (and instructive for Americans) as anything you'll read....

Editorial—*The new law will even override the basic requirements of freedom of speech, one of the pillars of our democracy. All comedy, entertainment, TV, books and radio will be subjected to this new regime if it comes into existence, no doubt rigorously enforced by an army of boot-faced, unsmiling commissars desperately trying to find some infringement of their rules.*

The politically correct censors will be our own British version of the East German Stasi. Under this proposed new orthodoxy, almost any colourful display of theatrical high camp could be presented as stereotyping of gay life and would therefore fall foul of the law. Those of us who have made something of a habit of taking to the stage as pantomime dames will be living in fear of the knock at the door, wondering whether we will be charged with wearing wigs, high heels and lipstick in a public place.

This might all sound absurd. The proposers of the new law would, no doubt, claim they are only seeking to ban extreme abuse of gays and lesbians. But the road to hell is paved with good intentions. New laws so often have unintended consequences, especially when they are introduced not to combat a genuine crime but to establish the state's view of orthodox thinking.

I sometimes have to ask myself what is happening to dear old Britain. Humour is meant to be part of our national DNA. Yet the politically-correct brigade is behaving like a bunch of Cromwellians, cracking down on any signs of laughter.

Supporters of this change like to pose as the protectors of the gay community, but they are nothing of the sort. The idea that we are all such enfeebled victims that we cannot take a single joke is actually an insult. Most gay men and women love self-deprecating humour and camp exaggeration of stereotypes. That is why drag artists are so popular on the gay scene.

Showbiz, camp theatrics and dazzling wit helped to pave the way for gay rights. They should be cherished, not suppressed. It is bitterly ironic that, in the name of tolerance, the Government should be marching towards such a culture of intolerance.

The politically correct bigots should not be allowed to have it both ways. They cannot say, on one hand, that gay lifestyles should be accepted as a perfectly normal part of life, and then, on the other, demand special treatment for gay people to shield them from everyday humour.[176]

Hear, hear! A fresh voice, dressed in high camp! As Biggins astutely observes, there's nothing funny about gay-rights legislation undermining the hallowed freedom of speech long cherished in both Britain and America.

If you think Biggins' comments apply only to professional comedians against whom, surely, no law would be enforced, think again....

News Item—*Conservative councillor Jonathan Yardley thought he was making a humorous quip at a Police liaison meeting he was chairing. As the meeting began, one of the organizers instructing the audience about using the electronic answer machines did a test run: "Press A if you're male or B if you're female." When a member of the audience piped up—"What if you're transgendered?"—Yardley responded (to much laughter) "You can press A and B together!" For that remark Yardley was hauled before the police for a two-hour dressing down for his "homophobic comments."*[177]

Does that send shivers down your spine? *It should!* Can you imagine police officers in America grilling a local city official over an off-handed joke like that? Wake up, America. Quicker than we can dial 911, "thought police" will not be simply a metaphor but a chilling reality!

Would that the only issue was high-handed government regulation of comedy. For Christians who still believe in the moral authority of Scripture, the issue of religious free speech is fast becoming a humorless joke, both in Britain and in the States. Here's just a sample of what lies ahead if we don't take immediate action to stop this creeping outrage....

Official government oppression of faith-speak

News Report—*During parliamentary debates on the homophobic hatred offence, a number of cases were presented to show the importance of a free speech protection:*

Miguel Hayworth, a street preacher in Manchester, was forcibly placed in the back of a police van, questioned and detained for over an hour following a complaint of "homophobia" for doing nothing more than publicly reading from Romans 1:17-32.

Stephen Green, a Christian campaigner, was arrested for handing out tracts containing biblical quotes about homosexuality at a gay pride festival in Cardiff. Mr. Green was held at a police station for four hours, questioned, charged and eventually committed for trial. The case against Mr. Green was subsequently dropped by the Crown Prosecution Service.

A Member of the Scottish Parliament asked Strathclyde Police to investigate remarks made by the Roman Catholic Archbishop of Glasgow who, in a church service, had defended the institution of marriage and criticised civil partnerships.

During a radio talk show about civil partnerships for homosexuals, Lynette Burrows, a family-values campaigner, said she did not believe that adoption by two gay men would be best for a child. Subsequently, a policewoman telephoned Mrs. Burrow to say that a 'homophobic incident' had been reported against her and that records of it would be kept by police.

Pensioners, Joe and Helen Roberts, were interrogated by police because they had expressed opposition to their local council about spending public money on 'gay rights' projects.

The Christian Union of the University of Cambridge was reported to the police following its distribution of the Gospel of John and hosting a meeting where the Dean of Sydney Cathedral put forward "a traditional biblical view on homosexuality."

The Rt Rev Dr Peter Forster, Bishop of Chester, was investigated by Cheshire Constabulary after he told his local newspaper that some homosexuals re-orientated to heterosexuality with the help of therapy. A complaint was made to the police that his remarks were a "hate crime." Thereafter the Chief Constable berated the bishop in the local paper, and the police passed a file to the Crown Prosecution Service, who decided not to prosecute because the Bishop had not broken any "current" laws.[178]

So far, the assaults on religious free speech launched by the police in Britain have failed to muster official support in the courts. But the amazing thing is how often attempts have been made to bring the heavy hand of the law down on anyone daring to criticize homosexual conduct.

In the debates which took place over the free speech clause, former government minister Tom Harris MP (Labour) said: "I am speaking against the Government for the first time since I became a Member in 2001." Later in a blog he explained his decision, saying, "If it is not the Government's intention that people of faith who criticise homosexual practice should be prosecuted for doing so, why are they insisting on the removal of this [free speech] phrase?

"If this phrase is removed from the Act tonight, it will be seen as a green light to all these who believe they can silence anyone who disagrees with them. There are a great many things in the Bible—the New as well as the Old Testament—which many people would find objectionable if they only bothered to read it. If it already hasn't happened, I can see, in the not too distant future, a complaint being raised with the police because a quote from the book of Leviticus or I Corinthians on a placard outside a church is 'incitement to homophobic hatred'."

During the same debate, Conservative MP Ann Widdecome said: "The religious hatred and sexual orientation laws, and myriad other laws that seek to bring equality, have an oppressive heart. The face may be liberalism, but the heart is oppressive."[179]

Join together the comments of those two MPs from across the political aisle and what you see is both a foretaste of things to come right here in America and the kind of twisted, oppressive heart that lies behind them. As Ann Widdecome suggests, classic liberal thinking—of the type that is truly tolerant of dissent—is hardly characteristic of today's liberal-Leftist thinking.

One can only be grateful that the House of Lords overwhelmingly rejected the Government's attempt to hit the mute button on free speech...at least for now. Until the next attempt (and it will come), the Government's sexual orientation hatred law at least includes a protection for the free speech of those who wish to express their objection to sexual misconduct.

So again comes the question for the ACLU: Which side of this debate are you on? Will you be America's staunch defender of religious free speech, or the most active and visible protagonist for the homosexual cause—even if it means running roughshod over religious free speech? Your abysmal record so far betrays your vaunted claim to be American's greatest defender of civil liberties. If you have any trace of libertarian conviction left, now is the time to step forward and show us what you've got.

Targeting Britain's youth

Just take a rough guess. What role do you think the police ought to play in society? Crime prevention? Crime detection? Apprehending thieves, burglars, robbers, and rapists? Protecting the elderly against home invasions, and the rest of us against street crime? Actually, in Britain these days, you'd be mostly wrong. As you may already have gathered from article after article, these days Britain's famed "Bobbies on bicycles, two by two" are more focused on enforcing political correctness than dealing with the growing crime problem. Never is this truer than when it comes to advancing the gay and lesbian political agenda....

News Item—*Schoolchildren aged 13 and 14 have been invited by Kent police to write an essay on their feelings about homosexuality as part of lesbian, gay, bisexual and transgender history month. A £25 book token is on offer as the prize for the best essay under the title: "All Different, Same Respect," the force's slogan for a series of events marking the history month.[180]*

And then there's the rainbow flag (a symbol of the gay rights movement) being flown from police stations around the country in honor of LGBT history month. At least one courageous senior officer from a London police station signaled the neutrality of his force on political issues by ordering the removal of a rainbow flag. What ought to be flying are red warning flags. Already the liberal-Left gestapo has targeted the Union Jack as the next flag to be lowered. It's that red cross in the middle, you know, like the one in the Red Cross flag that has become so offensive to secularists.

Naturally, it will take time for the general population to come around to this twisted thinking. The older generation sees it for what it is. After all, they and their parents and grandparents fought two great wars to repel such totalitarianism. So what's there to do but brainwash the young—in precisely the same way as all totalitarians before them....

News Report—*The Government has announced that lessons on homosexuality will be mandatory in schools throughout England but parents can withdraw their child if they wish, at least until further review. Faith schools must also comply, but they will be allowed to cover the material in a way which accords with the school's religious ethos.*

Terry Sanderson of the National Secular Society, said it was "unfortunate" that the Government is allowing faith schools to teach sex education in line with their religious beliefs.[181]

Anyone want to take bets on how long it will be before Britain's parents are no longer permitted to opt out of the national compulsory curriculum? The parents threatened with sanctions for pulling their children out of locally-mandatory homosexual classes in East London (as reported at the beginning of this chapter) wouldn't be giving you long odds. They've already had a bitter taste of a loony-Left local council pushing the gay agenda down the throats of ten-year-olds in defiance of their parents' wishes.

And how about that generous concession to faith-based schools, allowing them to cover the material in a way that accords with the school's religious ethos? You mean, faith-based schools can teach their pupils that homosexual behavior is against God's will? C'mon! You know that isn't going to fly! So what, pray tell, is the Government saying?

One can only guess that faith-based schools are already teaching their students to respect people of other faiths and lifestyles. If not always practiced as any of us might want, that's the Christian message, through and through. Know any mainline Christian, Muslim, or Jewish schools that don't teach their students to respect others as they would wish to be respected? But what can they say about homosexual relations (and immoral heterosexual relations) that doesn't involve the word "sin." Can they actually use the word *sin*? Would that fit comfortably with the compulsory curriculum?

To get a sense of time-line trajectory, read again Terry Sanderson's argument that faith-based schools should *not* be permitted to teach about homosexuality consistent with their religious beliefs. Chilling words for America where religion is on the wane and secularism is on the ascent.

For Christian parents in America, what's happening today in Britain ought to set off deafening alarm bells. How much longer do you really think this won't be happening in the school your children or grandchildren attend—whether public or private, secular or religious? Indeed, it's already happening in liberal pockets of America from coast to coast.

Equality Bill, a civil liberties Trojan horse

There is something else about which Americans should be fore-warned. We must resist with all the might we can muster any attempt to introduce a generalized Equality Law, even if it presumes to include equality of religious convictions. Already, our Equal Opportunity laws come dangerously close to crossing the line. If ever we pass an Equality Law like the one being brought into force in Britain, rest assured that certain rights, individuals, and causes, will be more equal than others, included among which will be the superceding rights of homosexuals.

If there is any doubt about the imminent danger on America's own horizon, simply note from a gay-sponsored website in Britain (www.equalitybill.com) how comprehensively the "equality principle" operates....

Web Blog—*The Equality Bill is now going through its final debate in the Commons. After this, the bill will move to the Lords, where we will be seeking amendments. As you may have read already in the papers, our primary focus will be on lifting the current ban on Civil Partnership Ceremonies from taking place in religious buildings. This is something that a lot of you had got in touch about, and something that we feel can easily be reversed by the Equality Bill. We will be working with Stonewall and others to ensure that we have the votes to get the amendment through.[182]*

Web Blog—*Over the last few days, members of a group called 'Pride In Canterbury' have come to us looking for help. Since 2002, they have been lobbying Canterbury City Council to help them in encouraging the local LGBT community, through simple means: promoting the city's LGBT tourism potential or staging performances of interest to the Gay Community at the council-owned city theatre.*

Despite their best efforts, the group has been ignored, shut out and fobbed off by the council-members. In direct correspondence with the director of culture and communications of Canterbury City Council, they have been told that it would be their responsibility, not the council's, to encourage LGBT dance or drama at the council-run Marlowe Theatre.

The details go on. But the message is clear: the council is refusing point-blank to engage with the LGBT community. They have no interest in the issues, and no desire to even consider the proposals. It is unacceptable. With an Equality Duty, this behaviour would be made quite literally illegal.[183]

Can't get through the front door? Try the back door. At the back door, hardly anyone notices you're breaking in.

Who could possibly argue against equality...unless it's anyone who understands the Fifth Law of Thermodynamics. Pursuant to the Fifth Law of Thermodynamics—by which perversion squared equals social, political, and moral inversion—religious liberties, among all other liberties, will always be at bottom of the pile.

Still think that, when society around you has surrendered its fundamental moral values, your religious conscience at least can take refuge in the church? Think again....

News Report—*According to deputy equalities minister Maria Eagle, the Labour government's Equality Bill will prohibit churches from refusing to hire active homosexuals even if their religion holds such behavior to be sinful. British churches will be forced to accept practicing homosexuals or "transsexuals" in positions as youth workers and similar roles. Eagle indicated at a conference called "Faith, Homophobia, Transphobia, & Human Rights" that the legislation "will cover almost all church employees."*

The bill allows a religious exemption for roles deemed to be "for the purposes of an organised religion" but restricts this definition to those who conduct liturgical celebrations or spend their time teaching doctrine.[184]

Back home in the States, the U.S. Supreme Court has recently held, in its decision in *Hosanna-Tabor Evangelical Lutheran Church and School v. Equal Employment Opportunity Commission*, that there is a ministerial-exception to discrimination protections. This ought to give some solace to churches facing challenges from gay activists, but if it hasn't yet hit you full force, *this* is what the fuss is all about! Nothing less than the homosexual lobby (including both homosexuals and out-and-proud heterosexuals on the liberal-Left) taking control of government, culture, schools, churches, and even private religious conscience. It's a revolution, folks. A *totalitarian* revolution. No more Mr. Nice Guy. It's not just high camp, but high treason. With the demise of civil liberties in the very name of civil liberty, democracy itself is at risk! Is anybody listening?

Leading politicians leading the way

It's tempting to think that the gay lobby is composed only of radicalized rabble on the extreme Left of society. (Indeed, not even all practicing homosexuals are either Leftists or gay activists.) But "the gay lobby" includes all those in government and politics who are openly and intentionally advancing the cause—including members of the British Parliament, the U.S. Congress, Presidents and Prime Ministers.

Perhaps no one in British politics in recent years has done more to promote the homosexual agenda than former Prime Minister Tony Blair. Under his watch, the homosexual revolution progressed by leaps and bounds. Now that Blair is no longer in office, he is using his global recognition as a "bully pulpit" to press the cause even further—even daring (as a newly converted Catholic) to lecture the Pope on the fine points of theology....

News Analysis—*Tony Blair has challenged the "entrenched" attitudes of the Pope on homosexuality, and argued that it is time for him to "rethink" his views. In an interview with the gay magazine, Attitude, Tony Blair said that he wanted to urge religious figures everywhere to reinterpret their religious texts to see them as metaphorical, not literal, and suggested that in time this would make all religious groups accept gay people as equals.*

Asked about the Pope's stance, Mr. Blair, himself a Roman Catholic, said: "There are many good and great things the Catholic Church does," said Blair, "and there are many fantastic things this Pope stands for, but I think what is interesting is that if you went into any Catholic Church, particularly a well-attended one, on any Sunday here and did a poll of the congregation, you'd be surprised at how liberal-minded people were."

He also thought that in Islam there would eventually be a change of heart. "I believe that, ultimately, people will find their way to a sensible reformation of attitudes."

"When people quote the passages in Leviticus condemning homosexuality, I say to them—if you read the whole of the Old Testament and took everything that was there in a literal way, as being what God and religion is about, you'd have some pretty tough policies across the whole of the piece." Blair continued: "What people often forget about, for example, Jesus or, indeed, the Prophet Muhammad, is that their whole raison d'être was to change the way that people thought traditionally."

Conventional wisdom is not necessarily wise, he said. "It can be wrong and it can be just a form of conservatism that hides behind a consensus. If you look back in time, through the suffragette movement, the fight against slavery, it's amazing how the same arguments in favour of prejudice crop up again and again and again."

Referring to his contacts with evangelical groups in the US and elsewhere through the foundation, Blair said: "I think there is a generational shift that is happening. If you talk to the older generation, yes, you will still get a lot of pushback, and parts of the Bible quoted, and so on. But if you look at the younger generation of evangelicals, this is increasingly for them something that they wish to be out of—at least in terms of having their position confined to being anti-gay."[185]

Wow, where to begin? Perhaps with the obvious, that when leading politicians have bought into the homosexual agenda to this extent, culture in general has pretty much lost the plot. Blair's comments also highlight the bait-and-switch argument that so easily fools the public: that the homosexual movement is all about equality. Certainly equality was the core issue in the battle over workplace opportunity (a question now firmly decided), but equality has nothing to do with the morality of homosexual conduct itself.

With rare exceptions, those who on religious grounds believe that homosexual conduct is immoral do not reject the fundamental human equality of homosexuals anymore than they would reject the human equality of those who engage in heterosexual sin. Indeed, the belief held by people of faith that we've all been created in God's image is precisely what motivates the concern about how that divine image is besmirched by sin of all kinds, including the confessed and unconfessed sins of those who vociferously object to homosexual relations.

"Equality" as defined by Tony Blair and the gay lobby fails at the hurdle of moral equivalence. No, not that homosexual sin is any more grievous a sin than any other. If by its very nature homosexual sin ought to be an obvious deviation from the moral order, it nevertheless remains a fact that sin is sin is sin. On the other hand, neither immoral heterosexual relations nor homosexual conduct can be sanitized of its immorality simply by government fiat or public consensus, as Tony Blair seems to believe in chiding the Pope on that point.

It's the niggling problem of immorality that plagues government-sponsored gay marriages and the faux marriages disingenuously called "civil unions." To decriminalize immoral sexual behavior of all types—whether adultery, fornication, or sodomy—is one thing. It leaves morality where civil libertarians would insist it be left—in the privacy of one's own conscience, answerable only to God (or no God at all, if one insists). But it's another thing altogether for the state to put its official stamp of approval on relationships that are inherently immoral, and to promote the homosexual lifestyle as if it were the moral equivalent of legitimate heterosexual expression.

When Tony Blair begins to talk about Holy Scripture and how passages relating to homosexual behavior ought to be interpreted metaphorically rather than literally, he is clearly out of his depth. Argue however you wish regarding the current applicability of the laws of ancient Israel, or the writings of Christ's apostles, but is Blair seriously suggesting there is a way to think of those passages *metaphorically*? What is metaphorical about: "Do not lie with a man as one lies with a woman; that is detestable?"[186]

Worse yet, Blair's treatment of Scripture is arrogantly dismissive, as seen first in his reference to the older generation from whom we get "parts of the Bible quoted, and so on" (as if the biblical passages quoted are wholly insignificant). Blair is further dismissive in his failure to engage the Scripture text in any meaningful way, making light of the complexities any serious student of Scripture would take into account. Blair's ultimate dismissive swipe comes when, along with all gay activists, he denigrates conscientious moral objection as nothing more than bigoted homophobia. What conscientious objectors bring to the table is not a fear of homosexuals, but a fear of public immorality triumphing over moral order.

There is, then, Blair's swaggering co-opting of both Jesus and Mohammed, whose "whole raison d'être," says Blair, was to change the way that people thought traditionally"—as if either part of that compound argument had an ounce of truth to it. Whatever else he taught or did, Jesus' raison d'être ("the Lamb slain from the beginning of the world") was to save mankind from sin. "For God so loved the world he gave his one and only Son, that whosoever believes on him shall not perish but have eternal life."[187] And although Jesus did rail against human traditions embroidered onto divinely-inspired religious ritual, never once did he treat moral prohibitions as mere cultural tradition. Nor for that matter did Mohammed.

And what in heaven's name is Blair thinking when he blithely assures us that Islam eventually will have a change of heart about homosexual behavior? Does he understand so little about Islam? Dare he be so patronizing to a people who (unlike Britain's mostly-secularized, nominal Christians) take their religious beliefs seriously? Has it completely escaped him that one of radical Muslim's best recruiting tools is the moral corruption of that Great Satan—the Christian West—as best seen, not in its crass materialism or immodest dress or rampant divorce, but in its widespread public condonation of homosexual conduct? If the aim of Blair's Faith Foundation is to promote understanding of the world's major religions, Blair has misunderstood both the Christian and Muslim faiths by a factor something on a scale of his misunderstanding the existence of WMDs in Iraq.

Yet in the midst of all of this utter nonsense, Tony Blair is certainly right about two things. The first is that "conventional wisdom is not necessarily wise." To change but a single word of his own assertion, "It can be wrong and it can be just a form of *liberalism* that hides behind a consensus." That is precisely why eternal truth (preeminently revealed in Holy Scripture) trumps the kind of conventional wisdom that would deem homosexual behavior to be morally acceptable.

It is that same eternal truth to which William Wilberforce and other anti-slavery advocates appealed in order to overcome the conventional wisdom of their day regarding slavery. Not one of the anti-slavery campaigners ever would have confused the supreme righteousness of their hallowed cause with today's debased homosexual agenda. One's race is not a moral issue; one's sexual conduct is.

Blair is certainly right in his assessment of how liberal-minded the person in the pew is these days. There is indeed a generational shift in which young Catholics, mainline Protestants, and even Evangelicals have washed their hands of the homosexual issue, relegating it to the realm of human rights, social equality, and even Christian tolerance. For many, sexual purity—whether heterosexual or homosexual—has become a complete disconnect from their formal religious faith commitments. From the swinging '60s onwards, believers almost as much as non-believers have been seduced by the sexual liberation of our time. The crucial difference now is that sexual impurity has become guilt-free and openly declared off-limits to moral censure. What we once recognized as sinful about our own sexual misconduct, we now comfortably rationalize in both ourselves and others.

More later on this tectonic shift in religious thinking, especially in America. For the moment, it's worth noting how even "conservative" politicians have swallowed the Great Lie—hook, line, and sinker....

A Janus-faced redefinition of marriage

News Report—*"It is remarkable," said David Cameron, "to have a Conservative leader standing on a Gay Pride platform. Five years ago, not many gays would have turned up."*

In Cameron's four years as Tory leader the atmosphere has changed so markedly that on Tuesday 180 people, male and female, crowded into a smart London bar for a Gay Pride rally at which the last rites of Section 28 were administered. In a brave speech, the Tory leader formally said "sorry" for his party's policy.

Meanwhile Cameron's former Oxford compatriot, the maverick Conservative Mayor of London, Boris Johnson, was also seen cavorting in a Gay Pride parade, giving all the political sanction to the homosexual cause that his high office could command. And these are Britain's *conservative* leaders. "We've come a long way, baby!"

But forget the parties and parades for a moment. Look what's being paraded about....

Magazine Interview—*David Cameron, recalling his first Conservative Conference as leader of the party in an interview with Total Politics magazine, said: "I stood up...and said that I believe in the importance of marriage, and that as far as I was concerned it didn't matter whether it was between a man and a woman, a man and a man or a woman and a woman."* [188]

Only in a postmodern, post-thinking world can politicians get away with asserting two contradictory concepts simultaneously without the slightest embarrassment, or perhaps even consciousness of the logical inconsistency. David Cameron, who describes himself (again postmodernly) as a "liberal-conservative," just doesn't get it. "I believe in marriage—*whether between a man and a woman, a man and a man, or a woman and a woman*"? Cameron might just as well have said, "I believe in horses—whether they are cows, chickens, or pigs." Or, "I believe in democracy—whether it's totalitarian, communist, or Stalinist."

Reminds one of the conversation between Alice and Humpty Dumpty:

> *"When I use a word," Humpty Dumpty said, in a rather scornful tone, "it means just what I choose it to mean—neither more nor less."*
> *"The question is," said Alice, "whether you can make words mean so many different things."*
> *"The question is," said Humpty Dumpty, "which is to be master— that's all."[189]*

Winning arguments by mere redefinition is a classic debate ploy, but it doesn't change the reality of what lies behind the redefined words. ("Gay" doesn't necessarily mean one is truly happy, and "pride" often masks a deep-seated angst which is anything but proud.) Once we are permitted to redefine reality as we wish it to be, words lose all meaning. And when meaning is lost, no words can be trusted.

A rose by any other name might still be a rose, but a carnation is not a rose. Nor is a tulip, petunia, or daffodil. Marriage between a man and a woman has a dynamic complexity that simply cannot be duplicated by same-sex partners, no matter what you call it. "Gay marriage" is an oxymoron of the highest order.

Any culture willing to maintain a distinction between male and female toilets must surely still have the capacity to understand that there are some things so basic they need not be explained. (Believe it or not, even *gender-specific toilets* are now under attack!) That anyone should have to spell out why marriage is inappropriate for members of the same sex tells us just how far we've come—not higher into enlightened liberalism, but downward into a deep, dark hole of unenlightened ignorance.

The redefinition of marriage is as good an illustration as any to highlight the overarching issues touching on the danger of secularist, liberal thinking. When secularism invades sacred space, there is an inexorable slide from *moral order* (divinely ordained by God for the good of his Creation) to an *amoral order* (in which God is erased from the picture while only a residue of moral order remains) to an *immoral order* (which finally devolves into personal, social and political chaos).

"Gay marriage" is not merely a political, social, or legal question, but first and foremost a moral question. It's not simply that marriage between a man and a woman has the time-honored stamp of approval as custom in virtually all cultures throughout history, but rather that the "custom" of heterosexual marriage conforms to a fundamental moral principle transcending custom. Even if custom were to change, the moral principle wouldn't.

Nor is marriage defined primarily by procreation, as normative as that is for heterosexuals and as impossible as that is for homosexuals (*as homosexuals*). The octogenarian widow and widower who tie the knot are as legitimately married as in their first marriages when producing offspring was a natural part of the package.

The issue of "gay marriage" is nothing more or less than plain and simple *morality*. Both definitionally and conceptually, "marriage" is exclusively the union of a man and a woman, having a moral imprimatur in both reason and revelation that no immoral relationship can ever hope to command. The personal moral imprimatur homosexuals seek in lobbying for "gay marriage" will never be theirs, whatever the laws of the land. That imprimatur cannot come from the state, social approbation, or even the church. For homosexuals, the insurmountable problem is not *man-made* law, which can always be changed, but *man-discovered* law, which is changeless.

Language certainly evolves, but divorcing intrinsic meanings from value-laden words undermines both public trust and moral certitude. To speak of marriage as inclusive of any conceivable combination of genders is (to continue the Lewis Carroll theme) moral Jabberwocky at its very worst. "Beware the Jabberwock, my son! The jaws that bite, the claws that catch!"

Back home in America...a President speaks

News Report—*President Obama delivered an unprecedented message to the Human Rights Campaign Saturday night. Sounding more like a homosexual activist than a sitting president, Obama went well beyond his expected message of "I'm here with you" on the homosexual agenda.*

"My expectation is that when you look back on these years, you will see a time in which we put a stop to discrimination against gays and lesbians— whether in the office or on the battlefield," Obama told an estimated audience of 3,000. "You will see a time in which we as a nation finally recognize relationships between two men or two women as just as real and admirable as relationships between a man and a woman."

Even Human Rights Campaign President Joe Solmonese was stunned at the breadth of Obama's statement, calling it "something quite remarkable. This was a historic night when we felt the full embrace and commitment of the President of the United States," Solmonese said in a post-speech statement. "It's simply unprecedented."

But Peter LaBarbera, president of Americans for Truth About Homosexuality, called the president's remarks "appalling." Said LaBarbera, "Barack Obama is declaring that these relationships are basically equal to the real thing," LaBarbera told CNSNews.com. "I think this is the ultimate Obama audacity play. For him, just declaring it seems to make it so."

The president pointedly used the pronoun "we," not "you," throughout much of his speech. "Do not doubt the direction we are headed and the destination we will reach," Obama said at one point. "For despite the real gains that we've made, there's still laws to change and there's still hearts to open," the president said at another juncture.

Obama also talked about homosexual "families"—two men and children or two women and children.

"If we are honest with ourselves we'll admit that there are too many who do not yet know in their lives or feel in their hearts the urgency of this struggle. That's why I continue to speak about the importance of equality for LGBT (lesbian/gay/bisexual/transgendered) families—and not just in front of gay audiences," Obama said.

The president said he and his wife Michelle had made a point of inviting homosexual "families" to the White House to participate in events like the Easter Egg Roll—"because we want to send a message." Obama noted that his administration had extended benefits to the domestic partners of homosexual federal workers and that he had appointed an open homosexual, John Berry, to serve as director of the federal Office of Personnel Management.

As expected, he also mentioned his support for a laundry list of homosexual activist issues, including bringing an end to the military's "Don't ask, don't tell" policy on homosexuals serving in the military and overturning the federal Defense of Marriage Act, which defines marriage as being between one man and one woman.

But the president also characterized those who oppose the homosexual agenda in terminology reminiscent of last year's presidential campaign, when then-candidate Obama, campaigning in Pennsylvania, referred to "bitter" residents of small-town America who "cling to guns or religion or antipathy to people who aren't like them." Obama told Saturday's event that there are still people "who hold fast to outworn arguments and old attitudes; who fail to see your families like their families; who would deny you the rights most Americans take for granted."[190]

When the American people elected Barack Obama on a platform of change, change is what it got. Mind you, not much change in the usual lobby-driven, vote-buying, back-room-dealing politics of Washington, but unquestionably a seismic shift in ideology at the very pinnacle of American political life. With the inauguration of President Obama, American made a sharp *Left* turn.

Debate all you wish about the economy and the wisdom of massive economic bailouts; or how to handle terrorism and the war in Afghanistan; or whether "Obamacare" is a smart idea or a dumb mistake. As important as all those issues and battles may be, the sleeper issue (with the potential for adversely affecting all of the above) is how America views its collective soul.

Above all, it is important to remember that the issue here is not simply the radically-Leftist instincts of one man—Barack Obama. The President was elected by a wide margin of voters, including blacks, Latinos, whites, Catholics, Protestants, Evangelicals, Jews, older folks and fanatically-energized college kids. Maybe they didn't all understand just how far Left they were turning. Maybe they just fell in love with a charismatic leader who empowered them to say (to any issue of their choice), "Yes we can!" But on social issues, certainly, America is now a far more politically-liberal nation than one ever thought possible.

That said, would all of Obama's admiring throngs agree with his assertion that "relationships between two men or two women are just as real and admirable as relationships between a man and a woman?" If an overwhelming majority of states with laws explicitly prohibiting homosexual marriages (including those with recent constitutional amendments stating that marriage is between a man and a woman) is anything to go by, the answer is a resounding no. Despite ongoing generational shifts in attitudes, Americans are not yet ready to open the floodgates to publicly-recognized homosexual unions.

The intriguing question is: Why? What continuing unease do so many Americans sense, even if they might not be able to articulate it? If the answer is not sheer bigoted homophobia (and for the most part it's not), what explains our great cultural divide on this sensitive issue?

Why the gay-rights debate is so pivotal

Have you ever wondered why, of all possible hot-button social issues, it's abortion and homosexual behavior that find themselves most often in America's political spotlight? The reason is that abortion and homosexual behavior are both iconic. They're bellwethers. They're easily recognized symptoms. Why? Because if *they* are not obviously, intrinsically, unequivocally, and definitively wrong, then *nothing* is definitively wrong.

When something as fundamentally immoral as homosexual behavior becomes socially acceptable, there is no illicit conduct or behavior, public or private, that over time cannot become acceptable—whether heterosexual cohabitation, cheating on exams, cooking the books of giant corporate audits, or even the breathtaking abuse of Parliamentary expenses. (London headline: "I've done nothing wrong!")

Of all the moral dangers associated with the acceptability of homosexual behavior, the most to be feared is the inability to discriminate properly between good and evil. Blurred gender lines blur peripheral moral vision as well. Having been told so often and for so long that discrimination is wrong (in legitimate cases of race, gender, and age), we no longer have the ability to discriminate between good causes and bad causes; between that which is moral and that which is immoral.

Nor, by extension, can we make good judgments between proper concerns for child protection and the over-the-top regulation of every citizen as if they were a pedophile. Or between, on one hand, a proper concern for teen pregnancy and, on the other hand, government programs which end up giving young people the green light. Or between the primary role of parents in education and the supportive secondary role of government. Or between legitimate concerns about public health and safety and loony laws attempting to eliminate all risk. Or between limited surveillance aimed at public safety and the intrusive, Stasi-like violation of civil liberties of ordinary citizens.

In every aspect of social interaction, the wise balancing of competing interests ultimately is dependent upon sound moral judgment. Get morality wrong and you'll get the balance wrong. Worse yet, get morality wrong on fundamental moral issues like abortion and homosexual behavior and a nation might never again regain its balance.

In the larger frame, both private and public morality are tied inextricably to government, politics, law and order. Government does not exist in a morals-neutral vacuum. If it might be possible in the short term to have good public morals without having particularly good government, it is nigh unto impossible to have bad public morals without having bad government. Put simply, good government depends on good morals.

If by chance you believe the conclusions in this chapter to be wrong, *why* are they wrong? On what basis are they wrong? To what standard of right and wrong do you appeal to reach such a conclusion? Indeed, why is discrimination against homosexuals wrong? Why is the bullying of sissies on the playground wrong? Why is pedophilia and child abuse wrong? By what higher law is it to be known that it is wrong to offend religions other than your own?

With every answer you might give, there are yet more *why's* to be asked...all the way back to God and his divine moral law. By that moral law, pedophilia *is* wrong. By that moral law, intentionally offending worshipers of other faiths *is* wrong. By that moral law, bullying sissies on the playground *is* wrong. By that moral law, treating the homosexual as less than the "neighbor" whom Christ said we should love *is* wrong. But by that very same moral law, homosexual behavior falls below the standard which God himself has established. And by that same moral law, the institution of marriage is reserved exclusively for a man and a woman.

But some would ask how any moral order could possibly deny one's natural tendencies. For those who care what Jesus taught, there is that intriguing line (in the context of his discussing a question on divorce) about those who become as eunuchs for the sake of the Kingdom.[191] For all others, there is this question to be asked: Does a heterosexual's natural tendencies automatically give free license for any and all heterosexual expression, no matter the context? (How about adultery?)

Without making any comparison whatsoever with homosexuals, on principle would you be willing to accept the "natural tendency" argument from a pedophile? The point is that natural tendencies alone do not silence all moral considerations. (Witness the many heterosexuals who have committed themselves to a lifetime of celibacy.)

The problem of Burger King morality ("Have it your way") is shared by all who are on the liberal-Left, including those who profess faith. In God's moral order, it is not left to us to pick and choose. If a Christian gay rights activist can choose which part of God's moral order to ignore, what prevents a gang member from doing the same? Or a sadist or a pedophile? Or, for that matter, anyone who chooses to ignore the morality lying generally behind all calls for non-discrimination?

Yet pick-and-choose morality is not the biggest problem for anti-religious secularists among the liberal-Left who would deny the very existence of God and any higher moral law. Their biggest problem is having no universal standard to which they can appeal for the rightness of their cause. Without a universal moral law (which can't simply appear from out of the blue), there is no legitimate basis for insisting that discrimination against homosexuals is "wrong." Without a higher moral law, nothing is *definitively* "wrong"—not murder, robbery, rape, pollution, bullying, health-and-safety negligence, teen pregnancy, religious bigotry, or hate crimes.

Without a higher law motivating individuals to behave in socially cohesive ways, the state is left with nothing but sheer political will, arbitrary rules, and endless regulations whereby to maintain order. And in a vicious cycle, the less the moral law, the more the rules; the more the rules, the less the moral law, and thereafter follows even more rules. Explains a lot about a rules-obsessed bureaucratic nanny state, doesn't it?

Two tough questions

At the end of the day, there are really only two questions needing to be asked. The first is more personal for homosexuals. If the time should come when every law has been changed, every institution completely transformed, and society so accepting of homosexual behavior that the word *homophobia* is no longer in the lexicon, will you be at peace *with yourself*?

The second question is for the rest of us. If the time should come when every law has been changed, every institution completely transformed, and society is strictly forbidden to object in any way to homosexual relations, will sufficient civil liberties remain to stave off some future generational regime change whose leaders might be both anti-religious *and* anti-homosexual?

10

The Evolution of the Loony Gene

Let us understand Darwinism so we can
walk in the opposite direction when it comes to setting up society.

—RICHARD DAWKINS

Advance warning here that this chapter will take on a rather different flavor compared with the preceding chapters, only because it drills down far deeper than the others, right down to the philosophical assumptions undergirding much of the liberal-Left politics we've been discussing.

If you see cracks in the walls of a house, you'd do well to examine closely the underlying foundations. Same with troublesome fissures in a society. The larger they are, the more likely it is that bedrock foundations have shifted. No use trying to patch up distressing social and political cracks if the philosophical underpinnings have crumbled. So this chapter is all about what lies beneath the surface of hyper-regulated, bureaucratized, nanny-state cultures. It's about the big picture. About the cosmic fork in the road. About fundamental assumptions to which most folks have never given the slightest passing thought, but upon which everything else hangs—literally *everything*.

News Report—*The Government has announced that Darwin's theory of how life evolved through natural selection would be a legal requirement in science teaching from September, 2011, at least "in the later stage of primary education."*

The new curriculum requires Britain's schools "to investigate and explain how plants and animals are 'interdependent' and are diverse and adapted to their environment by natural selection." The change is supported by more than 500 scientists.

Church and other faith schools will be required to educate their pupils about the theory of evolution, although it can be taught in a context that reflects a school's ethos, said a spokesman for the Department for Children, Schools and Families.

Professor Sir Martin Taylor, vice-president of The Royal Society, said: "We are delighted to see evolution explicitly included in the primary curriculum. One of the most remarkable achievements of science over the past 200 years has been to show how humans and organisms on the Earth arose through evolution. Learning about evolution can be an extraordinary, exciting and inspiring experience for children. Teachers should aim to explain why evolution by natural selection is the only known way of understanding all the available evidence."[192]

What's so groundbreaking about this latest initiative? Only that Evolution is specifically being highlighted in an expanded national curriculum...and also being forced on all of Britain's state schools, including faith-based schools. Of course, there is the usual mumbo-jumbo about faith-based schools being able to teach Evolution "in a context that reflects a school's ethos." It's déjà vu from the same mixed-signals relating to the sex-education courses which faith schools are now required to teach. ("Premarital sex is immoral, children, but do be sure and use a condom!")

As for faith-based schools teaching Evolution, one can hear it already. "So, children, God created man in his own image, a living soul which survives death to face eternal judgment. But think of it this way: Forces of nature acting selectively and capriciously over time produced the human beings we now are, but just as easily might not have been, given even the slightest change in natural conditions and occurrences millions of years ago." Does that about cover today's lesson? Are there any questions, anyone?

Of course, some faith-based schools will be more than happy to combine the two explanations of human existence, content to prattle on blithely about God creating humankind using an evolutionary process of natural selection to achieve his intended goal of a soul fit for eternity. The immediate problem for any thoughtful person, of course, is how a process of purely *natural* selection can simultaneously be a matter of *supernatural* selection. Even while tipping his hat to the simple beginnings "breathed by the Creator," the last thing Darwin would wish anyone to think is that his famed "natural selection" had anything whatsoever to do with God somehow pulling the strings even periodically along the way.

And then there's that niggling matter of the soul. For anyone of faith who wishes to retain a belief that men and women are essentially spiritual souls wrapped in human flesh, the problem remains how to explain the existence of spiritual beings who survive physical death, which no biological theory even begins to address. Did God create the soul and, at some point in evolutionary history, infuse that soul into a physical body that just happened to have developed over time by random forces (and happily was a perfect package for the soul)? Does it take any less faith to believe *that* highly-problematic scenario than to believe in special, divine creation of humankind—body and soul?

If you think the existence of the human soul is a huge problem for Christians and Jews, how about the Buddhist problem of reconciling Evolution's purely naturalistic hypothesis with reincarnation? The Dalai Lama (pop idol of the liberal-Left) says the theory of Evolution fails to account for the idea of karma, by which Buddhists believe the balance sheet of reward and punishment carries over from one lifetime to the next.[193] As long as Evolution is in charge of the universe, no metaphysical dimension is in charge. The spiritual can inform biology, but biology has no capacity to inform the spiritual.

And, of course, it's not alone a question of biology. What shall we teach the children about the origin of the *light* necessary for all that evolution to occur? And *gravity*? And *air* and *water*? And the land and the oceans and the skies above? And chemicals, quarks, protons, neutrons, electricity, mass, color, and on and on? How shall we explain the fact that the Earth with its sheerly fortuitous moon just happened to be perfectly aligned with the sun so as to be neither too hot nor too cold for evolution to occur? Or how all those immensely complex phenomena came into being at just the right time and place to cradle and nurture evolution? Or how a non-intelligent, unpredictable process produced such an organized universe? Or by what alchemy *life* could have come from *nonliving matter*?

In the end, our search for a Theory of Everything becomes a desperate attempt to cobble together a duke's mixture of disparate speculative theories lacking any semblance of coherence. So are we simply to say, "Well, children, one day there was a "big bang" emerging from absolute nothingness, and unlike the typical chaos which results from explosions, we find ourselves in a vast, elegant cosmos of exquisite beauty, infinitely intricate complexity, and with such mathematical order that we can engage in the intellectual pursuit of science beyond our wildest imaginations?" Naturally, young people love fairy tales, but—if all "myths" are suspect—why is a fanciful "science-of-the-gaps" myth to be trusted, even if it is perpetuated by the scientific community?

Despite the plethora of crucial issues on the table about which science freely admits to having tentative answers at best, we have the Royal Society's Professor Taylor adamantly insisting that "teachers should aim to explain why evolution by natural selection is the *only known way* of understanding all the available evidence." Guess Taylor missed Darwin's own words in the introduction to *The Origin*: "I am well aware that scarcely a single point is discussed in this volume on which facts cannot be adduced, often apparently leading to conclusions directly opposite to those at which I have arrived. A fair result can be obtained only by fully stating and balancing the facts and arguments on both sides of each question, and this cannot possibly be done here."

One might not agree with the explanation offered by those who believe the evidence points, instead, to a grand design (and thus to a Creator God), but it takes incredible hubris to declare— even to (or especially to) young minds—that there is only one possible way to interpret the evidence. Worse yet, to boorishly castigate Creationists as polemicist Richard Dawkins has done, saying: "Anyone who chooses not to believe in evolution is ignorant, stupid or insane."[194] Convince if you wish. Persuade all you want. But winning an argument of this magnitude by sheer dismissive edict is neither educational, scientific, fair, or intellectually honest. Speaking of which....

Evolution never was quite as sexy as made out to be

Since the afternoon class on Evolution follows the mandatory sex-education class in the morning, what if one of the bright ten-year-olds asks the obvious question (as children are wont to do) about how sex got started in the first place? When you rewind the whirring tape of evolutionary history and play it again in stop-action slow motion, how did it happen that—at some definitive point, for the very first time—suddenly there was a male and a female? If we assume Evolution's hypothesis that the first primitive organisms were asexual, how did they suddenly acquire distinctively male and female reproductive organs? *Complex* reproductive organs! And it *would have to be sudden*, wouldn't it? Like in one generation? Otherwise, how would things ever have progressed to the second generation by *sexual* reproduction?

Think about it. For *sexual* reproduction to have gotten out of the starting blocks, it would be necessary in some *actual, historically-factual, single generation* somewhere back down the line for two asexual beings (or even hermaphrodites, if you wish) to have developed into separate, fully-developed male and female sexual beings capable of procreation—at the very same time...in the very same place...under the very same conditions...within a single lifetime. And after all that (gasp!), what if those two hadn't been *attracted* to one another!

In the controversy over Evolution, time is always the magic bullet used to overcome all objections. "Anything can happen, given enough time!" (Never mind that over time entropy tends towards disorder, not order. Or that over time things tend to rust, rot, corrode, and decay rather than improve.) But if there's ever a case where the usual mantra of "millions of years" simply can't mask the obvious, it's the case of the missing sex link. As useless as half of a wing for a bird, merely half of a uterus or only part of a penis would not have advanced the cause.

And that's only the *human* reproductive dilemma. The same problematic process would have been required for each and every species which reproduces by male/female copulation—whether cats, dogs, horses, or sheep. A sheep without fully developed reproductive capabilities would not, first of all, be a "sheep," just *sheepish*! More crucially, a not-yet-fully-evolved sheep still *sheepish* about sex could not possibly reproduce another sheep of any sort, much less one that could replicate itself to produce the next generation.

Faced with this seamy sex scandal, concepts such as natural selection, survival of the fittest, variety, and genetic mutations suddenly all come to a screeching halt! What they each can do *within limits* cannot be done *beyond those limits*. Can a rubber band stretch? Of course. But not when stretched so far that it breaks!

Not even cleverly-inventive theories of "punctuated equilibrium" (a kind of leap-frog concept introduced by Harvard's late Steven Jay Gould) can rescue this crisis, which Darwin himself recognized as a huge, huge problem. Darwin never felt satisfied that he had an answer, nor has anyone since. So are we really going to tell schoolchildren the dirty little secret about evolutionary sex? The truth, the whole truth, and nothing but the truth, so help me...oops, can't go there!

The great "similarity" scam

While we're being intellectually honest, maybe we should talk about the argument that *similarity* proves *sequence*. It's the old "all living things are built from the same genetic toolbox" ploy. "And the more genetic material species share, the more closely related they are." So, for example, if humans and chimps share 96 percent of their DNA sequence, then (surely, logically, irrefutably) one must have evolved from the other, or—at the very least—there was common ancestry somewhere back down a long line of evolution. A matter of irresistible logic? At least as logical as saying that, given their shared traits, one twin surely must have evolved from the other! In the case of twins, of course, common ancestry certainly works, though the odds of either one of them beginning a separate line of descent ending in some distinctly non-human creature are roughly as good as Richard Dawkins becoming a fundamentalist Christian.

Could we bring in our bright ten-year-old again? "Care to play with these Lego® pieces? See what all you can build with this bucket of a thousand plastic bricks. Be as creative as you wish. Let your imagination run wild!"

At day's end, we come back to find dozens of fanciful, intricate creations—some similar, some completely different—but all with the same red, white, blue, and yellow pimpled plastic bricks. "DNA," if you will. Interestingly, our young student has used 100 pieces to make a rather boxy-like man, and 96 pieces to make what could pass as a chimpanzee, which conclusively proves, of course, that the chimp came first, then the man—or, at the least, that they had a "common ancestor" in some prototype that our student first constructed, then cannibalized to build the "man" and the "chimp"!

Why is the "common-DNA" argument thought by Evolutionists to be so persuasive? Doesn't the flip-side play just as well? If God created all living creatures, would it be surprising if he used the same molecular building blocks in creating a vastly divergent world of similar and dissimilar creatures? As we can tell, it sure works!

The simplistic explanation Britain's children undoubtedly will be given in their classes about similarity proving both sequence and progression is less disturbing than the more troubling variation on theme: "If *similar*, then the *same*." Which is to say that there are no real qualitative differences between similar species. If we are separated from "lower species," they will be told, it is only *by degree*, not *in kind*. (The "lower animals" are merely distant *cousins!*)

Which brings us back to our Lego® illustration. If all we're talking about is DNA (pimpled plastic bricks), then there *is* a sameness to human and animal DNA. Bricks is bricks! But what accounts for the obvious *differences* between humans and animals, especially considering the *sameness* otherwise? Is it just being arrogantly speciesist to suggest that only humans would engage in this very conversation we're having about the origin of species? Or read and write books containing ever-changing ideas communicated by complex and varying languages? Or speak of history and the future, and of life after death? Or debate whether there is a God, or discuss truth, justice, and equality? Since there is no indication that the "lower animals" do any of the above, one might be excused for thinking that a shared DNA pool is not the end of the story.

At some point, denying a profound difference *in kind* is to be in denial about the whole of human history as it relates to man and animals. Campaign against animal cruelty all you wish, be a vegan if you choose, talk to your pets and even mourn their loss when they die. But not even the most radical campaigners can overturn a universally assumed distinction between humankind and all other living beings.

Richard Dawkins may detest fox hunting and contribute money to shut down Spain's infamous bullfighting, but not even Dawkins is prepared to elect one of his "distant cousins" as Prime Minister, or permit them to perform brain surgery. Or call for pet owners to liberate parakeets from their cages, or take all dogs off their leads. Or cry over a dead fly.

You want to talk about speciesism? The real speciesists are those who attempt some arbitrary distinction between cute foxes and destructive termites, or between raging bulls and pesky ants. If we all came from a common ancestor and thus are not in the least qualitatively different, such whimsical distinctions can't possibly be justified. In practice, of course, not even animal rights activists take to the streets to save unsavory critters, and human life still trumps even gray whales (barely). That we humans are qualitatively different from every other living being—large or small, cuddly or repulsive, noble or ignoble, faithful companion or deadly foe—is a distinction maintained at the practical level by both Christians and atheists, both Evolutionists and Creationists.

Dawkins and other Evolutionists might at least plead professional privilege. The scientist—as a scientist—is not professionally equipped to talk about any differences *in kind* that might possibly accommodate a spiritual dimension. By definition, the scientist is looking only for *natural* explanations, not *supernatural* explanations. The trouble is, if you have only one drawer in which to look for complete answers, you might well come up short. Is it not possible there are other drawers to be opened? Perhaps drawers one knows about, but is unwilling to open...perhaps fearful of where the answers might lead? If that charge can be laid at the feet of Creationists, why not Evolutionists?

Evolution: true *and* false

Let's clear the air just a bit. Does biological evolution occur in all living organisms? Yes. Are there mutations which, over time, result in changes within known species? Yes. Is that a process which occurs naturally, depending on internal genetics and external forces of nature? Yes. In the course of that evolutionary process do species sometimes (or even frequently) become extinct? Yes. Is the definition of "species" sufficiently fluid to encompass "new species" developing from "former species?" Yes. Is the process of evolution from one "former species" to a "new species" observable? Yes. Does this observable evolution explain the wide variety of organisms within the plant and animal world from peas to petunias to dogs? Yes. So was Darwin right about observable evolution? Yes. Is there any reasonable doubt about any of this? No. Any objection from any camp? No. Any objection to teaching school children about how observable biological evolution works? No.

So what's the beef? Why is Evolution so controversial? Why the bitter war, usually between religious folks and secularists, over the question of Evolution? Perhaps you've noticed the capital "E" in Evolution, meant here to indicate the larger, *amoeba-to-man*, General Theory of Evolution first articulated by Darwin and, with variations on theme, widely (though not universally) accepted today within the scientific community. Ideologically, call it "Evolutionism" in parallel with "Creationism." Both are belief systems on the level of religious faith.

"Houston, we have a problem!"[195] When "evolution" is always spelled the same, and no distinctions are specifically articulated, no one has a clue which kind of "evolution" we're talking about. Is it *observable evolution within normally recognizable species* (such as horses, elephants, bananas, and orchids)? Or is it the hypothesized *"big-picture" Evolution* (from simple cells to complex; from simple animals to complex; from invertebrates to vertebrates; from amphibians to birds and mammals; from primates to homo sapiens to humans)? Without knowing which kind of evolution/Evolution we're talking about, we end up talking past each other. (Pollsters, beware!)

"So, Mr. Witness, do you believe in evolution—*yes* or *no*?" "Objection, Your Honor, compound question." "Sustained. Rephrase your question."

As a General Theory, Darwinian-style Evolution hypothesizes from the observable to the unobservable. It's the "then" of any number of fallacious if-then arguments. *If* observable evolution, *then* also unobservable evolution. If *any* variety by evolution, then *all* variety by evolution. If *any* species by evolution, then *all* species by evolution. If *micro*, then surely *macro*. If *current*, then *historical*. If *provable*, then... And that's where Evolution suddenly runs out of room. From that point forward, observable, *provable*, biological evolution become only a working *hypothesis*. Maybe it's a valid hypothesis. But good or bad, right or wrong, it's incapable of the same level of proof as the variety-producing evolution we easily can observe.

For Kool-Aid drinking true-believers such as Professor Taylor, "capital-E" *Evolution* as opposed to "lower-case" *evolution* is all bait-and-switch. A cosmic shell game. A not-so-funny play on words. A *trompe d'oeil*. For the rest of us, the *amoeba-to-man* Evolution hypothesis begins with a reasonable-enough assumption but ends with a highly speculative, hardly-provable, and most likely false conclusion. Say again?

What Darwin theorized was logical enough, but quite arguably wrong. Think about it this way. If a car is detected by police radar traveling 90 m.p.h., one might reasonably conclude that the car was actually 90 miles away an hour earlier. Although that reasoning has a certain logic to it, it's probably not true. It's more likely that the driver is a fairly local resident who simply sped up to 90 m.p.h. only a few miles back down the road. Right?

The point is that we can be completely logical, reasonable, and scientific—and still be wrong. Believers as well as unbelievers. What we must do is put the various hypotheses on the table and carefully test each one. Which is more reasonable? Which best fits what we know of our universe and of ourselves? Which explains the most while encountering the least difficulties? Which best resonates with the "big picture" of human existence, including language, creativity, the arts, and even such seemingly unique human traits as faith and scientific inquiry?

No room for compromise

If it's true that "the fool has said there is no God," one is tempted to refer to Richard Dawkins as the King of Fools. Yet at least it can be said that Dawkins is consistent in saying that there is no divine back-story lurking behind the scenes of Evolution—which is more than can be said for those who say they believe in both Darwin-like Evolution and divine Creation. Trying to hold hands with both Evolution and Creation is to misunderstand both. Attempting to reconcile the irreconcilable is foolish indeed, though it's obvious that many would disagree....

News Item—*According to a survey carried out by the British Council seeking opinions from more than 10,000 people in Britain and elsewhere, 54 percent thought that science and religion are compatible—that it is possible to believe in both God and evolution. Only 19 percent of those questioned said it is impossible to believe in a God while also holding the view that life on earth evolved as a result of natural selection.*[196]

Did you catch the indiscriminate mixture of observable micro-evolution and merely hypothesized macro-Evolution? God and "evolution" are compatible; God and "Evolution" aren't. Rarely are pollsters or their subjects sufficiently sophisticated even to attempt a distinction.

What are the 54 percent in the survey really saying? First, that *they personally* believe in God. Second, that they also accept the view widely propagated by the scientific community that over vast periods of time humankind has evolved from lower species through a non-directed process of natural selection. And because they maintain these two beliefs simultaneously, *for them personally* science and religion must be compatible.

It would have been far more enlightening had the survey asked: Do you believe that science's theory of amoeba-to-man Evolution over millions of years is compatible with divine Creation, as in the biblical account of Adam and Eve appearing suddenly and fully-formed? Think there would still be 54 percent saying yes? Probably not. And yet, there *are* many folks (notably, liberal theologians) who think there's a way to reconcile the seemingly irreconcilable, believing in so-called "theistic evolution."

Despite the wishful thinking, "theistic evolution" is a classic oxymoron. Certainly, there is nothing inherently unreasonable or impossible about a Creator God forming mankind in a purposeful, deliberate, step-by-step process over time. Even over millions of years, if he so chose. But that wouldn't be either "lower-case" evolution *or* "capital-E" Evolution. It wouldn't be *natural* selection by blind, random forces in nature which could turn out just as easily one way as another. It wouldn't be upward progression by survival of the fittest in a chaotic, unplanned, and undesigned universe. So there's no way that step-by-step creation comes anywhere close to being the kind of biological evolution accepted by the scientific community or mandated to be taught in Britain's schools.

Don't overlook the obvious. If God really and truly had been behind the scenes, orchestrating the outcome of the amoeba-to-man process and directing it intentionally and divinely from Point A to Point B—even if by a "law of natural selection" that he himself had set in motion—it would be *Creation*, not *Evolution!* If that is what you believe happened, then you are a *Creationist*, not an *Evolutionist*. Not even a *theistic Evolutionist!*

Far more important than terminology and labels, if there *is* a Creator God powerful and wise enough to create humankind by a step-by-step (or even so-called "evolutionary") process, then by definition he is powerful and wise enough to create humankind in an instant, at the sound of his voice, as in the Genesis account. So what's to be gained by futilely attempting to reconcile two mutually exclusive hypotheses? It's not a win-win, but a lose-lose.

Loony assumptions, loony conclusions

A separate issue is the one most crucial to this book: What are the implications naturally flowing from each hypothesis? Which theory of origins bodes best for government, culture, and society? What are the upsides and downsides? Is it all just a tempest in a teacup, or is the question of origins fundamental to all other discussion? More specifically, is there any connection between Evolution and liberal Looney-Tunes, or is our attempt to connect those dots the looniest of the loony?

Just for openers, is it mere coincidence that the more politically Left a person happens to be (whether a professed Christian or a hard-core secularist), the more likely Evolution is accepted? It virtually goes without saying that most secularists don't buy into divine Creation, and certainly no card-carrying atheist does. Nor would many dispute that Creationists are far more likely to be politically conservative. So can we not all agree that at least those particular dots do in fact connect?

To move even closer to the point of our discussion, what do you think? Out of all the various categories of folks just mentioned, who is pushing the liberal agenda in Europe, Britain, and the United States—*Evolutionists*, or *Creationists*? No prizes for guessing! So the real question is: What, if any, is the connection between an acceptance of Evolution and the liberal-Left legislation and policies showcased in this book?

Evolution's cruel cudgel

To get us started, perhaps it's time to revisit the opening chapter quote from Richard Dawkins: "Let us understand Darwinism so we can walk in the opposite direction when it comes to setting up society." Is Dawkins really saying what it looks like he's saying—that a strictly Evolutionary society would not be a *good* society? The immediately preceding sentence confirms it. "I am a passionate Darwinian when it comes to explaining how things are," says Dawkins, "but I am an even more passionate anti-Darwinian when it comes to politics."[197]

So does this explode any notion of a link between Evolutionists and political liberals, or does it just muddy the water?

What Dawkins finds so troubling about the implications of Darwinism is the same thing that troubled Darwin himself—the cruelty of natural selection and survival of the fittest. "What a book a Devil's Chaplain might write on the clumsy, wasteful, blundering, low and horridly cruel works of nature," wrote Darwin. (Merely consider wasps paralyzing caterpillars segment by segment so their larvae may feed on live meat.) It's a cruel world out there! As Dawkins puts it, "The sheer amount of suffering in the world that is the direct result of natural selection is beyond contemplation."[198]

Certainly it would be easy to blame God for all this cruelty and suffering—if you believed in a God who brought it all into existence. Even believers have to struggle with that troubling issue. Indeed, Darwin's own belief in the Christian God was dinted—not as much by his newfound faith in Evolution as by the tragic death of his ten-year-old daughter, Annie. Darwin is not the only grieved parent to have asked how a loving and good God could allow that to happen.

Evolutionists are quick to cite cruelty and suffering as reason enough not to believe in a God of nature. In Britain, no naturalist is better known than the highly respected, widely-watched Sir David Attenborough, whose television programs have taken viewers into nature, into the wild, into Evolution...and into disbelief. Listen to how he uses nature's cruelty as an argument against belief....

News Item—*Sir David Attenborough says the question his correspondents generally ask him is why he doesn't "give credit" to the Lord for having created such wondrous beauty in nature.*

"They mean beautiful things like hummingbirds," says Sir David. "I always reply by saying that I think of a little child in east Africa with a worm burrowing through his eyeball. The worm cannot live in any other way, except by burrowing through eyeballs. I find that hard to reconcile with the notion of a divine and benevolent creator."

Of his own lack of faith, the 82-year-old Sir David tells the Radio Times: "It never really occurred to me to believe in God."[199]

Consider this: Would that worm burrowing through the child's eyeball think it is cruel to do what it does? Would the wasp think it cruel to paralyze a caterpillar segment by segment? Would the lion think it cruel to attack and devour a wildebeest? Of course, not. But that raises the separate question about cruelty itself: *What is cruelty*, and where did we get that concept?

You can be sure that we didn't get it from nature, or any supposed evolutionary process. Is it *cruel* for bacteria to evolve into resistant strains—even when it requires the death of those less quick, less strong, and less smart? Without that process, so it is said, we wouldn't have the grace of the cheetah, the beauty of a butterfly's wings, or the complexity of the very human brain which contemplates the question of cruelty.[200] To be sure, evolution is raw, ruthless, and unrelenting. It is destructive, deadly, and uncaring. But *cruel?* Absolutely not. It just is what it is!

Neither moral nor immoral

Despite being strictly "scientific," Evolution is an operating system which comes shrink-wrapped together with its own philosophy. A *disturbing* philosophy at that, even for Darwin. Given its obvious potential for invalidating religion and cherished moral assumptions, Darwin told a friend that publishing his theory was "like confessing a murder."

In some respects, what Darwin "confessed" was indeed a mortal wound to religion and morality. Yet, unlike murder, which is plainly *immoral*, Evolution itself is *amoral*—which is to say neither inherently moral nor immoral. So when Darwin, Dawkins and Attenborough speak of *cruelty*—a term of moral judgment—they don't get that concept from their closed, naturalistic, scientific system. For Evolutionists, morality is a borrowed concept.

About one thing, both Dawkins and Darwin are absolutely right. Once you overlay Evolution with a moral template, then it *does* seem to be cruel. If you apply external moral standards to what happens in the process of evolutionary progression (extinction in particular), nature gets away with doing things humans would be sent to jail for! Nor is Evolution interested in the least in social justice. It discriminates against the weak and the vulnerable, is intolerant of non-procreative sex, and couldn't be bothered about inequality of any kind. In fact, it *thrives* on inequality! And don't even mention health and safety to nature. With Evolution, risk is the name of the game!

No wonder Dawkins says that, if we want to create and maintain a good society, we must do better than what an amoral system such as Evolution would teach us to do. Dawkins is spot on when he asserts that we can (and must!) rebel against nature's mechanistic indifference (read *moral indifference*). Who could live with it? Who could survive? Where would be the hope?

Tellingly, Dawkins readily acknowledges that human beings are the only creatures on the planet capable of creating a more compassionate world than Evolution could ever produce on its own. And why would that be? Is it just because we're more intellectually developed than our "distant cousins?" (Or does that sound suspiciously speciesist!) More to the point, isn't this a classic inconsistency—at first denying any qualitative difference between species and then assuming the very qualitative difference we've just denied?

Never underestimate the implications of Dawkins' admission that Evolution's cruel, dog-eat-dog philosophy is antagonistic to good society. If an amoral system is not good for society and politics, *why* is it not good? The answer lies in a little-known, and even less appreciated, corollary to the theory of Evolution: That which is amoral in nature tends over time to mutate in the human species into that which is immoral unless resisted by that which is moral.

That corollary has plenty of observable data. For example, when "nature" kills, it is always *amoral*, with no exceptions. When humans kill, it is always *immoral*, unless the killing falls within certain built-in justifications (like self-defense) which themselves are moral considerations.

There are no rights on the Serengeti Plain. No idealistic notions of tolerance or fairness. No issues of unfair discrimination. The "noble" lion which pounces on the weakest and most vulnerable prey does so with no fear of being hauled before a Court of Animal Rights.

Likewise, human rights, with their corresponding duties and responsibilities, come not from Evolution, but from moral mandate. The notion of equality comes not from Evolution, but from the self-evident truth, confirmed in Scripture, that all humans are created equal, and in God's image.

But what if you happen not to believe that? It's not that Evolutionists aren't moral or ethical people. (Richard Dawkins is scrupulously law-abiding, stopping his bicycle at red lights even when there's not a cop in sight.) It's just that Evolutionists don't get their morality from their Evolution, which Dawkins as much admits. He donates to disaster relief efforts, clearly something he recognizes is totally "un-Darwinian."

So if Evolutionists don't get their morality from Evolutionist philosophy, where do they get it...?

News Item—*John Denham, the Communities Secretary whose department oversees policy on religion denied that there was a "conspiracy" by the state to marginalise faith, arguing that the Government should recognise the work that believers did in volunteering, preserving the environment and standing up to extremists.*

Mr. Denham admitted that he himself is a "secular humanist" and does not believe in God. He added, however, that his values and "moral precepts" owed something to his Church of England upbringing.[201]

At least Denham was honest enough to acknowledge the beneficent moral influence of his upbringing in the church. But he would be kidding himself to think he could have any moral framework whatsoever if he carried his atheistic humanism to its logical conclusion. Where do atheists get their morality? Not from a godless natural world but from religious faith that in its many forms permeates society, culture, and human thinking. Want to test that theory? Just get rid of religion—lock, stock, and barrel—and see what morality remains.

Despite all the evil perpetrated in the name of religion (and it has been horrendous), what would the world be like with *no* religion? Take away the church, both buildings and believers. Obliterate the Bible, the Koran, the Vedas, and all other writings held to be sacred so that not a single copy remains. Drop "God" and its many variants from all vocabularies. Suck every thought of a higher power from the human mind. Speak not a word of morality, transcendence, or the divine. Command that there be no duty, virtue, or grace higher than instinct. Ban human conscience. Wipe out any notion of a soul that survives death. Forbid parents to instill standards of right and wrong.

Let nothing remain but nature itself—wild, untamed, uncivilized, uncaring, nature—and man will be a beast. Not a noble beast, just a beast. Acting like beasts act.

The wishful lyrics of John Lennon's peace anthem, "Imagine," would have us think that if only we imagined there's no heaven or hell, and no religion, the world suddenly would be as one and we would all live in peace. "You may say I'm a dreamer," Lennon chides, but in truth he *was* dreaming! In the dog-eat-dog universe of natural selection and survival of the fittest, there is no room for "the brotherhood of man." In a world without religion and transcendent morality "nothing to kill or die for" turns into *everything* to kill for—for whatever reason one might conjure. Indeed, in the amoral jungle that is natural selection, even Lennon's own tragic murder would not be *tragic* at all. Just what happened. Just part of a value-free, mechanistic process. Evolution sheds no tears.

Secular humanists and atheists have the luxury of denying or diminishing God, faith, and religion as long as there are still believers around to keep morality alive for society. Elton Trueblood described it best with his powerful image of a "cut-flower civilization." Thinking that morality can last forever apart from its proper roots in faith and religion is as futile as trying to make cut flowers in a vase live forever. Even more foolish is thinking that morality ever could have emerged in the first place from an amoral world of godless Evolution.

Darwin himself is the perfect example of the struggle to accommodate social morality with the amorality of his scientific findings. In his *Decent of Man*, Darwin is ambivalent at best as to whether and how morality might somehow have evolved from natural selection....

> *With civilised nations, as far as an advanced standard of morality...natural selection apparently effects but little; though the fundamental social instincts were originally thus gained.*

As if to say, *since* we can observe morality, and *since* all things have evolved from natural selection, the only conclusion is that social morality *must also have evolved*, though how it possibly could have occurred by natural selection cannot be known.

Yet notice Darwin's "fall-back" position as to how morality is learned and propagated:

> *But I have already said enough, whilst treating of the lower races, on the causes which lead to the advance of morality, namely, the approbation of our fellow-men, the strengthening of our sympathies by habit, example and imitation, reason, experience and even self-interest, instruction during youth, and religious feelings.*

If a case might possibly be made for a kind of "naturalistic, pragmatic, reasoned morality," what possibly could be the origin of "religious feelings" under a purely naturalistic system? Truth be known, what Darwin is expressing here is nothing more than a reflection of *his own* "instruction during youth, and religious feelings." Left to the amoral Evolutionary system Darwin unearthed, religion and religious feelings never would have been conceived, much less given birth. And without them, morality would have been a non-starter. Nothing from nothing leaves nothing.

Like our secular-humanist John Denham, Darwin may have come to believe in a value-neutral system of origins, but he could never fully escape the spiritual morality that pervades this universe and beyond. A morality which natural selection never could have produced. A transcendent morality that both Darwin and Denham were taught as youngsters.

Which brings us back to the critical bottom line...the children.

The lessons children will learn

Teach children that they are created in God's image—as is everybody else—and you've got a shot at their not acting like animals. Transcendent, divinely-ordained morality sends clear signals about the social virtues of fairness, justice, equality, tolerance, respect, obedience, duty, honor, and courage—all without the synthetic faux-morality of political correctness.

But teach children that they are nothing more than highly-evolved animals, and they will have little incentive for not acting like animals. Especially is that true if you hit them with the double-whammy of denigrating faith in every way possible and eroding what fragile moral standards remain after social approval of abortion, homosexual conduct, heterosexual promiscuity, and so on down the line. If morality is what keeps nature's amorality in check, this generation is being served a lethal cocktail of evolutionary amorality and morally-vacuous secularism.

The danger lies in how school children in Britain and America will connect the dots they are given to work with. It's not difficult to predict. Let's see...I'm taught that I am the product of natural selection, not divine Creation. So if there is a God, he has little or no relevance to my life. If I am not qualitatively different from other animals with which mankind has evolved, then I must not have a soul that survives death, and if I don't live beyond this life, then I'm not answerable to any Supreme Being when I die. If there's no eternal accountability, then I can choose on my own to be noble, honest, and kind, but equally I can choose to act however I wish, subject only to the risk that society will punish me if I'm caught. If there is no God, then there is nothing that is inherently immoral. Marriage is a mere convention; sexuality is as much a non-issue as sex in the jungle; and the sanctity of life is up for grabs, whether in the womb or on violent streets.

Is that so far-fetched? Is there a better explanation for an increasingly uncivilized civilization requiring more and more arbitrary rules and regulations to fill the moral vacuum? (Shades of Tacitus: "The more corrupt the state, the more it legislates.")

In the absence of a spiritual dimension, there is nothing for the next generation but a material, naturalistic world, tempered only by ever-shifting political correctness imposed heavy-handedly by micro-managing secularist governments. Want a picture of where that all ends up? Try the godless communism of North Korea, China, and the former Soviet Union. It's a stark choice: Either you have faith-based morality and political freedom, or you have secularism and tyranny.

To be sure, there's also *religious* tyranny, as best seen in the rise of extremist Islam with its often-brutal Sharia law. But secularism is not to be preferred, especially now when militant Islam is threatening Western culture. It's the West's immoral secularism, not its Christian doctrine, that provides Muslim extremists with their *raison d'être*. But extremists need not obsess about destroying us. Given enough time, we will self-destruct from within. By the laws of nature, whenever there's a moral vacuum, social implosion is a natural phenomenon.

Evolution no friend of liberal causes

Don't you just love the irony? It's the liberal-Left always demanding the teaching of Evolution in the classroom. Never can get enough of that natural selection and survival of the fittest, you know. It fits hand-in-glove with the atheists among them and seems so wonderfully *progressive* for those who still pay lip-service to faith. Evolution is all about progress. Upward and onward!

There's just a tiny problem here. If you take Evolution seriously, some of your favorite liberal causes don't make a lot of sense. Abortion does, of course. A mother killing her own offspring can sometimes be observed in nature, so why not with humans? *Must* be a morally-neutral amoral act. Couldn't possibly be immoral.

Same again on the other end of life with euthanasia. In a purely naturalistic system, how could hastening death for the elderly and the infirm be immoral? Isn't that nature's way, really? Despite even Darwin's observation about humans not following nature's course when it comes to how we treat the dying, evolutionary philosophy is not lost on liberal activists. But other reasoning is indeed lost....

Have you ever wondered how Evolutionism possibly coexists with Environmentalism, that other great religion of the liberal-Left? Surely, something's missing here. Save the planet? Save the whales? *Why?* For what? *From* what? From extinction? Extinction is evolution's road to progress! An Ice Age here and there is nothing to the planet. An extinct dinosaur here or there causes nary a ripple in the evolutionary stream. *(We're* here, aren't we?) And even if it did cause a ripple, what would it matter? In Evolution's closed, naturalistic, amoral system, no species is any more or less valuable than any other.

If Creationists are guilty of being speciesist, Evolutionists are guilty of being "generationist," as if *our generation* is more important than any other wafer-thin generation in the long history of evolutionary progress. How ironic that liberal environmentalists are trying to save species—and even a planet—that, in the billions-of-years scheme of Evolution amount to absolutely nothing.

When you move from biology to cosmology, vast stars dwarfing the size of Earth live and die with no funerals, no epitaphs, and no footnotes. If Earth came into existence by random forces and is just as vulnerable as the stars to ending up in some black hole, what is that to us or to some future generation that might never come to pass? Are we "highly-evolved animals" getting just a tad bit sentimental here? Is there room in Evolutionism for sentimentalism? Or is there just some human hubris going on here?

Creationists have not done a particularly stellar job being stewards of God's pristine Creation (to put it mildly), but at least the divine mandate of stewardship fits far more comfortably in the Creationists' camp than in the camp of environmental activists whose only gospel is that the universe, the planet, and man are all just lucky ever to have seen the light of day.

A most un-social Darwinism

At the heart of Britain's quintessentially liberal legislation known as the Equality Bill is, supposedly, legal protection for the weak and the vulnerable (other than the unborn and the elderly, of course). Does "social Darwinism" have anything to add to the conversation about the weak and the vulnerable? Indeed it does, but Evolutionists turn absolutely livid when you bring it up! And who wouldn't...?

In his *Descent of Man*, it was Darwin who first grappled with the profound social implications of his revolutionary theory. Counterintuitively, Darwin observed how (mercifully) civilized society operated in an opposite way from the process of natural selection...yet to society's detriment:

> *With savages, the weak in body or mind are soon eliminated; and those that survive commonly exhibit a vigorous state of health. We civilized men, on the other hand, do our utmost to check the process of elimination. We build asylums for the imbecile, the maimed and the sick; we institute poor-laws; and our medical men exert their utmost skill to save the life of every one to the last moment.*[202]

Exactly *why* "civilized societies" are counter-evolutionary, and precisely *how* that break with evolutionary philosophy came about in the process of natural selection, Darwin does not venture far to say. But

Darwin is happy enough that "noble" man has come to the point of protecting rather than destroying the weak and the inferior...yet would be happier still if, on their own, the weak in body or mind would simply refrain from marriage!

> *Hence we must bear without complaining the undoubtedly bad effects of the weak surviving and propagating their kind; but there appears to be at least one check in steady action, namely the weaker and inferior members of society not marrying so freely as the sound; and this check might be indefinitely increased, though this is more to be hoped for than expected.*[203]

Contrary to rumor, Darwin was not the father of eugenics, only the godfather. Beyond question, Darwin's theory of man's evolutionary origin was all about the strong weeding out the weak. About the superior replacing the inferior. But when some of his contemporaries took that theory to its logical extreme and applied social Darwinism to those whom they viewed as inferior races, Darwin did not hesitate to challenge the validity of their thesis.

When, for example, Darwin's cousin, Francis Galton (the true father of eugenics, in the steps of Malthus and Spencer) pointed to the "careless, squalid, unaspiring Irishman" and the "inferior" Celt who multiplied faster than the "frugal, foreseeing, self-respecting, ambitious" Scot and Saxon, Darwin didn't join either side in the budding battle over eugenics. Instead, Darwin noted that Galton had not taken into account all of the relevant data which might militate against his conclusions, maintaining that the social implications of natural selection were far more complex than what might seem obvious.

In the aftermath of Darwin's *Origin of Species* and *Descent of Man*, that which came to be known as "Darwinism" has become all things to all people. In the same way that many Calvinists are more Calvinistic than Calvin, many Darwinists are more Darwinian than Darwin! It's a risk shared by all who offer seminal ideas through their writing. Start the ball rolling, and you can never be sure where it might end up.

Merely consider that single famous line from Darwin when he stated simply as a matter of dispassionate observation that it would be helpful to civilized society if "the weak in body and mind refrained from marriage." As reported in the opening chapter about Kerry Robertson and Mark McDougall who were not allowed to marry because of mental impairment, many in positions of authority today are more than eager to turn Darwin's academic musings into harsh reality. Ideas have consequences, not all of them intended. But the consequences in the Robertson/McDougall case are tame compared with how others have employed the logical extension of Darwin's research.

For those who took up the social Darwinism banner in Nazi Germany, evolutionary ethics found nightmarish expression in the ghettos and concentration camps of a society enamored with evolutionary philosophy. Even with other complex social factors contributing to the Holocaust, for Hitler's "socially progressive" regime, committing genocide in aid of racial purity was simply the most natural way to produce a master race. (Why else the films showing beetles fighting in a lab, as demonstration of survival of the fittest?) It had taken almost no time at all for Darwin's timid fear that his theory was "like *confessing* a murder" to evolve into a fascist society brazenly *committing* murder!

No doubt Darwin himself (who was personally outraged even by slavery) would be appalled beyond belief—and all the more so to think he had contributed in any way to such an atrocity. Unfortunately, it was his biological theory, more than all the other non-scientific ideas about social struggle advanced before him, that opened Pandora's box to those who were far less scrupulous than he. And sometimes even to the scrupulous and well-intended, who are still blind-sided by the logical implications of Darwin's now-widely-accepted hypothesis. Such would include Britain's liberal-Left, intent on indoctrinating Britain's children regarding a theory which is rife with potential social danger. And you can add Obama and friends to that list as well. Evolution with a capital-E is the bedrock creed of all who are liberal-Left.

Not all worldviews are created equal. Some evolve into inferior social mores, weakened citizens, and grotesque governments.

And we truly don't expect bright school children to run with the ball they are being thrown? Richard Weaver was right: Ideas do indeed have consequences!

When the church buried Darwin...

Charles Robert Darwin died on April 19, 1882, at his home in Kent. His funeral was held a week later on April 26, and Darwin's body was interred in a place of honor at Westminster Abbey. The funeral was attended by fellow scientists, philosophers, naturalists, and dignitaries of all sort—including, of course, leading members of the Anglican Church.

It did not seem to bother the Church that Darwin's famed theory was, at the very least, problematic for the existence or nature of God; was troubling in its implications for morality, divine judgment, an immortal soul, and the afterlife; and was laden with potential for undermining faith in Scripture, the Church, and Jesus Christ himself.

Nor did it seem to matter that Darwin had not attended church from the day he buried his precious Annie; nor that by the end of his life Darwin had become an agnostic with no pretense of faith in a personal God; nor that Darwin would have made no claim to Jesus Christ being his Lord and Savior. The Church was more than happy to say grace over the man who was Britain's greatest naturalist—with few, if any, questions asked.

As indelicate as it may seem to say so, when the Church of England buried Darwin at Westminster Abbey, it quietly and imperceptibly dug its own grave. Not that it wasn't already spiritually moribund in many respects, but there is a very real sense in which the Church's celebration of Darwin's life and work was a significant nail in the coffin of its spiritual influence in Britain.

One can only wonder how different things might have been for the Church had Darwin ended up in the clergy as his father had hoped (since Plan A for his being a medical doctor had failed miserably). Darwin initially liked the idea, since many clergymen were as interested in natural history as he was, and being in a small parish church would afford him the time to study the flora and fauna of the local countryside. However, an unexpected opportunity to be a naturalist aboard H.M.S. Beagle on its two-year survey of South America changed the course of Darwin's life...the course of history...and likely the course of the Church.

Not surprisingly, Darwin's bold new idea was met initially with official outcry and dismay by the Church. The debates were infamously fierce. One in particular, lasting four hours at Oxford University's Museum Library, pitted Bishop Wilberforce against Thomas Huxley and Joseph Hooker. But in time many Anglican theologians in the nineteenth century positively embraced Evolution. It was a time of discovery, exploration, and scientific enthusiasm. It was a time of progressive, enlightened thinking.

More recently, most of the leaders in the Church of England have shed any doubts they may have had about Evolution, qualified only by their staunch belief in God and traditional faith concerns that would be expected of the Church. There's no better snapshot of that theological and philosophical mishmash than when an archbishop dared to take on Richard Dawkins....

News Item—*The former Archbishop of Canterbury, Lord Carey, accused Richard Dawkins of evolving into a "very simple kind of thinker." Said Carey, "His argument for atheism goes like this: either God is the explanation for the wide diversity of biological life, or evolution is. We know that evolution is true. Therefore, God doesn't exist.*

"I'm an evangelical Christian, but I have no difficulties in believing that evolution is the best scientific account we have for the diversity of life on our planet."[204]

What can one say? If Lord Carey believes that eternity-bound spiritual souls wrapped in humanity and "made in the image of God" are included in "the wide diversity of biological life" resulting from *evolution* (by definition, wholly and solely naturalistic), then Dawkins is no more a "simple kind of thinker" than Carey. In fact, Dawkins' position is far more consistent....

If naturalistic *amoeba-to-man* Evolution is a scientific fact (which both Dawkins and Carey maintain), there is still theoretical room for God to exist (which Dawkins denies and Carey asserts), but not an *involved* God who had anything to do with the existence of man (with which Dawkins reasonably agrees and Carey unreasonably disagrees). Certainly not the providential Creator or Christian God in whom Carey fervently believes. In the end, they are both being naively simplistic. Dawkins stubbornly doesn't want to eat any cake, so he insists against all evidence that there isn't one; whereas Carey foolishly wants his cake and eat it too!

For Dawkins' part, he would be well-advised not to tie the knot quite as tightly between Evolution and atheism. Folks may be "pig-ignorant about science," as he puts it (rather speciesistly!), but if forced to choose between Evolution and God, Dawkins might be surprised how many people, including the non-religious, will begin to have their doubts about Evolution. God was around a long time before Darwin ever hit the scene.

For Lord Carey's part, he would be well-advised to loosen the knot between Evolution and belief. Folks may be ill-informed as to the fine distinctions of the origins debate, but if forced to hold hands with both Evolution *and* God, Cary might be surprised how many believers will begin to have their doubts about God. A God languishing in the shadowy margins is hardly worth believing in.

But that's just a highly interesting side-bar. Consistent with Evolution's ever-widening acceptance over time, it is now so fully embraced by the Church of England that, in 2009—celebrating two hundred years from Darwin's birth—the Church issued England's favorite son a formal apology....

News Report—*Nearly 150 years after Darwin published his most famous work, the Church of England will formally concede that it initially was overly-defensive and overly-emotional in dismissing Darwin's ideas. The Church's apology will call "anti-evolutionary fervour" an "indictment on the Church." It will also declare that, in their response to Darwin's theory of natural selection, Christians repeated the mistakes they made in doubting Galileo's astronomy in the 17th century.*

The formal apology reads: "Charles Darwin: 200 years from your birth, the Church of England owes you an apology for misunderstanding you and, by getting our first reaction wrong, encouraging others to misunderstand you still. We try to practise the old virtues of 'faith seeking understanding' and hope that makes some amends."[205]

Wow, that's some evolution in the Church's thinking! But still no apparent concern about the negative spiritual implications of Darwin's theory. Or about how Darwin's hypothesis has unwittingly contributed to such evils as the Holocaust. Or about Darwin's own personal lack of faith. Does none of this mean anything to the Church? Does it not go to the heart of what Christian faith is all about?

And how quaintly odd, addressing the apology directly to Charles Darwin as if, somewhere in the Great Beyond, Darwin could hear, see, or somehow sense the apology! If there *is* a Great Beyond, the home of the soul, why would the Church apologize for wrongly reacting to a theory that fundamentally excludes both the soul and its otherworldly home? And what in Christian doctrine would suggest eternal approbation for someone who knowingly turns his back on God...and provides the perfect vehicle for millions of others to ride down the same road to unbelief?

Regarding the gratuitous Galileo reference (as if there were a parallel!), is the Church so daft as to miss the *real* parallels? From antiquity,

Aristotle had refuted heliocentricity (a sun-centered solar system), and by Galileo's time, virtually every major thinker subscribed to the geocentric (Earth-centered) view popularized by Ptolemy, the Greek mathematician and astronomer. So Galileo upset, not just the church, but what then passed for *the entire scientific community*—both Christian and non-Christian. Ptolemy's hypothesis was the entrenched Darwinism of his day—for centuries! Most importantly, it hadn't derived from Scripture at all, but from pagan (human) reasoning, which the Church foolishly baptized with legitimacy. Sound familiar?

Here's something else to think about. If the Church could get a major scientific hypothesis so terribly wrong *once*, why should we think it couldn't get another scientific hypothesis terribly wrong *again*? And the Galileo debate didn't even have the slightest implications regarding human nature, immortality, transcendent morality, Christian doctrine, or social issues of any kind.

In Darwin's day, the Church was established, comfortable, entrenched, and unchallenged. If you were British, you were "Christian." Regardless of what you happened to believe (or *not* believe), you were baptized "Christian," married "Christian," and buried "Christian."

Not much has changed in the Church since Darwin's era except that society's evolving political liberalism has been matched step-by-step with religious liberalism. In the classic language of evolutionary debate, it's pretty much been a case of monkey-see, monkey-do. Today the Church of England warmly embraces most liberal causes. The Church is happy to have women priests and increasingly is out and proud on homosexual issues—so much so that it has caused near schism among the Anglican fellowship world wide.

One can't conclusively say that, had the Church been more intransigent on the issue of human origins, it would not have evolved to be so theologically and politically liberal, but the whiff of cheap political correctness behind the "Darwin-apology" publicity stunt would appear to confirm it.

And some wonder how the Church of England has lost its moral authority in "Christian Britain?" Sadly, it's called *secularist compromise* and *spiritual abdication.*

Given what ought to be its powerful position of moral and spiritual influence in Britain, the Church of England bears great blame for much of the loony leftist liberalism that is now plaguing the nation. To its dismay, the Church is just now beginning to discover that the secularism it helped to unleash in Darwinian Evolution has evolved into a menacing political beast nipping at its own sacred heels. In vain doth it protest, and from a position of abject moral and spiritual weakness.

What can the Church of England do to reclaim the moral and spiritual high ground, both for itself and for Britain? Perhaps by bringing Charles Darwin back to faith...or at least those who would follow in his footsteps. Darwin may have died an agnostic—still confused about how science and faith could be reconciled. But, like millions of Britons and Americans who really aren't sure about all these ponderous matters, Darwin could not fully distance himself from the notion of a living soul that survives death—felt most keenly at the death of his own beloved Annie.

Just listen to these poignant words of lament which Darwin wrote in a personal memoir: "We have lost the joy of the household, and the solace of our old age....Oh that she could now know how deeply, how tenderly we do still & and shall ever love her dear joyous face."

Parted by death. Buried in a grave. Yet in her father's heart, Annie was still "she"—who, he wished, could *even now know* he loved her! Not some highly-evolved being that simply died and decayed. Not just a "noble" human bound to nowhere. But an immortal soul fit for eternity who, as Darwin intuitively knew, was far more than the sum of the parts of the grand scientific theory he had contrived.

For the Church of England, for Britain, and for all those who would hope the best for humankind, it's the *soul* that's key here. It's the *eter-*

nal soul that people desperately want to understand. The *troubled soul* that needs solace. The *guilty soul* that needs redemption. The *questioning soul* that needs answers. The *searching soul* that needs direction. The *lonely soul* that needs love. The *empty soul* that needs filling. The *longing soul* that seeks escape from a material world. And most crucial of all for the immediate purposes of this book, the *moral soul* that is the anchor for any society that would be just, caring, responsible, and free.

Make no mistake. That divinely created soul and its human body did not emerge from primeval slime, but from the creative hand of the One who is sublime. Forget the debate over the "six days" of Genesis. Argue all you want about the age of the earth or the universe. Feel free to explore the mystery of the dinosaurs and other extinct species. At the end of the day, only one thing really matters, both for ourselves and for the well-being of society: In the edenic miracle of the historical Adam and Eve, man and woman suddenly and supernaturally appeared on the planet—incarnate living souls, more immortal than mortal. Incarnate living souls tailor-made for society. Incarnate living souls morally attuned to their divine Maker.

If the Church feels a need to make an apology to Charles Darwin, it should apologize for failing to assuage his grieving soul in its greatest hour of need. And, in the wider frame, for abandoning its role as the proclaimer of truth to all doubting souls, proclaiming with no uncertain sound the Almighty Creator who, with eternal purpose, omniscient wisdom, and omnipotent power, deigned to make us in his own image.

How America has evolved

If Darwin himself was the great Evolution sensation for Britain, the Scopes "monkey trial" in 1925 was the backwoods-turned-Hollywood version for America. The widely-reported trial of science teacher John Thomas Scopes (a test case cleverly set up by the ACLU) had the practical effect of ushering Evolution into the American classroom, and kicking God out. In the wake of this bizarre case, state laws banning the teaching of Evolution fell like dominoes. More importantly, there was growing disapproval of any group of people imposing their religious views on others—an irony that would play out over the coming decades as Evolutionists turned the tables and began imposing their own fanatical secularism on everyone else.

Using the pretext of church-state separation (unknown to Britain with its established Church), the ACLU pressed the courts of the land from the lowest to the highest to censure any mention of divine Creation—or "creationism" as it was strategically cast to bring it within the realm of religion and thus more vulnerable to the Establishment Clause. In the 1968 landmark case of *Epperson v. Arkansas*, the U.S. Supreme Court struck down Arkansas' anti-Evolution statute as unconstitutional, prompting a spate of state legislation mandating "balanced treatment" of both Evolution and "creation-science."

No prizes for guessing the result when the Supreme Court considered the "balanced treatment" statutes in the 1987 case of *Edwards v. Aguillard*. Officially and finally, Evolution had had its way, and Creation had had its day. Taking a page from the "balanced treatment" approach, even the liberal-Left came to appreciate that calling your own sacred beliefs *science* rather than *religion*, served to stifle traditional religious belief while promoting the equally passionate religion of secularism.

Today, try going to court to stop secularist teaching in America's public classrooms, and you'll find no cause too liberal to withstand all objections. All the while, the ACLU sits on its civil-libertarian hands as academic freedom, freedom of expression, and religious free speech get thoroughly trashed...by none other than the ACLU!

In reaction to God-free-zone classrooms, believers in America began a home-school revolution and also established thousands of K-12 Christian schools. From kindergarten to high school, students finally could be taught biblical Creation without interference from the government. In the spirit of both fairness and academic inquiry, most Christian schools also teach "lower-case" observable evolution, as well as introduce students to "capital-E" Evolution as the alternative view held by many in society.

Among churches, the more mainstream (liberal) denominations quite happily accept "theistic evolution" in the fashion of Lord Carey. Not surprisingly, they also back the usual political causes of the liberal-Left. Equally predictable, the more conservative and fundamental the church, the more its adherents are both Creationists and politically right of center. Hence the great culture wars at the end of the 20th century, and the fierce battles over abortion, homosexual rights, and faith in the public square.

Numerically, the percentage of those who still believe in divine Creation far exceeds the percentage of those who would deny it—adjusted only by the large number of believers who think Creation and Evolution are easily compatible. If the generationally-reflective Emergent Church goes in the direction it seems to be headed politically (pendulum-swinging leftward from the culture wars fought by the religious right), that number might well explode. Now three generations into the secularization of America's classrooms, not even the church is immune to the liberal secularist tide with its dangerous undercurrent of Evolution thinking.

Have we mentioned that ideas have consequences? Few ideas in all of history have had more broad-sweeping and disastrous consequences for society than the belief that humankind has emerged from the amoral, naturalistic system known as Evolution. Where run-amok social Darwinism tragically contributed to the deaths of millions in the Holocaust, the political Darwinism of the liberal-Left sounds its own solemn death knell for civilized society.

For over a century and a half in both Britain and America, we have sown the winds of Evolutionary thinking. Little surprise that we are now reaping the whirlwind.

11

Revolution and Regime Change

*The marvel of all history is the patience with which
men and women submit to burdens unnecessarily laid upon
them by their governments.*

—William H. Borah

As we began this conversation, we spoke of the liberating American Revolution in which common, ordinary citizens summonsed the courage to rebel against tyrannical government. That their bold actions eventually spawned a new, sovereign nation is only incidental to that struggle. Regime change can also happen within an established nation, as witnessed by the Solidarity Movement in Poland and the overthrow of communism in Eastern Bloc countries at the fall of the Wall.

Regime change happens, but it doesn't *just* happen. There has to be a tipping point, a moment in history when the people have had enough. A time when an overbearing government runs out of excuses, and the people run out of patience. A day which dawns with the penetrating light that far too few political leaders have their constituents' interests at heart—and that politics is politics, no matter which banner you fly. That if there are Leftist "liberals," the alternative is usually no better than "liberals" on the Right, dressed in conservative clothes. That— whether in Britain or in the States—political *red* and political *blue* tend to fade into a pale, sickly purple. Tweedledum and Tweedledee.

One could have hoped that the near-miraculous, grass-roots election of Massachusetts Senator Scott Brown might have signaled such a tipping point, but—despite what would be the delicious parallel with Paul Revere's famed ride through the Massachusetts countryside heralding America's first revolution—surely that expectation was overly-optimistic. And yet...could it possibly be that, Tea Party and all, America is rousing from its deep slumber? Have Americans finally gotten their fill of intrusive government, mind-boggling deficits, daft liberal social policies, business-choking regulation, and officious meddling in every aspect of our lives?

Surprisingly, the short answer is *no*. Or at least *not yet*. It's one thing to grouse and complain; another to act. It's one thing to fight a skirmish here and there; another to gear up for an all-out political war. It's one thing to wish for a regime change; another to make it happen.

Listen to British citizens on the streets today and, along with mandatory complaints about the lousy British weather, you'll get an ear-full about Britain's loony Government—in precisely those terms. Political leaders of all parties and functionaries from Westminster to Whitehall to the local town council have little respect among the citizenry. Yet, through it all, the Brits' famed "stiff upper lip" seems not to quiver in the least. It's not so much a matter of seemingly-genetic British resolve as much as it's simply a lack of options.

After all, what's the person on the street to do about the flood of immigration, when the government won't turn off the tap? Or about exorbitant taxes at the petrol pumps? Or the burgeoning array of security and traffic cameras? Or the maddening delays one must endure on national health care? Or the affront to local parish councils when they are all but ignored by supercilious planning officers miles away in obscure cubicles, whimsically issuing edicts affecting village life about which they haven't the slightest clue. Or even the daily insolence of having to key in one's car registration number at the Pay-and-Display, apparently because being forced to pay for parking while patronizing struggling shopkeepers on your local High Street simply isn't insult enough?

Even if the average person on the street wanted to effectuate change through the political process, there is little hope of having any real influence, whether in Britain or America. As long as the major parties are mostly in the hands of political elites far removed from the realities of everyday life, John Q. Citizen is all but disenfranchised. Other than the perfunctory ticking of one box or the other on the occasional ballot, the average Joe or Jill is regarded as little more than fodder for voracious political machines. And it's not just political disenfranchisement that is so debasing. It's the constant, mind-numbing chipping away of personal autonomy by regulation upon regulation, and rule upon rule.

Maybe this pervasive sense of disempowerment explains the *bossy bureaucrat syndrome*, whereby disenfranchised, over-regulated minions in even low-level positions of authority from town councils to educational departments become, themselves, bossy bureaucrats in a desperate attempt to regain at least some modicum of personal empowerment, even if it means becoming as mercilessly autocratic over their fellow citizens as those higher up the bureaucratic food chain.

Perhaps, too, it explains the mystery of why millions of ordinary citizens seem to take all this nanny-state bullying lying down. Could it be a variation on theme from the so-called Stockholm Syndrome—a term derived from the notorious Swedish hostage crisis where four bank employees were held by an escaped convict and ended up fearing the police more than their captors? As disputed as that theory is (that hostages identify with their captors), there must be something similar going on when regulation-weary citizens offer such little resistance to the crazed nanny state holding them hostage.

Class wars and the warring classes

To best understand the compliance culture in Britain, one need only look a couple of generations back to a time when—outside large metropolitan areas—the nation was "ruled" by local Lords of the Manor. Acting somewhat as benevolent dictators, the Lords of the Manor were the local government of their day. If you've ever driven through the quaint, lost-in-time villages dotting the verdant English, Scottish, and Welsh landscapes, it's easy to forget that those villages were built by wealthy landowners in support of their enormous estates.

In addition to the delightful stone cottages which housed the workers, there were the shops, tithe barns, mills, forges, churches, and village halls. And don't forget the roads, dry stone walls, and other infrastructure—all maintained to a high standard, albeit by workers we today would call serfs. Not many of us would wish to trade places with them, yet on the upside it has to be said that all of their basic needs were satisfied. It was a cradle-to-grave culture in which (for the most part) kindly Lords of the Manor looked after their workers relatively well for the times in which they lived.

Still today, you can talk with villagers who themselves worked for the Lord of the Manor, and whose parents knew nothing else. It was an era of strict social strata in which everybody knew their place— whether to the manor born or to the hovel born. Stationed high or low, the story was always the same: cradle-to-grave status, cradle-to-grave provision, cradle-to-grave expectations.

Should anyone be surprised, then, that even today there is a compliance mentality in Britain? Or, indeed, an *entitlement* mentality? Or, more yet, a comfort zone with socialist governance?

If you're wondering what brought an end to this orderly social structure, the answer is simple. It's called class envy. Seems that not all the workers were content to live in their hovels while the Lord of the Manor lived in such a vastly different manner. In time, there was nothing less than a regime change. Quietly, bloodlessly, almost imperceptibly, the manor system began to disappear. And the weapon of choice? Taxes. When socialists ascended to power intent on leveling the classes, they simply taxed the Lords of the Manor (today's "1%") out of existence. Job done!

Now in more modern times, the new "Lords of the Manor" reside in London, Edinburgh, and Cardiff. They rule from a distance, with a heavier hand than their predecessors, and with hardly any more respect for the workers. Like most absentee landlords, they don't seem to notice the crumbling infrastructure all around, or haven't the money to do anything about it. Having dispossessed the evil landowners of their wealth, the envying class managed only to despoil the nation in the process.

It also goes without saying that most of Britain's current ruling class wouldn't be caught dead living in the inner-city hovels they provide for the teeming masses—their supposed equals. Instead, as recently revealed in the embarrassing expenses scandals plaguing Parliament, they pillage and plunder the public coffers with no less temerity than the worst of the Lords of the Manor...and ever so crassly. A so-called "classless society" may have emerged...but with little class.

In point of fact, it's not a classless society at all. Not even close. After decades of egalitarian politics and programs, there is now more of a social divide than ever before between the well-off middle class and the poor underclass, whether in terms of income, health, or education.

On the education front, the battle for absolute equality continues apace, permitting no class of students to truly excel if that means other children thereby are made to look like dunces. The result has been a disaster. Rather than lifting the lower classes higher, all that's been achieved is dragging the upper classes down to the lowest common denominator.

Even as far back as the war years, Oxbridge scholar and writer C.S. Lewis was decrying the folly of the egalitarian agenda (embodied so proudly in today's Equal Rights Bill). "What I want to fix your attention on," said Lewis, "is the vast overall movement towards the discrediting, and finally the elimination, of every kind of human excellence—moral, cultural, social or intellectual. And is it not pretty to notice how 'democracy' (in the incantatory sense) is now doing for us the work that was once done by the most ancient dictatorships, and by the same methods?"[206]

And just in case you thought the class wars were over in a new era of liberal tolerance, think again. When fox hunting—that colorful and quintessentially British tradition going back centuries—was banned on Tony Blair's watch, animal cruelty was not the pressing issue. The real prey being chased was the class of folks who dared participate in fox hunts. Those upper-middle-class toffs who can afford such an expensive sport. Those Sherry-swiging, fancy-dressing hoidy toidies with second homes in the countryside, you know. It hardly matters that many members of the hunt never fit that description, nor that the jobs of ordinary folks employed by the hunts were put at risk, nor that what the hunts contributed to the maintenance of the lands on which they hunted has since gone missing.

While the liberal-Left licks its chops like a fox over a meal of fine young lamb, the irony is that the hunts continue mainly unabated. For Britain's class-busters, it was satisfying enough simply to *prove* they could stick it to the toffs! (Would that they were equally satisfied to claim a Pyrrhic victory when it comes to legalizing the greatest of all cruelties—the dismemberment of babies in the womb. Now that they've successfully assured the availability of abortion, could the Leftists please just move on to other liberal battles so that moral reason might yet prevail and the unthinkable cruelty in the womb forever cease! In the liberal-Left's "classless society," the unborn are the only truly unprotected class.)

So what about America, you ask? Separated by an ocean from the mother country, the American colonies didn't exactly make a clean break with British precedents, but enough of a break to avoid the compliance and entitlement mentality characteristic of the British way of life. Self-determination, self-assurance, and self-reliance became hallmarks of the fiercely independent, frontier American spirit—except, of course, in the sub-culture of slavery, where an evil legacy of groveling compliance and cradle-to-grave entitlement (meager as it was) even now has stubborn memory rings going back generations.

And yet one day, somewhere along the line, even we Americans woke up to discover that we, too, had a compliance and entitlement streak in us. With the advent of massive government handouts, social security benefits, and Medicare coverage, we quickly cultivated a taste for entitlement, American-style. And with each additional encroachment of big government into everyday life, we have become increasingly compliant. Once-unfamiliar federal, state, and local regulations have become so commonplace that we simply shrug our shoulders and move on in the vain belief that it can't possibly get any worse. Which, of course, it does.

So what's a person to do but follow the line of least resistance? To go with the flow. Even to become personally co-opted by the system....

Goin' postal with compliance

Have you mailed a package at your local post office lately? No doubt you've heard the mandatory litany of questions from the weary clerk behind the counter:

> *Anything fragile, liquid, perishable, or hazardous?*
> *Need insurance? Delivery confirmation?*
> *Need stamps?*

If you want to see a furrowed brow, just try preempting their checklist by approaching the counter, saying, "Nothing fragile, liquid, perishable, or hazardous, and I don't need any stamps, thank you." Odds are, you will still get the dreaded questions...one after the other! (Try the pharmacy down the street with the friendly clerks in the post office at the back. Odds are they won't grill you like the robots at the official counter...and somehow, miraculously, your packages will still arrive at their destination!)

273

We wouldn't want to be too critical of the hard-working postal clerks. After all, they're "just doing their job." But does "goin' postal" inevitably mean the loss of all common sense, judgment, and discretion? Are rules never flexible enough to accommodate obvious exceptions?

There must be something in the air around post offices, whether in America or in Britain. The following conversation was overheard in a local village post office in the Cotswolds where the postmaster was obviously familiar with the woman at his counter:

> *Postmaster: "Hello Jean, how are you today?"*
> *Jean: "Very well, thank you, Simon."*
> *Postmaster: "How can I help you, Jean?"*
> *Jean: "I need to put in a change of address, please."*
> *Postmaster: "Do you have two forms of identification?"*

What's wrong with this picture! Of course, there was a time when no form of identification whatsoever was required for a simple change of address (and still isn't in the States...for now). People could be trusted back then. But times change and these days not everyone is to be trusted, so maybe identification is a good thing. But *two* pieces of I.D.? Okay, okay, *two* pieces. But for *Jean*, the dear old pensioner obviously well-known to Simon as one of his regular customers? What is Simon thinking! At this point, Simon the postmaster is the very embodiment of the Post Office—the living, breathing *face* of the Post Office across the counter from one of Her Majesty's humble subjects.

In this case, we're not talking about loony liberal politicians on the top rung of Government, or edict-crazy members of the European Parliament, or even the tyrannical train steward who refused to sell an egg sandwich to a delayed rail passenger on the pretense that the stranded passenger might choke on it if he had to evacuate the train! We're talking simply about a local postmaster so caught up in the compliance culture that he suffers a complete lapse in common sense.

Moving yet another level down, we're talking about an old-age pensioner who (obviously informed in advance about the latest bureaucratic nonsense) dutifully produced her pension card and a gas bill. What else could she have done if she wanted to get her mail? What option was left but to comply with a mischievous regulation, perfunctorily and stupidly administered by an unthinking postmaster?

It's for all the hapless "Jeans" of the world that both government bureaucrats and non-government technocrats should be tossed out on their ears! And that includes anyone at the bottom of the totem pole who refuses to use common sense in applying rules that make little or no sense in the moment. The problem is not just the ideological madness of the liberal-Left at the top levels of government, but the monstrous compliance culture it has created. Monsters *they*; thus monsters *we all*.

In a nanny state, whether British or American, it's good old-fashioned *discretion* that's in such short supply lately....

Letter to Editor—*Airline pilots complain about being subject to the same security measures as passengers (presumably, lest they violently seize control of their own aircraft!) These complaints are but a symptom of a far wider problem: That strict regulations invariably prevent the exercise of all discretion and common sense by minor officials.*

Doctors, once responsible for treating their patients according to their best medical judgment, are now required to make medical decisions in accordance with targets and set schemes having little to do with their patients' best interests.

Whenever there's a fatal highway accident, police rules say it must be investigated as a "potential crime scene," even if experienced officers can almost instantly tell the difference between a suspicious and non-suspicious accident. Thanks to the mindless rules, the investigation results in frustrating road closures, sometimes for hours, not to mention countless man-hours that otherwise could be spent investigating real crimes.

As a society, we can either employ only infallible, omniscient and omnipotent regulators, or give those enforcing the rules more discretion. If there is a being who meets the criteria for the first, I fear he is unlikely to apply for the job, having better things to do. The latter is also a problem as our schools seem unwilling to promote initiative and common sense in pupils.[207]

Choked by political legalism

What is it that produces a culture devoid of discretion? An addiction to rules! Rules, rules, and more rules. One could wish that when someone says, "The Brits love rules," they're only talking about the ever-popular Rules Restaurant in Covent Garden. But not likely.

Whether or not the Brits actually *love* rules, the fact remains that any highly regulated society like theirs tends to make legalists of all who are forced to live under such a system. When you think of legalism and legalists, what comes to mind? Religious zealots? Puritans? Ultra-orthodox Jews? Christian fundamentalists? The Taliban? You wouldn't be far off. But you might be surprised to learn just how much in common liberal, nanny-state governments have with religious legalists.

For political liberals, it's all about comprehensive, benevolent social planning. And social planning is all about rules: Policy upon policy. Regulation upon regulation. Rule upon rule.

Of necessity, rules require both *rulers* and *the ruled*. The more the rules, the more oppressive the *rulers* and the more compliant *the ruled*. If the first part of that equation seems obvious, it's the second part that often gets overlooked to our detriment. The problem is not simply that by virtue of living in a nanny state we necessarily have more and more rules; or that those rules increasingly become a nuisance to everyday life. The problem—indeed, the *danger*—is that we ourselves become more and more compliant and legalistic. Which is to say less free. Which is to say *dead*. Politically dead, for sure, but *spiritually* dead as well.

By this time, you won't be surprised to hear intentional connections being made between politics and the soul. And not simply some metaphorical "soul of the nation," though there is that, too. We're talking here about the metaphysical, spiritual soul of the individual, both yours and mine. The soul that groans when oppressed. The soul that's sad when it sees a nation headed in wrong directions. The soul that mourns the loss of public decency and morality. The soul that fears terrorists, huge national deficits, and loss of family and religious freedoms. The soul that bristles at the hypocrisy, corruption, waste, and arrogance of public officials who have relinquished their elective or appointive responsibilities for selfish aims.

When the soul cries for release, it is not simply wishing to be free from the shackles of rules, but from the conditions which make rules necessary. Anarchism is not the goal. Unfettered autonomy is not the aim. That for which the soul longs is a decent society respecting the bounds of moral constraint such that, were there no rules at all handed down by government, society would still be *good!*

Grant Gilmore summed it up elegantly in his Yale University lecture on "The Age of Anxiety":

> *The better the society, the less law there will be....The worse the society, the more law there will be....In Heaven, there will be no law, and the lion will lie down with the lamb....In Hell, there will be nothing but law, and due process will be meticulously observed.*[208]

Don't overlook the reverse implications: the more laws and rules, the more likely it's a corrupt society; the less regulated and controlled, the less likely it's a society *needing* rules.

More than just name-calling

We have spoken at length of the "liberal-Left" as if it were some monolithic social evil. Individually, of course, political liberals are no more evil than the rest of us, flawed as we all are. But make no mistake. No less than the evil done by extremists on the far Right (many of whom are staunchly religious people), one must never underestimate the profound evil done by the liberal-Left (as fervently dogmatic and evangelistic as any religious folks ever were).

Today, a younger generation is desperate to avoid extremist conflict and the tiresome culture wars which have ravaged our nation since the 1960s. They want nothing to do with the bitter tit-for-tat demonization of Left and Right. Can't blame them, really. On one level, it seems little more than a playground scuffle between two bullies. Yet, we can't just wish away real, true-to-life ideological differences as if they simply didn't exist. (For all we might wish otherwise, cancer is cancer, pregnancy is pregnancy, and unemployment is unemployment.) More important, it's no use lamely hoping that competing ideologies make no practical difference to ourselves, our children, our neighbors, and our communities—or even to our very souls.

Some will object to the whole premise of this book, with its much-repeated assault on the "liberal-Left" and "leftist liberals." Sounds too much like politics as usual doesn't it? Rest assured that if it were the religious-Right presenting the greatest threat at the moment, this book would have that as its target. (In fact, there's more to be considered momentarily.)

Think about it this way: Would anyone dare claim that the *religious-Right* is today's greatest threat in a plainly *secularist* Britain? Is it the religious-Right (particularly American-style), or even the *conservative* Right (of any style), that is responsible for the nanny-state madness witnessed in this book? And if not in Britain (in whose footsteps we Americans are following fast) then how could anyone reasonably suggest that all this "progressive" thinking is coming from the extreme

Right back here in America? So what else can we conclude but that the liberal-Left is primarily responsible for the political madness in both countries? And that secularist liberalism is currently the greatest threat to our nation's collective soul?

At the intersection of faith and politics

There's that word *secularist* again! Still not convinced that Britain's leftist Government is anti-religious (despite many liberals in the Government claiming a personal faith)? There's only a gossamer-thin line between being *irreligious* and *anti-religious*...and Britain is already *irreligious*. About the most that can be said of whatever British faith remains is that it is "fuzzy faith"....

News Report—*According to a recent European Social Survey funded by the European Union, Britain is one of the least religious nations in Europe. The survey of more than 30,000 people in 22 countries, found only five nations—Slovenia, Sweden, Norway, Holland and Belgium—reporting lower levels of church membership than Britain. Only 12 percent of Britons feel they "belong" to a church, compared with 52 percent in France.*

Professor David Voas, of Manchester University's Institute for Social Change, who led the project, said the UK was involved in a "long process of disestablishment, with Christianity gradually being written out of laws and political institutions. Christian faith will soon have no role among our traditional establishments or lawmakers," he said. "It remains to be seen for example, how much longer bishops will be allowed to sit in the House of Lords."

Professor Voas noted that Britain has one of the highest rates of "fuzzy faith," defined as an abstract belief in God and an ill-defined loyalty to Christian traditions. "Fuzzy faith," said Professor Voas, "is a staging post on the road to non-religion. Adults still have childhood memories of being taken to church, and they maintain a nostalgic affection for Christianity, but that is dying out. They still go along with some kind of religious identity but they're not passing it on to the next generation, and people who aren't raised in a religion don't generally start as adults."[209]

Participation in organized religion is never the whole story. Certainly that is true when it comes to the intersection between faith and politics. But it's a big start. Mark it down, underscore it, and flag it with a red flag: *A secularist nation is simply not the same as a faith-based nation*. It thinks differently, acts differently, rules differently, functions differently.

Apart from the unique historical precedents discussed above, the single most identifiable reason why Britain is so much farther down the nanny-state road from America is the faith factor. And the single most identifiable reason why America is fast catching up with Britain's present looniness is an ebbing away of our own religious faith.

By definition, secularists simply wouldn't "get it," but at base and at core, political looniness is a spiritual issue. It doesn't just come out of the blue with no warning, no reason, no cause, no antecedents. It doesn't happen in a vacuum. To the contrary, political looniness *fills* a vacuum—a spiritual vacuum that leaves government, politics, and society in a desert wasteland, lost and confused, vulnerable particularly to any Messiah who would come along offering *hope* and *change*. (Anybody we know?) Ah, the disappointing mirage!

Headline: Church contributes to loony cause

It is not only the secularists who don't "get it." Surprisingly, it is also those among us who would claim to be the most spiritual—America's churches. Theologically-liberal "mainline" churches offer nothing but tired, politically-liberal rhetoric. They've been so spiritually sanitized by their vacuous theology that they are virtually indistinguishable from the God-denying secularists with whom they are allies. Maybe they feel better paying lip-service to God, but they also feel pretty comfortable holding hands with those who deny God altogether. In their case, it's not politics alone that makes strange bed-fellows.

At the opposite extreme there's the religious-Right, often so focused on flag-waving that they forget the difference between *nation* and

Kingdom. Between saving a *government* and saving *souls*. Between fighting culture wars and "fighting the good fight." Between honoring the *Constitution* and submitting to *the Word*. Between being *Republicans* and being *Christians*.

And then there's that broad swath of Evangelicals who seem to have more theological balance and judgment, yet who have also lost their way. You see it in their frenetic attempts to capture the young with *entertainment* presented as *worship*. You see it when church leaders water down both religious doctrine and moral imperatives; who wink at immodesty even in the pew; who speak more about divorce recovery than about God hating divorce; who fit ever so comfortably within the surrounding materialist culture.

There are countless ways to become secularized. Just ask all those Christian young people who've been catered to for a generation, who now—being both biblically illiterate and jaded from all the megachurch hype—are fleeing the church, or at least ignoring it. Who now find faith irrelevant. Who are replacing faith with skepticism, or humanism, or even today's militant atheism. Who, alarmingly, will soon be active at every level of politics and government, making radically different decisions from their religious parents and grandparents.

Ever since Barack Obama arrived on the political stage, much talk has filled the airways about his religion. Ask many folks, and they'll insist to their dying day that Obama is a Muslim, not a Christian. Obama himself has contributed to that rumor by saying that he has warm feelings toward Islam, and that the Muslim call to prayer is one of the sweetest sounds on earth. But one would be hard-pressed to make a case that Obama is a practicing Muslim, or even a closet believer. Yet the Muslim-Christian debate hardly matters. Whatever he believes about Mohammed or Jesus Christ, first and foremost Barak Obama is a card-carrying, ideological, doctrinaire *secularist* through and through. And the same goes for most of his political cronies and allies, whatever their personal faith.

Across the Pond, that certainly goes for *Catholic* Tony Blair and *Anglican* David Cameron. Indeed, it goes for an incredibly high percentage of those who would call themselves "Christians" across the British Isles. "Christians" they may be (virtually by default since they are neither Muslim nor Jews), but first and foremost they are *secularists*. Even among Muslims, there are entire countries under the official banner of Islam which, despite countless adherents answering the muezzin's call to prayer five times a day, are at heart and soul *secularist*.

The point is that, in America today, among those today who regard themselves as "church-going Christians" are millions who have been baptized in secular thought no less than in the Christian faith. And that number is growing exponentially.

The *Christianization* of America has not always produced a *Christianized nation* of America. Compared with the "faithless Christian nation" that is modern Britain, America is not so much a *faithless* nation as an *unfaithful* nation. A "Christian nation" that speaks often of God, but just as easily takes his name in vain. A "Christian nation" filled with regular church-goers who take equal if not greater delight sitting in sports stadiums. A "Christian nation" *toying* with faith rather than *living* it. A "Christian nation" which is unashamed to speak of the Bible, but wouldn't have a clue where to find Obadiah or Zephaniah. A "Christian nation" with currency saying, "In God We trust" when it's mostly the currency itself in which we trust. A "Christian nation" with a surfeit of wealth and material comforts whose Lord and Savior had nowhere to lay his head. A "Christian nation" whose politicians routinely end their speeches with "God bless America," even as they're promoting a godless agenda. All of which begs the question: Why *should* God bless America?

If you happen to be a Christian who finds this book's British-inspired portrait of a looming Obama nanny state deeply disturbing, how disturbed are you by this brief snapshot of Christianity in America? Are you willing to concede that in profound ways we who claim to be followers of Jesus Christ have met the enemy and it is *us*? That *we ourselves* are contributing to our own undoing? That slowly but surely we are handing this nation over to secularists on a silver platter?

It's one thing to rail against the secularist, liberal, nannying philosophy that Barack Obama champions. It's another thing altogether to individually and collectively hold up to an increasingly-confused society a preeminently winsome portrait of the only One who truly can bring us *real* hope and *meaningful* change. The One who beckons us, rather than pushes us. The One who sets high standards, rather than micromanages us. The One who has every reason to treat us as mere puppets, but chooses instead to give us freedom. Genuine, real, true freedom!

In the end, there are only two portraits from which to choose. If the genuine is not presented as far more compelling, the fake will not just be *seen to be compelling*, but inexorably, militantly, and ruthlessly *will be compelled*.

The scariest of all thoughts

To be religious is not necessarily to be spiritual, or spiritually-minded. So to be a religious nation is not necessarily to be a spiritual nation. And *not* being a spiritual nation invites social disaster. Britain is the perfect poster child. America is fast joining the queue.

What's been your reaction to this book? Is it a "scary" book? It ought to be! If this runaway train we're on (with a precious cargo of children and grandchildren aboard) doesn't hit the brakes soon, there's no way we'll all avoid careening into the abyss ahead.

When all is said and done, you know what may be the scariest thought of all? It's that those on the liberal Left, fearlessly led in our nation by Barack Obama, really and truly think that they own the moral high ground. That they are on the side of goodness, truth, and justice. That what the rest of us sense as sheer madness is felicitous benevolence and near-divine wisdom—all in *our* best interests.

To which we'll let C.S. Lewis respond as we close this book....

> *Of all tyrannies, a tyranny sincerely exercised for the good of its victim may be the most oppressive. It may be better to live under robber barons than under omnipotent moral busybodies. The robber baron's cruelty may sometimes sleep, his cupidity may at some point be satiated, but those who torment us for our own good will torment us without end for they do so with the approval of their own conscience.*[210]

And so ends the lesson.

Recipe for social disaster

Take one dubious scientific hypothesis to explain the origin of human existence.

Remove as much faith and morality from the people as possible.

Replace fundamental morality with a giant heap of rules and regulations.

Stir in the artificial flavoring of political correctness.

Add a dash of arrogance.

Blend it all together using as much political force as necessary.

Bake for several generations, or until done.

Makes multiple layers of a problematic society, subject to crumbling.

Serve liberally, always from the Left.

Endnotes

1. "Mother who left children playing in park is branded a criminal," Nick Allen, *The Daily Telegraph*, July 13, 2009.

2. "Smacking kids like using electric fence, says QC," *The Belfast Telegraph*, February 3, 2009; "Commissioner loses appeal against law that allows parents to smack children," *Irish Times*, February 21, 2009; "Commissioner loses smack appeal," *BBC News*, February 20, 2009

3. "Mother trailed by policeman and warned by council for telling off son at checkout," Neil Sears, *MailOnline*, November 9, 2009

4. See "Nurse Susan Pope sacked from school after smacking son loses appeal against dismissal," John Bingham, *The Daily Telegraph*, August 19, 2009

5. "Father arrested and locked in a cell for smacking son," *The Daily Telegraph*, November 17, 2008

6. "Parents protest at Ofsted inspections for children taught at home," Joanna Sugden," *TimesOnLine*, September 14, 2009

7. "NSPCC 'doctored information' in Victoria Climbie case," *MailOnline*, December 11, 2009

8. "BBC slurs evangelicals in home school debate," *Chelmsford Anglican Mainstream*, October 21, 2009

9. "NH court orders home-schooled child into government-run school," http://www.alliancedefensefund.org/news/story.aspx?cid=5050, August 26, 2009

10. See "Oxford pupils to text school nurse for morning-after pill," Sam Lister, *The Times*, March 25, 2009; "The morning-after text: Girls of 11 will be able to send school nurse a message asking for contraceptive pills," Daniel Martin, *The Daily Mail*, March 25, 2009; "Morning-after pill is not to be taken lightly," Liz Hunt *The Daily Telegraph*, March 24, 2009

11. See "Parents should not teach children the difference between right and wrong in sex," Lucy Cockcroft, *The Daily Telegraph*, February 22, 2009; "Parents should NOT tell their children what is 'right or wrong' about having sex, say ministers," Steve Doughty, *MailOnline*, February 23, 2009, "Parents told: avoid morality in sex lessons," Jack Grimston, *Times Online*, February 22, 2009

12. "Social services to take newborn away from teenager 'too stupid to marry,'" Murray Wardrop, *The Daily Telegraph*, October 18, 2009

13. See "Government green guru Sir Jonathon Porritt calls for two-child limit," John Bingham, *The Daily Telegraph*, February 2, 2009

14. "What's good for our children is for us to say," Philip Johnston, *The Daily Telegraph*, October 18, 2009

15. See "Machetes by the door, drugs on the table - and mothers paid by the state to have babies with men they barely know. What HAVE we done to the British family?", Harriet Sergeant, *MailOnline*, September 21, 2009

16. "US births break record; 40 pct. are out-of-wedlock," Mike Stobbe, AP Medical Writer, March 18, 2009

17. "Ofsted told to leave friends to look after each other's children," Joanna Sugden, *The Times*, October 13, 2009

18. "Parents lose right over sex education," Graeme Paton, *The Daily Telegraph*, November 5, 2009

19. "Sex pamphlet for 6-year-olds horrifies family lobby," Rosemary Bennett, *The Times*, September 18, 2008

20. "Boys to get credit card for condoms," Marie Woolf, *Times Online*, July 7, 2009

21. "Children must be taught about the 'right to sexual pleasure', say government advisors," *Family Education Trust*, http://www.famyouth.org.uk/bulletin.php?number=137#children, Bulletin 137, Autumn, 2009

22. See "NHS viral video on teen pregnancy banned by YouTube," Mark Sweney, *The Guardian*, May 15, 2009; "You Tube bans shocking NHS sex education film," *The Christian Institute*, May 18, 2009

23. "Parents lose right over sex education," Graeme Paton, *The Daily Telegraph*, November 5, 2009

24. See "GCSE pupils studying 'soft porn' lads' magazines," *The MailOnline*, April 6, 2009

25. "Primary school curriculum shake-up attacked," Graeme Paton," *The Daily Telegraph*, November 19, 2009

26. "GCSEs marked 'generously', says watchdog," Graeme Paton, *The Daily Telegraph*, November 20, 2009

27. See "Girl, 5, told off at school for talking of God," *This Is Exeter*, February 13, 2009; "Christian primary school receptionist sues over

religious discrimination," Caroline Gammell, *The Daily Telegraph*, August 22, 2009

28. See "Druids, Rastafarians and atheists in new religious studies classes," Graeme Paton, *The Daily Telegraph*, March 24, 2009

29. See "Lib Dems back state faith schools," *BBC News*, March 7, 2009

30. See "Faith schools 'should be phased out to stop segregation', says teachers' union," Laura Clark, *Mail Online*, April 6, 2009

31. "Gypsy liaison officers 'in all schools,'" Graeme Paton, *The Daily Telegraph*, November 6, 2009

32. "Teachers need the law on their side," Boris Johnson, *The Daily Telegraph*, October 26, 2009

33. "Mother who left children playing in park is branded a criminal," Nick Allen, *The Daily Telegraph*, July 13, 2009

34. Letters to the Editor, *The Daily Telegraph*, September 12 and 22, 2009

35. "New vetting rules could end Scout jamborees in Britain," Lucy Cockcroft, *The Daily Telegraph*, October 12, 2009

36. "Child actors fall victim to weight of protection paperwork," Martin Beckford, *The Daily Telegraph*, October 6, 2009

37. "European exchange trip scuppered by safety rules," Graeme Paton, *The Daily Telegraph*, November 7, 2008

38. "Nearly 127,000 children forced to have records checks each year," Martin Beckford and Tom Whitehead, *The Daily Telegraph*, December 6, 2009

39. "Vetting stops pupils caring for elderly," Jack Grimston, *The Sunday Times*, November 1, 2009

40. Online responses to the article above, signed Johnski Williams

41. "Businessman sues BA 'for treating men like perverts,'" Sophie Borland, *MailOnline*, January 16, 2010

42. "Council Bans Parents from Play Areas," Tom Whitehead, *The Daily Telegraph*, October 29, 2009

43. "Father-of-three branded a 'pervert'—for photographing his own children in public park," David Wilkes, *MailOnline*, July 16, 2008

44. "Arizona couple sues Walmart after being accused of sexual abuse over kids' bath-time photos," *The Associated Press*, September 18, 2009

45. "Anti-paedophile vetting regime 'is ruing school life,' head teachers warn," Laura Clark, *MailOnline*, December 11, 2009

46. "The Nanny State Loses One," Hal G.P. Colebatch, *The American Spectator*, October 18, 2007

47. "Health-and-safety spoilsports stop pensioner selling home-made cakes for charity," *The Daily Mail*, August 15, 2008

48. "Plastic flowers banned from cemetery for posing a 'health and safety risk,'" *The Daily Mail*, August 8, 2008

49. "Fury at hospital plan to ban Bibles," *The Daily Mail*, June 3, 2005

50. "Station bosses ban fireman pole amid health and safety fears," *The Daily Mail*, August 4, 2006

51. "How 'crazy' new Health and Safety rules on ladders could add £1,000 to home repairs," *The Daily Mail*, August 30, 2008

52. "Circus acts told to wear hard hats under new EU law," David Sapsted, *The Daily Telegraph*, July 23, 2003

53. "Clown cannot wear giant shoes due to health and safety," Chris Irvine, *The Daily Telegraph*, April 23, 2009

54. "EU order buxom barmaids to cover up," *The Daily Mail*, August 4, 2005

55. "My tonsils on display," Brian Stephens, *The Daily Telegraph*, October 12, 2009

56. "Lollipop man's high-fives banned," *The Daily Telegraph*, October 6, 2009

57. "Have pies had their chips in leisure centres?", *The Daily Telegraph*, February 19, 2009

58. "Don't arrest drunks, they might get ill," Martin Beckford, *The Daily Telegraph*, September 12, 2009

59. "Eating biscuits, the health and safety guide," *The Daily Telegraph*, October 20, 2009

60. "Land of elf 'n' safety: EU Proms police order musicians to keep the volume down," Laura Roberts, *The Daily Mail*, August 28, 2008

61. "Music teachers should wear earplugs or stand behind noise screens," Chris Irvine, *The Daily Telegraph*, January 21, 2009

62. "Man banned from using wheelbarrow to take his recycling to rubbish tip—and told to DRIVE there instead," *The Daily Mail*, August 22, 2008

63. "It's for your own health and safety, honest," *The Daily Mail*, October 19, 2005

64. "Sandpits disappearing from playgrounds as councils blame health," Harry Wallop and Jeni Oppenheimer, *The Daily Telegraph*, June 5, 2009

65. "Traditional school ties 'banned' over health and safety fears," Graeme Paton, *The Daily Telegraph*, May 16, 2009

66. "Town mayor fires 400-year-old firing tradition because it might scare children," Richard Savill, *The Daily Telegraph*, November 27, 2008

67. "Wear goggles when using Blu-Tack: the safety rules ruining education," Graeme Paton, *The Daily Telegraph*, June 19, 2009

68. "Health and safety: a grave error of judgment," *Times Online*, April 21, 2009

69. "Don't touch that office chair! Health and Safety demand 48 hours notice to move it," Arthur Martin, *The Daily Mail*, April 2, 2007

70. "Health and safety snoops to enter family homes," Robert Watts, *The Sunday Times*, November 15, 2009

71. "Shortlist looks overseas thanks to 'risk-averse' UK," Charlotte Higgins, *The Guardian*, July 27, 2007

72. "Risk-averse teenagers create need for speed," G. Moore, *The Independent*, October 17, 2009

73. "No paddling on school trips, children told," Graeme Paton, *The Daily Telegraph*, November 6, 2009

74. "The NHS is ranked 14th out of 33 European healthcare systems," Rebecca Smith, *The Daily Telegraph*, September 28, 2009

75. "Health inequality has got worse under Labour, says government report," Andrew Sparrow, *The Guardian*, March 13, 2008

76. "Our cancer shame: Survival rates still lag behind EU despite spending billions," Jenny Hope, *The Daily Mail*, March 20, 2009

77. "Patients in half of trusts still struggle to see their GP," Kate Devlin, *The Daily Telegraph*, October 15, 2009

78. "Disabled children wait up to two years for wheelchairs," staff writer, *The Guardian*, March 4, 2009

79. "Cancer survivor confronts the health secretary on 62-day wait," Lyndsay Moss, *The Scotsman*, March 21, 2009

80. "Girl, 3, has heart operation cancelled three times because of bed shortage," David Rose, *The Times*, April 23, 2009

81. "5,000 elderly 'killed each year' by lack of care beds," staff writer, *The Daily Telegraph*, June 26, 2006

82. "Women in labour turned away by maternity units," John Carvel, *The Guardian*, March 21, 2008

83. "One in six trusts is still putting patients on mixed-sex wards," Daniel Martin, *The Daily Mail*, May 10, 2007

84. "Culture of targets prevents nurses from tending to patients," Claire Rayner, President of the Patients Association, *The Daily Telegraph*, March 21, 2009

85. "Patient 'removed" from waiting list to meet target," staff writer, *The Scotsman*, January 31, 2008

86. "Private healthcare managers could be sent to turn round failing NHS hospitals," Philip Webster and David Rose, *Times Online*, June 4, 2008

87. "Finger on the pulse: this health and safety regulation takes the biscuit," Max Pemberton, *The Daily Telegraph*, October 26, 2009

88. "UK health service 'harms 10 percent of patients,'" Kate Kelland, *Reuters*, July 6, 2006

89. "'Lives put at risk' by out-of-hours GPs, Care Quality Commission reports says," Rebecca Smith, *The Daily Telegraph*, October 1, 2009

90. "NHS chiefs tell grandmother, 61, she's "too old" for £5,000 life-saving heart surgery," Chris Brooke, *The Daily Mail*, February 28, 2008

91. "Top doctors slam NHS drug rationing," Sarah-Kate Templeton, *The Daily Mail*, August 24, 2008

92. "NHS patients told to treat themselves," Rebecca James Kirkup, *The Daily Telegraph*, January 4, 2008

93. "Pensioner, 76, forced to pull out own teeth after 12 NHS dentists refuse to treat her," Olinka Koster, *The Daily Mail*, April 4, 2008

94. "1,000 villagers wait for a dentist after just one NHS practice opens," staff writer, *The Daily Mail*, March 10, 2009

95. "Smokers and the obese banned from UK hospitals," staff writer, *Healthcare News*, May 2, 2007

96. "Chocolate should be taxed to control obesity epidemic, doctors are told," Simon Johnson, *The Daily Telegraph*, March 13, 2009

97. "Pupils told they have a 'right' to a good sex life: That's the advice for youngsters from the NHS," Daniel Martin, *MailOnline*, July 12, 2009

98. "Premature baby dies as guidelines say he was born too early to save," Laura Donnelly, *The Daily Telegraph*, September 9, 2009

99. "Sentenced to death on the NHS," Kate Devlin, *The Daily Telegraph*, September 2, 2009

100. "Pensioner died after being wrongly put on 'death pathway,'" Nigel Bunyan and Rebecca Smith, *The Daily Telegraph*, October 13, 2009

101. "New policy on sex change therapy," *BBC Online*, April 23, 2009

102. "Why should IVF be available on the NHS?", Ed West, *The Daily Telegraph*, August 6, 2009

103. "Dental Socialism in Britain," Llewellyn H. Rockwell, Jr., http://www.lewrockwell.com/rockwell/british-dentistry.html, May 9, 2006

104. "Britons Weary of Surveillance in Minor Cases," Sarah Lyall, *The New York Times*, October 24, 2009

105. "Binmen's 'rubbish profiles' of homes," Alastair Jamieson and Louise Gray, *The Daily Telegraph*,"

106. "Is there a bug in your bin?", Milo Yiannopoulos, *The Daily Telegraph*, March 15, 2009

107. "Every dog in Britain will have to be tagged with a microchip," Andrew Hough, *The Daily Telegraph*, September 28, 2009

108. "We have everything to fear from ID cards," Andrew O'Hagan, *The Daily Telegraph*, January 1, 2008

109. "Cameron's pledge to win over motorists," Robert Winnett and David Millward, *The Daily Telegraph*, October 6, 2009

110. "Nyman attacks 'CCTV Britain,'" *The Daily Telegraph*, February 20,2009

111. "Grimewatch: police set up CCTV spy in their own canteen," *The Daily Telegraph*, February 19, 2009

112. "Cambridge rejects surveillance cameras," *The Boston Globe*, February 3, 2009

113. "Photographers and anti-terrorism: The holiday snaps that could get you arrested," Philip Johnston, *The Daily Telegraph*, December 4, 2009

114. "How Big Brother watches your every move," *The Daily Telegraph*, August 16, 2008

115. See also "Is Big Brother watching your ORCA card?", Mike Lindblom, *The Seattle Times*, December 17, 2009

116. "Britain is 'surveillance society,'" *BBC News*, November 2, 2006

117. "What is institutional racism?", *The Guardian*, February 24, 1999

118. "Every phone call, email and internet click stored by 'state spying' databases," Richard Edwards, *The Daily Telegraph*, November 9, 2009

119. "Surveillance will cost more than £34 billion say Convention on Modern Liberty," Sean O'Neill, *The Times*, February 18, 2009

120. Kim Zetter, Email Author, *Wired.com*, December 31, 2007

121. "Big Brother is watching us all," Humphrey Hawksley, *BBC News, Washington*, September 15, 2007

122. "A Report on the Surveillance Society," For the Information Commissioner by the Surveillance Studies Network, September 2006, §2.5

123. "A Report on the Surveillance Society," For the Information Commissioner by the Surveillance Studies Network, September 2006, §2.8.2

124. "A Report on the Surveillance Society," For the Information Commissioner by the Surveillance Studies Network, September 2006, §4.3.2

125. "Christian health worker faces sack over crucifix necklace," David Barrett, *The Daily Telegraph*, May 23, 2009

126. "Cross purposes," *The Times*, May 8, 2009

127. "Calls for Red Cross symbol to be axed over links to the Crusades," Michael Lea, *MailOnline*, June 10, 2009

128. "Male nurse of 40 years is sacked after urging 'patient' to go to church (in a training session)," David Wilkes, *MailOnline*, May 26, 2009

129. "Council worker suspended for talking to terminally ill client about God," Emily Andrews, *Mail Online*, March 30, 2009. See also, "Council worker suspended for suggesting terminally-ill woman 'put her faith in God,'" Andrew Alderson, *The Daily Telegraph*, March 28, 2009

130. "NY nurse threatened, forced to assist in late-term abortion," *www.adfmedia.org*, July 22, 2009

131. "Christian foster mother struck off after Muslim girl converts," Matthew Moore, *The Daily Telegraph*, February 8, 2009

132. "Nurse suspended for offering to pray for elderly patient's recovery," Andrew Alderson, *The Daily Telegraph*, January 31, 2009

133. "Human rights row over town council prayer session," Natalie Stewart, *The Westmorland Gazette*, June 12, 2009

134. "'Faith row' Kendal town councillor resigns post," *The Westmorland Gazette*, December 11, 2009

135. "Brighton library in religious poster and mints row," *The Argos*, July 24, 2009

136. "You mustn't mention God...council bans church from putting up notices about its meetings," *MailOnline*, September 16, 2009

137. "Bible moved to library top shelf over inequality fears," Lucy Cockcroft, *The Daily Telegraph*, February 18, 2009

138. "Christian hotel owners hauled before court after defending their beliefs in discussion with Muslim guest," Jonathan Petre, *MailOnline*, September 20, 2009

139. "Humanists rejoice! BBC will consult them on religion," Emily Dugan, *The Independent*, April 19, 2009

140. See "How cash meant for promoting faith is going to an organisation that campaigns AGAINST Christianity," *The Daily Mail*, March 20, 2009. See also the BHA response: www.humanism.org.uk

141. "Atheist buses denying God's existence take to streets," Martin Beckford, *The Daily Telegraph*, January 6, 2009

142. "Scout's oath 'is religious discrimination,'" Jonathan Petre, *The Daily Telegraph*, April 12, 2008

143. "Political leaders must 'do God' to understand modern world, says Tony Blair," *The Daily Telegraph*, March 19, 2009

144. "Walking by on the other side," Melanie Phillips, *The Spectator*, March 5, 2009

145. "MEP: EU seen as cold place for Christianity," *The Christian Institute*, October 23, 2009

146. "Sayeeda Warsi condemns Labour's hostility to Christianity and warns against anti-Muslim hatred," Tim Montgomerie, www.conservativehome.blogs.com, October 6, 2009

147. "It's PC madness," *www.Express.co.uk* , March 26,2009

148. "EU bans use of 'Miss' and 'Mrs' (and sportsmen and statesmen) because it claims they are sexist," *MailOnline*, March 16, 2009

149. "EU's attempt to ban courteous salutations must be ignored," Gerald Warner, *The Daily Telegraph*, March 16, 2009

150. Stewart Lee, from *Heresy*, BBC Radio 4, May 16, 2007

151. "Barmy Britain through the looking glass," Philip Johnston, *The Daily Telegraph*, September 28, 2009

152. "Employment Law Update, The Christmas Party," Solicitor's memo, December 2, 2009

153. "Primary pupils told to compile swear list," Nick Britten, *The Daily Telegraph*, February 19, 2009

154. "Think like a bomber, children told," Duncan Gardham, *The Daily Telegraph*, February 20, 2009

155. See "Multiple wives will mean multiple benefits," Jonathan Wynne-Jones, *The Daily Telegraph*, February 3, 2008

156. "Cartoon strip aimed at under-12s depicts Christian boy as Islamaphobe thug," Jonathan Petre, *The Daily Mail*, April 4, 2009

157. See "HR must do more to understand and prepare for Ramadan and other religious festivals," www.personneltoday.com, August 19, 2009

158. "Don't eat near Ramadan fasters, Home Office staff told," Jason Lewis, *MailOnline*, September 19, 2009

159. "Apology over 'offensive' puppy police advert after Muslim complaints," Simon Johnson, *The Daily Telegraph*, July 1, 2008

160. "Worshippers quit church after council noise ban takes away their ability to praise God," *The Daily Mail*, October 8, 2009

161. "We must stop Muslim schools teaching that integration is a sin," Denis MacEoin, *The Daily Telegraph*, February 20, 2009

162. "Let's not die for timid and misguided political correctness," Douglas Murray, *The Daily Telegraph*, April 11, 2009

163. "Detroit terror attack: A murderous ideology tolerated for too long," *The Daily Telegraph*, December 29, 2009

164. "If only Joanna Lumley would fight Labour's idea of equality," Charles Moore, *The Daily Telegraph*, May 1, 2009

165. See "The Roots of America's Culture War," Lance Morrow, *Time*, February 1, 2001

166. "Muslim question persists in Army shooting," *The Washington Post*, January 18, 2010

167. "Gay 'Romeo and Julian' play sparks political correctness debate," Murray Wardrop, *The Daily Telegraph*, February 27, 2009

168. "Parents face prosecution over 'gay' education class protest," *Times Online*, March 7, 2009; "Parents face court action for removing children from gay history lessons," *The Daily Mail*, March 7, 2009; "Parents face prosecution over school gay week protest," *The Daily Telegraph*, March 6, 2009

169. "Homosexual couple sue Christian hotel owners for refusing them a double room," Lucy Cockcroft, *The Daily Telegraph*, March 22, 2009

170. "Registrar sues for right not to marry gay couples," Jonathan Wynne-Jones, *The Daily Telegraph*, May 18, 2008

171. "Registrar Lillian Ladele Loses Appeal," *National Secular Society*, www.secularism.org.uk., December 15, 2009; "Ladele appeal judgment expected by Christmas," *The Christian Institute*, November 6, 2009

172. "Christian registrar demoted to receptionist after she refused to preside over gay 'marriages,'" Urmee Khan, *The Daily Telegraph*, June 22, 2009

173. "Charity worker suspended over 'religious debate' with work colleague," Andrew Alderson, *The Daily Telegraph*, April 11, 2009

174. "Gay rights, gay wrongs?" Mathew Hywel, *Pink News*, April 20, 2009

175. See "New law could make gay jokes illegal," Toby Helm, *The Daily Telegraph*, November 8, 2007; "Labour's new gay hate laws dealt devastating blow by shock Lords defeat," Steve Doughty, *The MailOnline*, April 22, 2008; "TV star says defend free speech in 'gay hate' law," *The Christian Institute*, March 19, 2009

176. "Will they lock me up for playing Widow Twankey?", Christopher Biggins, *The MailOnline*, March 24, 2009

177. "Joke leads to 'homophobia' warning," *Express & Star*, March 30, 2009

178. "TV star says defend free speech in 'gay hate' law," *The Christian Institute*, March 19, 2009

179. "MPs reject 'gay hatred' free speech safeguard," *The Christian Institute*, March 25, 2009

180. "Police force invites young schoolchildren to write essays on homosexuality," *The Daily Telegraph*, February 11, 2009; "Why, instead of chasing criminals, are police asking children to write essays about gay pride?", *The Daily Mail*, February 11, 2009

181. See "Lessons about gays will be compulsory from age of 11," *The Daily Mail*, April 28, 2009; "Pupils aged 11 to learn about gay sex," *Times Online*, April 28, 2009

182. www.equalitybill.com , Theo Grzegorczyk, posted on December 2, 2009

183. www.equalitybill.com , Theo Grzegorczyk, posted April 27, 2009

184. "UK: Churches to be Forced to Hire Actively Homosexual Youth Workers?", Hilary White, *Catholic Online* (from www.lifesitenews.com), May 23, 2009

185. "Tony Blair tells the Pope: you're wrong on homosexuality," Ruth Gledhill, *Times Online*, April 8, 2009

186. Leviticus 18:22

187. John 3:16

188. "David Cameron says Tory party has 'work to do' on gay rights," Tony Grew, *Pink News*, February 16, 2009; "David Cameron backs same-sex 'marriage'," *The Christian Institute*, February 18, 2009.

189. *Through the Looking Glass, And What Alice Found There*, Lewis Carroll (Charles Lutwidge Dodgson), 1871

190. "Obama: Homosexual Relationships 'Just as Real and Admirable' as Heterosexual Marriage," Pete Winn, *CNSNews.com*, October 13, 2009

191. Matthew 19:12

192. See "Evolution to be compulsory subject in primary schools," Greg Hurst, *The Times*, November 20, 2009

193. "Eden and Evolution," Shankar Vedantam, *The Washington Post*, February 5, 2006

194. "Eden and Evolution," Shankar Vedantam, *The Washington Post*, February 5, 2006

195. A popularized misquotation of a radio transmission by Apollo 13's "Jack" Swigert, who said, "Houston, we've had a problem."

196. "Majority think it is possible to believe in God and Darwin," *The Daily Telegraph*, July 1, 2009

197. "Eden and Evolution," Shankar Vedantam, *The Washington Post*, February 5, 2006

198. "Eden and Evolution," Shankar Vedantam, *The Washington Post*, February 5, 2006

199. "Sir David Attenborough questioned on faith, naturally," Tim Walker, *The Daily Telegraph*, January 26, 2009

200. "Eden and Evolution," Shankar Vedantam, *The Washington Post*, February 5, 2006

201. "Communities Minister John Denham says he is a 'secular humanist,'" Martin Beckford, *The Daily Telegraph*, October 19, 2009

202. Charles Darwin, (1871) The Descent of Man, 1st edition, pages 168 -169

203. Charles Darwin, (1871) The Descent of Man, 1st edition, pages 168 -169

204. "Poll reveals public doubts over Charles Darwin's theory of evolution," Jonathan Wynne-Jones, *The Daily Telegraph*, January 31, 2009

205. "Charles Darwin to receive apology from the Church of England for rejecting evolution," Jonathan Wynne-Jones, *The Daily Telegraph*, September 13, 2008

206. C.S. Lewis, *The Screwtape Letters*, 1942

207. "Labour is still encouraging mortgages that borrowers can't repay," Mark Edwards, Witney, Oxfordshire, Letters, *The Daily Telegraph*, February 23, 2009

208. Grant Gilmore, "The Age of Anxiety," The Storrs Lectures, Yale University Law School, October 31, 1974

209. "Britons are believers of 'fuzzy faith', says survey," Lois Rogers, *The Daily Telegraph*, March 21, 2009

210. C.S. Lewis, *God in the Dock*, 1979